prefentatives, fhall have authority to make laws in all cafes for the
the principles and articles in this ordinance eftablifhed and declared
-houfe, and by a majority in the council, fhall be referred to the go
whatever, fhall be of any force without his affent. The governor
the general affembly, when in his opinion it fhall be expedient.

The governor, judges, legiflative council, fecretary, and fuch otr
fhall take an oath or affirmation of fidelity, and of office, the govern
officers before the governor. As foon as a legiflature fhall be formed in the diftrict, the council and houfe, affembled in
one room, fhall have authority by joint ballot to elect a delegate to Congrefs, who fhall have a feat in Congrefs, with a
right of debating, but not of voting, during this temporary government.

And for extending the fundamental principles of civil and religious liberty, which form the bafis whereon thefe republics, their laws and conftitutions are erected; to fix and eftablifh thofe principles as the bafis of all laws, conftitutions
and governments, which for ever hereafter fhall be formed in the faid territory;---to provide alfo for the eftablifhment
of ftates, and permanent government therein, and for their admiffion to a fhare in the federal councils on an equal footing with the original ftates, at as early periods as may be confiftent with the general intereft:

It is hereby ordained and declared by the authority aforefaid, That the following articles fhall be confidered as articles
of compact between the original ftates and the people and ftates in the faid territory, and forever remain unalterable,
unlefs by common confent, to wit:

Article the Firft. No perfon, demeaning himfelf in a peaceable and orderly manner, fhall ever be molefted on account
of his mode of worfhip or religious fentiments in the faid territory.

Article the Second. The inhabitants of the faid territory fhall always be entitled to the benefits of the writ of habeas corpus, and of the trial by jury; of a proportionate reprefentation of the people in the legiflature, and of judicial proceedings according to the courfe of the common law; all perfons fhall be bailable unlefs for capital offences, where
the proof fhall be evident, or the prefumption great; all fines fhall be moderate, and no cruel or unufual punifhments
fhall be inflicted; no man fhall be deprived of his liberty or property but by the judgment of his peers, or the law of the
land; and fhould the public exigencies make it neceffary for the common prefervation to take any perfon's property, or
to demand his particular fervices, full compenfation fhall be made for the fame;— and in the juft prefervation of rights
and property it is underftood and declared, that no law ought ever to be made, or have force in the faid territory, that
fhall in any manner whatever interfere with, or affect private contracts or engagements, bona fide and without fraud
previoufly formed.

Article the Third. Religion, morality and knowledge, being neceffary to good government and the happinefs of
mankind, fchools and the means of education fhall forever be encouraged. The utmoft good faith fhall always be obferved
towards the Indians; their lands and property fhall never be taken from them without their confent; and in their property, rights and liberty, they never fhall be invaded or difturbed, unlefs in juft and lawful wars authorifed by Congrefs;
but laws founded in juftice and humanity fhall from time to time be made, for preventing wrongs being done to them,
and for preferving peace and friendfhip with them.

Article the Fourth. The faid territory, and the ftates which may be formed therein, fhall forever remain a part of
this confederacy of the United States of America, fubject to the articles of confederation, and to fuch alterations therein
as fhall be conftitutionally made; and to all the acts and ordinances of the United ftates in Congrefs affembled, confform-
able thereto. The inhabitants and fettlers in the faid territory, fhall be fubject to pay a part of the federal debts contracted or to be contracted, and a proportional part of the expences of government, to be apportioned on them by Congrefs, according to the fame common rule and meafure by which apportionments thereof fhall be made on the other ftates;
and the taxes for paying their proportion, fhall be laid and levied by the authority and direction of the legiflatures of
the diftrict or diftricts or new ftates, as in the original ftates, within the time agreed upon by the United States in Congrefs affembled. The legiflatures of thofe diftricts, or new ftates, fhall never interfefe with the primary difpofal of the
foil by the United States in Congrefs affembled, nor with any regulations Congrefs may find neceffary for fecuring the
title in fuch foil to the bona fide purchafers. No tax fhall be impofed on lands the property of the United States;
and in no cafe fhall non-refident proprietors be taxed higher than refidents. The navigable waters leading into the Miffifippi and St. Lawrence, and the carrying places between the fame fhall be common highways, and forever free, as well
to the inhabitants of the faid territory, as to the citizens of the United States, and thofe of any other ftates that may
be admitted into the confederacy, without any tax, impoft or duty therefor.

Article the Fifth. There fhall be formed in the faid territory, not lefs than three nor more than five ftates; and the
boundaries of the ftates, as foon as Virginia fhall alter her act of ceffion and confent to the fame, fhall become fixed and
eftablifhed as follows, to wit: The weftern ftate in the faid territory, fhall be bounded by the Miffifippi, the Ohio and
Wabafh rivers; a direct line drawn from the Wabafh and Poft Vincent's due north to the territorial line between the
United States and Canada, and by the faid territorial line to the lake of the Woods and Miffifippi. The middle ftate
fhall be bounded by the faid direct line, the Wabafh from Poft Vincent's to the Ohio; by the Ohio, by a direct line
drawn due north from the mouth of the Great Miami to the faid territorial line, and by the faid territorial line. The
eaftern ftate fhall be bounded by the laft mentioned direct line, the Ohio, Pennfylvania, and the faid territorial line;
Provided however, and it is further underftood and declared, that the boundaries of thefe three ftates, fhall be fubject
fo far to be altered, that if Congrefs fhall hereafter find it expedient, they fhall have authority to form one or two ftates
in that part of the faid territory which lies north of an eaft and weft line drawn through the foutherly bend or extreme
of lake Michigan: and whenever any of the faid ftates fhall have fixty thoufand free inhabitants therein, fuch ftate
fhall be admitted by its delegates into the Congrefs of the United ftates, on an equal footing with the original ftates in
all refpects whatever; and fhall be at liberty to form a permanent conftitution and ftate government: Provided the conftitution and government fo ro be formed, fhall be republican, and in conformity to the principles contained in thefe
articles; and fo far as it can be confiftent with the general intereft of the confederacy, fuch admiffion fhall be allowed
at an earlier period, and when there may be a lefs number of free inhabitants in the ftate than fixty thoufand.

Article the Sixth. There fhall be neither flavery nor involuntary fervitude in the faid territory, otherwife than in
punifhment of crimes whereof the party fhall have been duly convicted: Provided always, that any perfon efcaping into the fame, from whom labor or fervice is lawfully claimed in any one of the original ftates, fuch fugitive may be lawfully reclaimed and conveyed to the perfon claiming his or her labor or fervice as aforefaid.

Be it ordained by the authority aforefaid, That the refolutions of the 23d of April, 1784, relative to the fubject of
this ordinance, be, and the fame are hereby repealed and declared null and void.

DONE by the UNITED STATES in CONGRESS affembled, the 13th day of July, in the year of our Lord
1787, and of their fovereignty and independence the 12th.

Cha Thomson fec'y

THE ORDINANCE OF 1787, July 13, 1787, PCC No. 59, I: 229-230,
RG 360. 12¾ x 8 in. Broadsheet attefted by the signature of Charles Thomson
2 pages.

THE AMERICAN
TERRITORIAL
SYSTEM

NATIONAL ARCHIVES

CONFERENCES / VOLUME 5

Papers and Proceedings of the
Conference on the History of the Territories

of the United states. Washington D.C. 1969

SPONSORED BY
THE NATIONAL ARCHIVES AND RECORDS SERVICE

November 3–4, 1969
The National Archives Building / Washington, D.C.

THE AMERICAN

TERRITORIAL

SYSTEM

EDITED BY

John Porter Bloom

OHIO UNIVERSITY PRESS

ATHENS, OHIO

Published by Ohio University Press for the
National Archives Trust Fund Board
National Archives and Records Service
General Services Administration
Washington, D.C.

Printed in the United States of America

Library of Congress Card Catalog No. 72–96397
ISBN 8214–0130–0

Contents

Foreword

THE NATIONAL ARCHIVES and Records Service has inaugurated a series of conferences for the exchange of ideas and information between archivists and researchers. These conferences are designed to inform scholars about the wealth of useful research materials available in the National Archives and Records Service, as well as to provide an opportunity for researchers to suggest ways in which their use of these records could be facilitated.

The National Archives and Records Service, a part of the General Services Administration, administers the permanently valuable, noncurrent records of the federal government. These archival holdings date from the days of the Continental Congresses to the present.

Among the nine hundred thousand cubic feet of records now constituting the National Archives of the United States are hallowed documents such as the Declaration of Independence, the Constitution, and the Bill of Rights. However, most of the archives, whether in the National Archives Building, the federal records centers, or the presidential libraries, are less dramatic. They are preserved because of their continuing practical utility for the ordinary processes of government, for the establishment and protection of individual rights, and for casting light on our nation's history when subjected to the scrutiny of the diligent scholar.

One goal of the National Archives staff is to explore and make more widely known these historical records. It is hoped that these conferences will be a positive act in that direction. The papers of each conference will be published, in the belief that this lively exchange of ideas and information should be preserved and made available in printed form.

ARTHUR F. SAMPSON
Administrator of General Services

Preface

THIS VOLUME is made up of papers prepared especially for the first conference on the history of the territories of the United States, held November 3 and 4, 1969. This was one of a series of conferences on various subjects held over the years at the National Archives Building, Washington, D.C., sponsored by the National Archives and Records Service, General Services Administration. In addition to providing a forum for scholarly interchange, this and the other conferences have been especially useful in making archivist-scholars better acquainted with professional historians, their interests, and some particular research problems associated with their fields of study.

The editor of *The Territorial Papers of the United States,* John Porter Bloom, was conference director and editor of this volume. The *Territorial Papers* is one of the oldest and most distinguished continuing documentary publication series in America. The first editor, Clarence E. Carter, occupied the position from 1931 until his death in 1961, first in the Department of State and then within the National Archives, after 1950. Dr. Bloom undertook this assignment in 1964, and serves in addition as the National Archives senior specialist for western history.

His dual assignment is reflected in the great scope of the papers presented herewith. They bear on the earliest years of our national existence and also on the problems of today, and the geographical orientation is almost entirely to the West. They reflect wide utilization of the resources of the National Archives as well as many other repositories of the recorded heritage of the United States. Our hope is, in part at least, that the work presented here will prove to be a useful and inspirational starting point for many another scholar in the little-cultivated field of territorial history.

JAMES B. RHOADS
Archivist of the United States
1969

Introduction

IN VIEW of the great significance of the history of the American territorial system, it may seem unusual that no previous conference or comparable meeting has ever been devoted to this subject, so far as is known. The general plan was therefore to secure presentations on varied aspects of territorial history which give some reflection of the entire time span of the independent existence of the United States. Indeed, several papers reach back into the period of British rule for precedents and fuller understanding of the earliest political formulations for governance of the sometimes troublesome western regions. The concluding papers treat with contemporary aspects of territorial government, including problems in relation to United Nations trusteeship provisions. The volume will serve a useful purpose, in this manner, as an introduction to the subject and an indication of its richness and its importance to a thorough understanding of the overall development of the United States. It may be hoped that, in future conferences, groups of papers may be brought together to illuminate specialized aspects of the development of the American territorial system.

A possible definition of territorial history was given careful thought in planning this conference. United States territories exist still today, of course, and they have lineal ancestors directly back, throughout the entire span of American governmental history, to at least 1787 and the Northwest Ordinance. Insofar as a project of research may concentrate directly upon the history of this series of territories as such, or one or a group of them as entities, such a project will clearly fall within any definition of territorial history. Beyond this, however, the application of a definition may not be obvious. How to define the study of a commercial organization which existed partly or entirely in a territorial setting? A military campaign against Indians in or partially in an organized territory? An analysis of development in an urban center which originated during or before establishment of territorial government? A study of the sources of immigration into organized territories? The list of possibilities could go on indefinitely, with every one illuminating a different facet of human existence in the territories.

Taking this into account, it has seemed necessary to take a limited view of territorial history, falling back on the definition on which the published *Territorial Papers* series is based. Thus, the papers in this volume are rather strictly political history, illustrative of territorial administrative history, with the obvious exceptions of the personal memoirs of Clarence Carter. The administrative theme applies both to the national level, as in relation to the Ordinance of 1787, the role of Congress and federal land policy, and to the territorial level, as in the study of the functioning of territorial courts.

The order in which the papers appear in this volume is not the exact sequence in which they were delivered at the conference. Arthur Bestor, in the version of his paper delivered on November 3, 1969, gave major emphasis to the period following adoption of the Northwest Ordinance. In the revised version published here it makes better chronological sense to place it in sequence ahead of the essay by Robert F. Berkhofer, Jr. The papers of Thomas G. Alexander and Kenneth N. Owens were delivered at separate luncheon meetings during the conference. Relating mainly to the territories of the post–Civil War West, as they both do, logic seems to call for their placement following Kent D. Richards's commentary. Robert R. Robbins's "United States Territories in Mid-Century" was in fact the last major essay delivered at the conference, but it seems well to conclude the volume with the speech by the Honorable Harrison Loesch, assistant secretary of the interior, which gives great emphasis to the present circumstances of the territories of the United States as well as some insight into their future. The editor takes full responsibility for this rearrangement, accomplished solely in the interests of readership.

The cooperation and generous support of many persons made possible both the conference and this volume. An especially great expression of appreciation is due to Edward G. Campbell, assistant archivist for the National Archives, to James B. Rhoads, archivist of the United States, and to Robert L. Kunzig, administrator, General Services Administration, for their participation in person in the conference, and for their encouragement of both the conference and this publication. The contemporary members of the staff of the Territorial Papers project (Julia Ward Stickley, Harold W. Ryan, and W. Neil Franklin) were of course of invaluable assistance, as were persons too numerous to name from other National Archives offices. Carol Morgan and other members of the conference papers staff are to be commended for their roles as manuscript editors of this volume. Most of all, the editor's gratitude is due to the scholars whose contributions—a tremendous investment of time, energy, and inspiration by each one, both from outside and from the National Archives's own staff —will have given the conference and this publication everything of enduring value that it possesses.

JOHN PORTER BLOOM
Conference Director

THE AMERICAN
TERRITORIAL
SYSTEM

Clarence Edwin Carter: A Tribute

PHILIP D. JORDAN

ONE MORNING, when Clarence Carter was on leave from the editorship of the *Territorial Papers* to complete Miami University retirement requirements, I wandered, as was customary, into his office for our daily ten o'clock chat. His eyes brightened, and he puffed a pipe cloud which billowed like a smoky updraft from a steamboat funnel. "Phil," he chuckled, "have you heard this one?" I shook my head.

"Well," he said, "there was this backwoods preacher layin' on a powerful sermon at a camp meeting. He knowed all about hell, but damn little about paradise. And he was smack in the middle of picturing the fire and brimstone when his preachin' was interrupted by a loud dispute between two slightly liquored-up gentlemen. One was a Democrat and the other a Republican. They wuz arguing as to who was goin' to be the next president of the United States. Annoyed beyond all Christian patience, the preacher stopped his haranguing to address himself to the disputants. 'My dear friends, you are exciting yourselves unnecessarily an' wasting precious time in speculating as to the future president of the United States, for, before an earthly election takes place our blessed Lord will be president everywhere.' 'I'll bet you twenty-five dollars,' shouted the Democrat, 'he can't carry Kentucky.'"

Then Carter sank the barb. "You know some scholars," putting caustic emphasis on *scholars,* "you know some scholars don't have that much sense." He scratched aflame a kitchen match. "Congressmen," he twinkled, "don't either."

Those morning conversations of more than a quarter of a century ago

For a fuller account, see the author's "A Dedication to the Memory of Clarence Edwin Carter, 1881–1961," in *Arizona and the West* 10 (Winter 1969): 309–12; the present essay was also published in *Prologue: The Journal of the National Archives* 1. no. 3 (Winter 1969): 46–47.

followed no set pattern. The give-and-take stemmed from our mood of the day, from the concern of the hour, from the trust and confidence we had in one another, from both common and mutual interests. We chatted not only of cabbages and kings but also of codices and learned letters. As I remember and as my commonplace book indicates, Carter's favorite topics —the ones to which he returned again and again—dealt with the problems of historical research, the practical problems involved in the editing of the *Territorial Papers,* and, finally, what use scholars would make of the papers.

Carter felt that, generally speaking, too many historical harvest hands garnered the chaff and not the grain and that, as a result, graduate students could not distinguish between root and fruit. He was always deploring the fact that insufficient attention was given to the use of primary documents. Too many historians, he once said, follow the lazy way. And he named names and gave examples. When the conversation turned to the vexing, practical problems which he himself had to solve as editor, he was apt to gee and haw, not because he did not know what he wished to accomplish, but because he had not as yet formulated the principles of historical editing which he eventually brought together and published as a monograph and which, in my considered opinion, is still the best handbook to place in the hands of students. Yet when his *Historical Editing* was published in 1952, he wrote me, saying: "I'm not sure I made my point even if anybody reads it—which I doubt." The organization, arrangement, and editing of the papers could—and perhaps should—have been done differently. Carter himself was discontented with some of his results and methods. He was aware of faults. He fashioned his own heavy cross from the weight of his own self-criticism and, for the most part, bore it without complaint. Yet he was extremely resentful of a few reviews of earlier volumes.

The major worry—one that he kept rather well hidden—but which festered in Carter's mind, was that the *Territorial Papers,* which he had sweated to finance and had struggled to edit, would not be consulted sufficiently by researchers. He held a nagging fear that his blue-bound volumes would stand in an unbroken row on library shelves, disturbed only now and again by some rare breed of researcher who glimpsed promises of fresh approaches. Perhaps his hunch was right, although I feel he was overly pessimistic. Yet, an informal and a by no means scientific survey of graduate students in United States history in two universities and one college revealed that less than one percent had ever heard of the papers and that not a single student had consulted them. And within the past month a public library with a reference department serving a community with an area college and three junior colleges tossed away as wastepaper a set of the *Territorial Papers.* This, I am sure, is atypical.

Carter was inordinately impatient with sloppy work performed by students, colleagues, or members of his staff. He said he did not know of a single person capable of producing anything but an inferior first draft. To this he added the comment that the finished manuscripts of too many historians read like a preamble to a first draft. He was equally hard on those researchers whose bibliographical skills—if one may use the term "skills" in this sense—were more like thumbs than fingers; who read documents far too casually and hence jumped to false conclusions; who were inept at textual criticism; who did not check and recheck sources and citations; and who, as he said, skimmed historical cream with a coal shovel. "If I could only teach my staff," he said wistfully, "to take the time to work with care— to see the wisdom of collating every damned item that needs it."

He more than once spoke of the "slick" historian whom he defined as urbane, insipid, and as dishonest as an undertaker trying to peddle a thousand-dollar funeral—"We supply everything"—to an impoverished widow. Carter believed that whenever an historian felt he knew everything, he had better take down his shingle. To him, perhaps, the search was more significant than the finding.

I suspect that relatively few members of the profession ever realized that hidden behind the drive for perfection, the dedication to hard work, and the frequently salty and crusty comments there stood a shy, sensitive person. A man frustrated beyond all belief, an individual attempting to compensate for a rural background, a Calvinistic upbringing, a conservative ambience. He was a hard-earth boy who never was able to forget that the day's farm chores began early and who, even when it was no longer necessary, continued to punish himself by being at his desk long before his staff arrived. Tranquility was denied him his whole, long, frustrating, private and professional life. He was in my room an hour before he delivered his presidential address in Indianapolis at the old Mississippi Valley Historical Association. As he left, he drew me aside so that others present could not overhear. Even today, although his words have nagged me through the years, I still am not quite sure of their meaning. Perhaps you can help. He said, "I am an ass with a tarnished bit in my mouth." Then he left, closing the door quietly, to deliver a memorable and inspiring address.

Today distinguished scholars, some following leads furnished in Carter's *The Territorial Papers of the United States: A Review and a Commentary,* and others originating their own approaches, mine the rich veins which Carter so ardently hoped would be worked. This conference, so well conceived and planned by John Porter Bloom, is not only an outward manifestation of the immense and exciting contents of *The Territorial Papers of the United States* but also, I am happy to say, a tribute to that puzzling little man of boundless energy whose scholarship was balanced with a sense of humor and who, to the best of his ability, made available to the historical profession a magnificent collection of root documents.

Clarence Edwin Carter: A Memoir

HAROLD W. RYAN

DR. JORDAN'S REMINISCENCES about Dr. Carter have brought back my own many memories. I went to work in the office of the *Territorial Papers* publication on the first working day of 1941 and, except for three years in the army during World War II, I continued my association with Dr. Carter until his death in 1961. And here I might insert a warning that I have always been a great admirer of his complete professionalism.

If there are two words that could be used to describe Dr. Carter's professional life they would be "attention" and "industry." By this I mean his attention to detail, attention to form, attention to result; and the industry to carry through on each. I have seen him rewrite a footnote or a paragraph for a book review four or five times, striving to arrive at an exact phrasing that would be to his liking. For several years he was a sort of guest lecturer for the archival courses given at the National Archives under the auspices of American University. His object was to acquaint the students with uses for archival material—the same sort of missionary work he had been engaged in for many years. One would think that a standard discussion would suffice for the changing classes. But no! Each year the talk must be rewritten—a new idea incorporated, a new phrasing devised, a new emphasis introduced—to bring home the message with greater effect.

Dr. Carter, being an old country boy, was awake with the first streak of light each morning. He had special permission to be at his desk earlier than regular hours, usually by 6:30 A.M., with a corresponding shortening of the afternoon hours. I do not doubt that if this permission had been withheld he would have come in at the earlier hour just the same.

It was a traumatic experience, however, for an employee to arrive at the regular time, perhaps not yet up to the realities of the day, and to encounter

The present essay was also published in *Prologue: The Journal of the National Archives* 1, no. 3 (Winter 1969): 48–50.

this man at full steam, throwing off ideas and instructions like sparks. His correspondence was a memorable operation and he usually had it arranged into two parts by the time we arrived. First the crank letters and those that exhibited an excess of stupidity—these were usually turned over to me to be answered according to his instructions to "Tell the damn fool 'No'—but in a nice way." The second group of letters was composed of those from good buddies and from those persons making serious and sensible enquiries. To most of these Dr. Carter would draft the reply—sometimes rather earthy—to the aforesaid good buddies. He would write the drafts in his own unique and crabbed hand which, even after years of decipherment, on occasion still needed his expert translation. Mrs. Margaret Ansley who, in addition to her other duties, took care of most of the correspondence, would nearly go into a frenzy in her efforts to unravel his meaning; on occasion she would absolutely refuse to make the attempt. She used to ask him at what stage in his doctoral program did he include the course in bad handwriting.

Dr. Carter had private and informal words that would curdle milk and peel paint from walls. He attributed them to his mule-driving days on the farm in Morgan County, Illinois. His public, formal writing and speaking, however, utilized a vocabulary that was clear, direct, and exact. No doubt it derived from the strong Latin education that he had received; in fact, during his undergraduate days at Illinois College in Jacksonville he taught Latin at the nearby Whipple Academy. And woe be unto the one who misused a Latin phrase in his presence. Forthcoming would be a detailed lecture on the proper construction of the phrase and its derivation.

The good doctor did crib a bit, however, in the preparation of his writings and speeches. After his death Mrs. Ansley and I were clearing out his desk and we found some cards on which he had entered certain word usages that had caught his fancy. Usually these excerpts were from editorial pages of newspapers but some were copied from the sports and entertainment pages. Below each entry was a paraphrase in which he had changed the wording or word sequence to fit into his own style. These notes were discarded by us, and no check was made to see if the phrases ever appeared in his writing.

Dr. Carter had a fantastic memory—not, of course, as to the place where he had deposited one of his ferocious pipes three minutes previous. But his recall was almost total for something that he had read or discussed weeks, months, or even long years before. When he gave instructions to recheck some fact one soon learned to do it immediately because at a later date one would be faced with the query through an enveloping cloud of smoke— "Did you verify that date on galley 140 MM?" Embarrassing if one had forgotten the matter completely!

Sometimes I would come into the office with some "brand new" (to me) discovery that I had made among the documents. When I acquainted Dr. Carter with this new knowledge he would more often than not reply: "Oh yes, What's-His-Name did a rather good monograph on that in 1923." And usually he employed the expression "What's-His-Name." But shortly thereafter he would come up with the name of the author and the title of the work with instructions to see that the information was included as a footnote. Much of the printed material was in his own personal library of some six hundred fifty titles that could very well have served as the early American history section of a college library.

Dr. Carter had definite ideas on history and historians. His favorite definition of history was a quote from Dr. James Harvey Robinson, professor of history at Columbia University—"History is everything that man has done or thought or felt." But he tended to exercise great caution in the uses of history. He leaned toward the ideas of his friend and mentor Clarence Alvord, who held that there were lessons indeed to be learned from history but that humanity in its development was as yet much too close to the primordial ooze to recognize them. Against the time when this recognition would come, the records of the past must be preserved as pristine as at their origin. To Carter each document was unique; it was created by an individual, who was also unique, at a certain moment under circumstances that could never be duplicated exactly. In any examination of a historical document all of these elements had to be considered: the circumstances, the chronology, and especially the personality of the originator.

Dr. Carter had another favorite quote in regard to the role of historians. It is the first line from Vergil's *Aeneid: "Arma virumque cano."* "I sing of arms and the man." This, he felt, is the purpose of the historian. Of course, he would have preferred to consult the original documents used by Vergil but would have to content himself with the secondary work. He had a healthy skepticism for all secondary sources. No matter how learned or reliable the authority, every footnote and every quote must be collated— to the original, if possible. And this held equally true for previous volumes of the *Territorial Papers* publication. Many a time I had to run down a quote we had lifted from a previous volume and compare it, not to the said volume, but to the original document itself. He seemed to think that there was a possibility that later knowledge and greater expertise in the work might change the reading of a previous time.

During my years with Dr. Carter we had but few arguments and, strangely enough, they always came during the presidential election years. He was an unreconstructed conservative, so unreconstructed in fact that at one time I told him that he seemed to consider William Howard Taft a screaming radical.

This conservatism was only in the area of politics. He was always ready to make use of any new machine or procedure that would speed our work. Early in his career he learned to type, two-fingered, on a blind Oliver typewriter and, although not expert, he continued to use such a machine until the end. The office was always full of photostats and other photographic reproductions. When the proposal was made to microfilm the territorial documents in the National Archives he was all for it, although he would not completely accept the result because he was fearful that the camera operator might miss something vital. Besides, he seemed to gain a sort of extra incentive from personally handling the old documents.

Dr. Carter was a man of many surprises. He had conferences on the work many times, and after he had completed our business he would lapse into random discussion. On one of these occasions he said something about "when I worked my way to Europe on a cattle boat." Further enquiry elicited the information that his first trip to Europe was spent in the care, feeding, and sanitation of thirteen head of cattle—through the auspices of a Chicago beef dealer. Another time he told me about being in the entertainment room at a convention of the American Historical Association when ex-President Theodore Roosevelt was the center of attraction. After a few potions of hospitality Mr. Roosevelt was asked about Panama. "Panama," exploded the ex-president, "Hell, I took Panama." Dr. Carter said that he had always suspected as much.

There were many sessions of this sort—many that, regretfully, I cannot recall. I do remember one morning when I came into the office to see him meticulously tearing some pages into inch-square bits, and by the looks of the wastebasket there must have been quite a few sheets at the beginning. I waited, curious. "There," he said as he finished the last page, "That is the end of a project that Solon Buck and I started at Wisconsin many years ago. We were going to change the thinking of the entire historical world." It was a half hour too late to protest. It would have been of great interest to explore the mental processes of these historians at the fledgling stage.

Of all the memories that I have of Dr. Carter, the most vivid is the statement he made just after we had received delivery of one of the *Territorial Papers* volumes and he had paged through it:

Almost anyone can publish a collection of documents but we
are trying to produce a work of art. We may not succeed every
time; we may never succeed, but we must keep trying just the same.

THE NORTHWEST
ORDINANCE

EDITOR'S NOTE

The following two essays, with the ensuing discussion of sources, constituted the first session of the conference. Julian P. Boyd made general remarks in introducing the session, identifying himself particularly with Thomas Jefferson, setting forth "something of my understanding of his purpose, his aims, in respect to territorial history." "We are concerned," Boyd continued, "with one of the great achievements of the American people . . . ." "The problem they faced has been called the supreme problem of politics—that of achieving a just balance between the rights and interests of the various members of the body politic and those of the whole."

Boyd discussed the difficulties involved and cited eighteenth-century authorities on the impossibility of a solution. Hope was seen by the American leaders, however, by "looking to inward realities rather than to the outward forms of government," and in fact "this was the strongest government on earth because it rested on the consent of the people." He concluded, stating that "in this period of strife and confusion . . . they brought forth out of apparent weakness the proposition that thenceforth the people of all the territories to be acquired by the nation could look forward to participation as equals in the same political society and under guarantees of republican forms of government. This was something the world theretofore had not witnessed."

Constitutionalism and the Settlement of the West: The Attainment of Consensus, 1754–1784

ARTHUR BESTOR

"THE CONSTITUTION, in all its provisions," declared the Supreme Court in 1869, "looks to an indestructible Union, composed of indestructible States."[1] As this orthodox formulation makes clear, a constitutional lawyer ordinarily views the American form of government as dualistic. A constitutional historian, by contrast, is obliged to recognize that the United States has exhibited, during most of its history, a three-part structure. Besides the Union with its own Constitution and sphere of action, and the states with theirs, a third component has usually been in evidence—the territories. Though their powers of self-government were circumscribed and restricted, the conterminous continental territories were never regarded as mere possessions. Their inhabitants unhesitatingly described themselves from earliest days as "citizens of the United States, resident in this Territory."[2] In a very real and compelling though not easily definable sense, territories formed an integral part of the American Union, even though the latter was, by strict letter of law, a union solely of *states.*

Prior to 1787 constitution making went on as a separate and independent process at each of these three levels of government—state, federal, and territorial. There were three loosely connected constitutional systems, embodying different and sometimes contradictory political principles. With respect to the principles to be embodied in state constitutions a consensus was quickly reached, and with the ratification of the Constitution in 1788 a viable solution was finally provided to the intricate problems of *federal* constitutionalism. No such definitive answer was ever given to the even more complex problem of extending principles of constitutionalism to new political communities being established in the American West. To extend such principles to territories in the course of settlement was, however, an imperative obligation if the new Republic were not to turn its back upon doctrines it had advanced in its struggle for independence. A succession of landmarks was produced in the form of solemn congressional resolutions, formal territorial ordinances, and even more obligatory statutes known as organic acts. All throw light upon the processes through which constitutional principles win acceptance and become established.

The first major document that can be said to embody an American consensus on the principles of territorial constitutionalism was a set of resolutions adopted by the old Congress on October 10, 1780.[3] They constituted, in the first place, a final acceptance of the idea that constitutional policy for territories ought to be made, not by states individually nor by the first-comers to the frontier, but by representatives of the nation as a whole. In the second place, the resolutions amounted to a solemn commitment on the part of the nation that its ultimate aim was creation in the West not of a dependent empire but of republican states that would ultimately join their fellows on the plane of equality in the Union.[4] The resolutions of October 10, 1780, were the foundation upon which territorial institutions were gradually erected in years that followed. They constituted a final meeting of minds on fundamental issues of territorial policy which had been the subject of bitter controversy. To examine these issues—long antedating the Revolution and explicitly formulated as early as the Albany Congress of 1754—must be our first concern.

The plan that Benjamin Franklin drew up for the Albany Congress on July 10, 1754, proposed a confederation of American colonies under one "General Government," which would assume major responsibility for common defense. This implied careful, coordinated handling of relations with Indians, and the Albany Plan proposed to give the general government overriding authority in this realm. But westward expansion of white settlement, involving purchases of—and often lawless encroachments on—Indian lands, created problems that were inextricably intertwined with the handling of Indian relations. Facing this fact squarely, the Albany Plan proposed to transfer to the new general government full responsibility for developing an orderly and humane program "for Extending the British Settlements in North America." It was proposed to give the general government exclusive authority to "make all Purchases from Indians for the Crown, of Lands not within the Bounds of Particular Colonies." These bounds were, however, to be curtailed. The Albany Plan made frank mention of lands "that shall not be within [the] Bounds [of particular colonies] when some of them are reduced to more Convenient Dimensions." Furthermore, effective control over the pace and direction of westward expansion was placed in the hands of the general government by a clause authorizing it to "make New Settlements on such Purchases [from the Indians], by Granting Lands in the Kings Name." Finally, the general government was empowered to "make Laws for regulating and Governing such new Settlements, till the Crown shall think fit to form them into Particular Governments."[5]

The Albany Plan won approval neither from individual American colonies nor from authorities in Great Britain, and affairs in the West continued to be handled sometimes by individual colonies, sometimes by land speculators operating almost as petty sovereigns, and sometimes by officers of the crown.

The French and Indian War of 1754–63 was fought in much the same uncoordinated fashion. Victory, however, created a situation which could not be handled without some systematizing of policy for the West. By the Treaty of Paris of February 10, 1763, Great Britain received from France and Spain Canada, East and West Florida, and the long-disputed eastern half of the Mississippi valley from the river to the Appalachians. The British thus came into some sort of suzerainty over numerous Indian tribes who responded to the new situation by a formidable rebellion under Pontiac.

The British ministry's program for the Indians and for the unsettled regions was unveiled in a royal proclamation of October 7, 1763. The first task was to organize governments. Colonies in the past had come into existence from time to time according to no preestablished pattern. The Proclamation of 1763 set forth for the first time a blueprint to guide the process. Recognizing that political maturity was achieved by stages, the proclamation made provision at the beginning for nothing more than appointment of certain executive officials and establishment of courts where cases would be decided "as near as may be, agreeable to the laws of England." Legislative organs would be created at a second, more advanced stage, and "representatives of the people" would thereafter participate in the making of "laws, statutes, and ordinances for the public peace, welfare, and good government" of the colony.[6]

Of far greater importance, from almost every point of view, were provisions of the Proclamation of 1763 that dealt with Indian affairs. The underlying principles were the same as those of the Albany Plan, but stated more forcibly. The proclamation forbade all purchases of land from the Indians by private persons, and prohibited colonial officials from making grants or even permitting surveys beyond boundaries of their own particular colonies. The boundaries themselves were to be sharply constricted. Royal governors and other officials were forbidden to make grants or approve surveys "for any lands beyond the heads or sources of any of the rivers which fall into the Atlantic Ocean from the west or north-west,"[7] no matter what the legal boundaries might be.

One purpose of the Proclamation of 1763 differentiated it sharply from any plan that had originated, or could be expected to originate, in the American colonies themselves. Stated in the clearest language was the aim of creating a permanent Indian country throughout the entire interior of the continent, and of diverting migration into newly acquired Quebec or the Floridas.[8] The attempt to impose these arrangements by simple fiat destroyed any possibility of their being considered on their merits in the colonies, and they became an item in the American catalogue of grievances.

On July 21, 1775, after hostilities had begun at Lexington and Concord and after George Washington had taken command at Cambridge, Benjamin Franklin presented to Congress a draft Articles of Confederation in which he incorporated certain features of the Albany Plan. In particular, he reiterated the requirement that purchases of land from Indians by private persons should cease and that the Indians should be assured that "their land [was] not to be encroach'd on." Franklin unhesitatingly assigned to the general government "the Power and Duty" of "Planting . . . new colonies when proper."[9] On these particular matters, however, Franklin's views were those of a minority.

The precedents furnished by the Albany Plan and Franklin's proposal of 1775 were honored at the outset, for the first authorized committee draft of Articles of Confederation followed their lead. This draft, reported by John Dickinson on July 12, 1776,[10] proposed a comprehensive delegation of authority to Congress to deal with the whole range of problems involved in westward expansion. Consideration was given to rights of Indians in their lands, and Franklin's liberal phrases of 1775 were drawn upon.[11] With respect to extension of governmental institutions into the West, the Dickinson draft did more than borrow from earlier proposals; in many instances it went beyond them. Instead of expecting that states would voluntarily set western limits to their claims, the draft bestowed upon Congress the express power of "Limiting the Bounds of those Colonies, which . . . are said to extend to the South Sea." Like the Albany Plan, it gave the general government the power of "Assigning Territories for new Colonies . . . in Lands to be thus separated," and it spelled out the concomitant power of "Disposing of all such Lands for the general Benefit of all the United Colonies." But instead of authorizing the general government actually to govern new settlements (as the Albany Plan had done), it gave recognition to a right of self-government.[12] As a quid pro quo to states whose western claims would be extinguished, Dickinson's draft proposed a guarantee of the territorial integrity of each state by all others.[13]

John Dickinson, of Pennsylvania and Delaware, represented the views of seaboard states that could lay no claim to western lands. Even within his committee, however, the clauses just described met opposition, and in the margin Dickinson indicated that they were to be "submitted to Congress" rather than recommended outright.[14] Once the draft reached the floor of Congress the clauses in question produced a sharp debate, which extended through July 25 and 26 and August 2, 1776. Samuel Chase of Maryland said bluntly, "No Colony has a right to go to the South Sea; they never had; they can't have."[15] On the other side, speaking for the state with the largest claims of all, Benjamin Harrison stood firm for vested rights: "By its charter, Virginia owns to the South Sea. Gentlemen shall not pare away the Colony of Virginia."[16] Though conciliatory voices were heard, the proposal to curtail western claims went down to defeat and with it all provisions for establishment of new states on the frontier. The secretary of Congress made the notation "postponed" opposite four relevant clauses in his copy of the first draft of the Articles, and when a second version was printed,[17] incorporating the decisions reached by Congress prior to August 20, 1776, all four had disappeared.[18]

A final attempt to reinstate some provision concerning western lands was made on October 15, 1777, precisely a month before Congress completed work on the Articles. Three propositions were voted down. The mildest—a mere request that states lay before Congress the documents on which their claims were based—received votes of only three states out of eleven voting.[19] The most forcible, which Maryland alone supported, would have empowered Congress to fix the western boundary of every state claiming western lands and to "lay out the lands beyond the boundary, so ascertained, into separate and independent states."[20]

As a result of these adverse votes, the Articles of Confederation were submitted for ratification with no provision for handling problems connected with westward expansion. Even the most elementary constitutional question of all was left unsettled, the locus of power to establish governmental institutions in western territories. The only real alternative to chaos was recognition of Congress as the sole national body competent to reconcile conflicts and develop a responsible program. When in the 1780s Congress at last undertook to make constitutional policy for the West, it was obliged to act as a kind of constituent assembly,[21] working out constitutional arrangements to control the progress of western settlement, seeking agreement from state legislatures, and embodying resulting arrangements in a complex of documents which, in their totality, defined a constitutional system for territories. Just as the nature of the English constitution must be gathered from a medley of charters, coronation oaths, petitions, and statutes, so the nature of the American territorial constitution must also, for the earliest period, be sought in diverse documents such as deeds of cession, acceptances of the same, resolutions announcing policy, and ordinances setting up governmental machinery.

The form was comparatively unimportant. It was the substance that counted, and in the end these various documents provided answers to a number of crucial questions. Some, it is true, were never satisfactorily resolved—notably the question of the validity of private purchases of Indian lands made in the past. Three fundamental questions, however, which received definitive and final answers in the early 1780s, became in effect the principles of the constitutional system that was created for the territories.

The first question masqueraded as a question of property: to whom did the territories belong? In reality it was a question about the locus of authority to prescribe and control settlement. Was this power to be vested in whatever state might be able to claim a jurisdiction by virtue of some early charter, drawn up in vague and expansive terms? Or was the West to be regarded as the common patrimony of the American people as a whole?

In the second place, when political units came to be established in the West, would they be given the character of dependent colonial administrations? Or fully self-governing states? Or would some middle ground be found?

In the third place, if new western settlements were to become selfgoverning, would they also be admitted as full-fledged voting members of the Union, and if so under what conditions and safeguards? None of these was a simple question, and none could receive a simple answer.

The ultimate solutions were all set forth by one spokesman or another during the early months of independence. A clear-cut stand on the first two questions was taken by the convention that drew up the original constitution of Maryland. On November 9, 1776, that body resolved:

that the back Lands claimed by the *British* Crown, if secured by
the blood and treasure of all, ought in reason, justice, and policy, to
be considered as a common stock, to be parcelled out by
Congress into free, convenient, and independent Governments, as
the wisdom of that body shall hereafter direct.[22]

An equally clear answer to the third question was set forth in a clause that Jefferson vainly attempted to insert in the Articles of Confederation. The latter document promised full membership in the Union to Canada if it should choose to join in the measures under way. Jefferson moved to extend the same promise to "all new colonies to be established by the United States assembled."[23]

In 1776 these were minority positions. As we have seen, the articles submitted to the states next year for ratification included no provision bestowing upon Congress the kind of authority that would be needed to carry any of these proposals into effect. Silence, however, was hardly an answer, for the problems were real and would not go away. Furthermore Maryland, the state most insistent upon treating the West as "common stock," held a trump card which she was quite willing to play. To go into effect the Articles of Confederation required unanimous ratification, and Maryland refused to ratify. The fate of the Union depended—and by no means for the last time—upon a satisfactory solution of the territorial problem.

Until agreement could be reached on the first question it was useless to discuss the other two. Prior to 1780, accordingly, the constitutional issue that dominated every discussion of the West was the issue of state versus federal control. The positions taken on this issue were profoundly affected by interests and activities of speculators in western lands. Land companies with political ties to states possessing western claims naturally opposed cession of such claims. Companies and individuals whose political and economic base was in one of the landless states, and who in disregard of state claims were making purchases on their own from the Indians, naturally lobbied for vesting control in the United States.[24]

Weighty interests often depended on phrases that seem insignificant. Maryland, for example, in demanding that ownership of western lands be vested in the Confederation, was careful to exclude lands already "granted to individuals at the commencement of the present war"[25]—a formula that would in effect have validated claims of an important Maryland-based company.[26] To prevent appropriation by private interests of portions of the domain supposedly destined to become a common fund, Virginia insistently demanded that "all purchases and deeds from . . . any Indian Nation . . . made for the use of any private person or persons whatsoever, shall be deemed and taken as absolutely void."[27]

The fact that economic interests were obviously at stake does not make the constitutional issues themselves any less real or important. Constitutional issues so abstract as to have no bearing on economic and other vital interests would indeed be unreal issues. Constitutional issues are real precisely when and precisely because other issues become involved with and depend for their solution upon the decisions reached in the constitutional realm.[28] The question of the locus of control over western settlement was a genuine and momentous constitutional question for the nascent Republic. Whatever the motives of those who made the decisions—and statesmanship is not necessarily absent just because economic interest is present—the decisions themselves not only affected contemporary interest groups but also had an impact, vastly wider and more prolonged, upon future institutions and thus upon the life of many segments of the population. As such they were constitutional decisions of the gravest import.

Not until 1780 did the deadlock over state versus federal control begin to be broken. In May 1779 Virginia proposed to abandon the quest for unanimity and to establish a confederation without Maryland.[29] The latter state retorted with a sharp blast at "states who are ambitiously grasping at territories, to which in our judgment they have not the least shadow of exclusive right," and reiterated its demand that the "unsettled" lands should "be parcelled out by Congress into free, convenient and independent governments."[30] In communications to their own state officials, the Virginia delegates described the document as "intemperate" and "indecent" and urged a "counter declaration."[31] Tension built up during the summer thanks to Virginia's decision to open its own land office,[32] an action which Congress in October asked the state to reconsider, describing it as "attended with great mischiefs."[33] In December Virginia replied to its critics in a "remonstrance," which was duly presented to Congress on April 28, 1780, and which vehemently denied the right of Congress to "assume a jurisdiction, and arrogate to themselves a right of adjudication" with respect to the state's western claims.[34]

By the time the remonstrance was put on record, however, the situation had begun to open up. New York, which possessed some shadowy though extensive claims by virtue of treaties with the Iroquois, had in the past expressed only mild opposition to proposals to fix western boundaries. That state was in a position to make the kind of gesture that was needed to start things moving,[35] and it did so February 19, 1780. The New York legislature offered to relinquish all its claims west of a meridian line which it proceeded to specify. Congress was officially informed on March 7,[36] and on June 26 it appointed a committee to consider the offer of New York, along with the declaration of Maryland and the remonstrance of Virginia.[37] In a report presented four days later,[38] the committee took the sensible position that it would be futile at that moment to attempt revision or amendment of the Articles of Confederation. Instead it pointed to the New York offer as "an example which . . . deserves applause, and will produce imitation," and "earnestly recommended" to all the other landed states "a liberal surrender of a portion of their territorial claims."[39] The Virginia delegate on the committee, Joseph Jones, immediately threw himself into the task of convincing his own state to make such a cession.[40] The mood of Congress was obviously favorable and on September 6, 1780, the committee's resolution was adopted with only minor alterations of language.[41]

The other basic constitutional questions involved could now at last be fruitfully considered. Serious discussion was inaugurated by a motion which the Virginia delegates offered on September 6, 1780, immediately after passage of the resolution urging cession of western claims.[42] In its original form the motion was primarily a reassertion of Virginia's position on certain matters of special concern to her. Fearing that cession of western claims might be the first step in dismembering older and larger states,[43] Virginia insisted that Congress guarantee the remaining territory of any state which should cede its "Unappropriated" lands. Furthermore, the long-standing opposition of Virginia to any validation of private land purchases from Indians found voice again in the motion. By contrast, there was far less force and precision in phrases of the motion that dealt positively with future arrangements for organizing and governing the ceded territory. Nothing was stated explicitly about the character of institutions to be established or about full and equal membership in the Union.

It was a committee, appointed three days later,[44] that shaped these and other ideas into a system which can properly be described as a constitutional one. The committee report retained clauses guaranteeing the territorial integrity of any state that ceded western claims, and forbidding private purchases from Indians. But when Congress came to vote on the measure on October 10, 1780, these two provisions were struck out.[45]

Of permanent and enduring importance was the elaboration that the committee gave to the phrase of the original motion alluding to "separate and distinct States" to be created in the West. The committee transformed the vague first paragraph of the Virginia motion of September 6 into a threefold promise with respect to the future. In the first place, the revised resolution guaranteed (as the original one had done) that "the unappropriated lands that may be ceded or relinquished to the United States" would be "disposed of for the common benefit of the United States." In the second place, a new clause in the document promised that ceded territories would "be settled and formed into distinct republican states." And in the third place, the resolution pledged that these states would, in due course, "become members of the federal Union and have the same rights of sovereignty freedom and independence as the other states." When Congress adopted the resolutions with this paragraph intact, these three promises became the basic principles of American constitutionalism as extended to the western territories.

A stable constitutional system represents, in effect, a set of promises about the future, secured by institutional arrangements that command general assent and respect. Now a promise is not so much an exercise of power as a deliberate relinquishment of power. Promising to act in one way means, quite simply, giving up the right to act in ways contrary to or incompatible with the pledge thereby made. In the promise given in 1780 three parties were involved, and therefore the freedom of action of all would be curtailed in the future, if the words were not to be empty ones.

Thus the promise to the older states that lands they ceded would be "disposed of for the common benefit of the United States" was a limitation not only upon Congress but also upon new governments in the West, whose actions might be harder to restrain. This particular limitation was eventually spelled out in specific detail in the Ordinance of 1787, which provided that the new states should "never interfere with the primary disposal of the soil by the United States."[46]

Similarly, the promise that the West would "be settled and formed into distinct republican states" was not only a promise by Congress and the older states to settlers, but also a restriction upon the latter. Their privilege of self-government was curtailed to the extent that they were forbidden to establish institutions "incompatible with the republican principles, which are the basis of the constitutions of the respective states in the Union."[47] Such phrases about a republican form of government have figured in many basic American constitutional documents, with many diverse implications. In the resolutions of October 1780 the clause in question signified, above all, a promise to states with western claims that Congress would establish nothing but republican forms of government in territories they might cede. As later embodied in the Ordinance of 1784, the scope was enlarged so that the clause became in part a restriction upon settlers in their erection of new governments. When the phrase reappeared in 1787 in the federal Constitution, it had become a guarantee of protection by the federal government to states as well as to territories: "The United States shall guarantee to every State in this Union a Republican Form of Government."[48]

The last of the three promises of 1780—that the new states "shall become members of the foederal Union"—could only mean that neither Congress nor the older states might rightfully block such admission indefinitely or impose discriminatory conditions.

How could this interdependent network of promises and limitations be given binding force over all parties concerned? This is a central problem—perhaps *the* central problem—in any constitutional system. The solution would have been relatively simple had individual states retained control (as many of them wished to do) over the establishment of new governments in the western reaches of the domains they claimed. Under such circumstances the constitution of the mother state would remain in force as fundamental law until and unless the settlers came up with an acceptable constitution of their own. Such careful supervision of western constitution making was envisaged by Jefferson in his draft constitution for Virginia in 1776. He proposed that the Virginia legislature should lay off "one or more territories . . . for new colonies," should make sure that the latter were "established on the same fundamental laws" as those of Virginia itself, and should then recognize them as "free and independent [*sic*] of this colony [i.e., Virginia] and all the world." Though Jefferson's forthright promise was eventually watered down,[49] the process by which Kentucky attained statehood in 1792 did preserve many features of his original concept.[50]

Another method of subjecting fundamental law of new areas to scrutiny would have been to require an approved constitution before settlers moved to the frontier. This was a congenial idea in New England, and it figured explicitly in the "Propositions for settling a new State" drawn up by Colonel Timothy Pickering in April 1783.[51] A device for preventing departures from established constitutional understandings, which Jefferson proposed and Congress accepted in 1784, consisted in instructing the settlers at the outset "to adopt the constitution and laws of any one of the original states" and only later permitting alterations of their own.[52]

All these proposals assumed that some "consent of the governed" was requisite if constitutional limitations were to be binding. By contrast, Thomas Paine was prepared simply to impose a democratic form of government. At the outset, he argued in a pamphlet of 1780 entitled *Public Good,* "a constitution must be formed by the United States, as the rule of government in any new state, for a certain term of years (perhaps ten) or until the state becomes peopled to a certain number of inhabitants; after which, the whole and sole right of modelling their government to rest with themselves."[53]

No proposal for federal supervision of the constitution-making process could have much relevance so long as Congress labored under the handicap of a denial of any delegated power in the matter. Even if authority to sponsor interstate agreements could be assumed, there was a conspicuous lack of power in Congress actually to enforce the terms of any compromises that might be arrived at. Furthermore, there was no possibility of giving territorial pledges and restrictions the status of enforceable fundamental law by writing them into the Articles of Confederation: the Articles were not, like the later Constitution, "the supreme Law of the Land," to be obeyed "any Thing in the Constitution or Laws of any State to the Contrary notwithstanding."[54] If long-term guarantees, long-term limitations, and long-term relinquishments of power in territorial matters were ever to be upheld, then some method would have to be found for creating an ad hoc body of fundamental law binding on all parties concerned with western settlement.

The final solution was formally proposed by Jefferson on March 1, 1784, when he reported to Congress a committee-approved "plan for the temporary government of the Western territory."[55] The measure spelled out the guarantees contained in the resolutions of October 10, 1780, by providing the machinery for actually establishing self-governing political units, prescribing that these new governments should be "in republican forms," and promising them ultimate admission to equal voting participation in the

Union. To turn these promises into binding commitments the final paragraph of the report prescribed the following procedure:

> That the preceding articles shall be formed into a Charter of
> Compact [,] shall be duly executed by the President of the U.S.
> in Congress assembled under his hand and the seal of the United
> States, shall be promulgated, and shall stand as fundamental
> constitutions between the thirteen original states, and those now
> newly described, unalterable but by the joint consent of the U.S.
> in Congress assembled and of the particular state within which
> such alteration is proposed to be made.[56]

Congress approved this device, adding a proviso that the compact should be unalterable only "from and after the sale of any part of the territory of such state, pursuant to this resolve."[57]

In laying the groundwork for a new set of commonwealths, Jefferson was deliberately returning to first principles, just as he had done when, in the Declaration of Independence, he set forth the philosophic foundations of the new Republic. To him, as to most contemporary believers in natural-law concepts, it was axiomatic that governments derived their legitimate authority from the consent of the governed, and that this consent was given, in theory if not in historical fact, by the people's entering into a primordial social compact, which was then continuously renewed through the tacit acceptance of succeeding generations. The draftsmen of the earliest state consitutions explicitly avowed this doctrine. Until Jefferson invoked the same principle in this report of March 1, 1784, however, proposals for establishing governmental institutions in the West had been conceived of in terms of the dominion and power vested in the older states as owners of the unsettled domain. Jefferson placed the matter on a new footing, and his idea was restated with even greater amplitude and precision by Nathan Dane in the Northwest Ordinance of 1787, which spoke of a "compact between the Original States and the People and States in the said territory."[58]

By 1784 the promises made in 1780 had been given greater definiteness through three and a half years of additional discussion. Much of the debate, to be sure, consisted of wrangling about terms of cessions that various states were offering to make. Part of the resulting clarification was of a negative sort. Two points which delegates from the land-claiming states hoped to make part of the fundamental law failed to win inclusion in the resolutions of October 1780, but the campaign for them did not cease. Thus Virginia continued to press its demand that all private purchases from Indians be invalidated.[59] The refusal of Congress to adopt such a clause in October 1780 angered the Virginia delegates, but Madison pointed out that it was still possible for "the Ceding States . . . to annex to their cessions the express condition that no private claims be complied with by Congress."[60] Accordingly, the Virginia act of January 2, 1781, offering to cede its claims to the area northwest of the Ohio River, included such a condition, expanded so as to call in addition for a voiding of royal grants within the ceded territory.[61] When Congress rejected this condition,[62] and when Virginia acquiesced five weeks later,[63] the clause was finally dropped from consideration. The end in view had thereafter to be sought through statutory rather than constitutional enactments. In theory at least it would be possible for Congress, by carefully prescribing the method of surveying and granting title to lands in the public domain, to prevent speculators from profiting from vague and irregularly acquired claims. In this sense, the ordinance of May 20, 1785, "for ascertaining the mode of disposing of Lands in the Western territory,"[64] and the long succession of later statutes and administrative orders relating to sales of public land possessed constitutional significance. But these were products of legislative or executive discretion; they never achieved the status of constitutional law or custom in even the most inclusive sense of the latter term.

The second provision that Congress definitely refused to write into fundamental law for territories was a promise that, after cessions were made and accepted, the Confederation itself would guarantee "the remaining territory" of the grantor state. Critics insinuated that states like Virginia and New York were offering to surrender what had never been theirs in the hope of securing undisputed title to "valuable territory which they now have no good claim to."[65] Congress in 1783 spoke decisively in opposition to such a guarantee,[66] which thereafter disappeared from among proposed constitutional stipulations for territories. In 1787, however, an equivalent assurance was written into the Constitution of the federal Union, where it more properly belonged.[67]

These two old and exacerbated controversies aside, the really crucial problems of territorial constitution making as defined in the resolutions of October 1780 were basically three: to make sure that territories would be developed "for the common benefit," that they would be given "republican" government, and that they would be hastened to full and equal membership in the Union. On these crucial matters there were hopeful signs of a growing unanimity of opinion, despite the wrangling that occurred between 1780 and 1784.

The most important contributor to the new spirit was obviously the coming of peace. In 1776 and 1777, when the Articles of Confederation were being considered, the discussion of territorial matters was unreal in some degree, for the fortunes of war might easily destroy not merely the claim to the West but the claim to independence itself. Even in October 1780, when territorial policy was first clearly formulated in resolutions, the surrender of Cornwallis was still a year in the future. Not until March 1783 did Congress know the shape and size of the western domain that the United States could expect to receive in the final treaty of peace.[68] When it became clear that the whole stretch of land from the Allegheny Mountains westward to the Mississippi River would belong to the United States, territorial policy making became at last really meaningful. News that the articles of peace had actually gone into effect reached America on April 9, 1783, and on that very day James Wilson moved that Congress appoint a committee to consider and report "the measures proper to be taken with respect to the Western Country."[69] It was the first motion that dealt with possessions actually in hand rather than in prospect. The ensuing eleven months produced many fruitful suggestions, products of the hope which peace had inspired.

Likewise significant in altering the mood and tone of discussion was a new point of view that emerged respecting the character of settlers who could be expected to migrate to the West. Many citizens of the seaboard states had looked upon the frontiersmen as shiftless wanderers, barely eking out a subsistence from lands on which they had probably trespassed, and sinking ever deeper in a mire of ignorance and irreligion. With the end of the war this image abruptly changed, as discussion centered more and more upon prospective large-scale settlements in the West by Revolutionary soldiers, whose lands were a compensation for services rendered their country. Viewed in this light, self-government and eventual statehood for western settlements began to be regarded not as a risk but as a reward. Indeed, the most precise and definite plan for the granting of statehood that Congress had ever seriously considered was proposed in a motion of June 5, 1783, dealing with land grants to army veterans. Included in the motion (made by Theodorick Bland of Virginia and seconded by Alexander Hamilton of New York) was a firm promise that when any district laid off in the West should attain a population of twenty thousand male inhabitants it would automatically be recognized as "a separate, Independent free and Sovereign state" and would be "admitted into the Union as such."[70]

A significant debate on October 14, 1783, showed how far Congress was at last willing to go in granting self-government to western settlers. Regarding the degree of self-government to be accorded, however, differences of opinion remained, and Congress had to make a choice among three subtly different formulations. There was common agreement that the time had come "to erect a district of the western territory into a distinct government." In dispute were the instructions that should be given to a committee charged with working out details. The resolution initially presented to Congress called simply for "a plan for the temporary government of the inhabitants and the due administration of justice, until their number and circumstances shall entitle them to a place among the states in the Union, when they shall be at liberty to form a constitution for themselves."[71] Unsatisfactory to most delegates was the absence of any safeguard against arbitrary rule prior to statehood, and a revision was voted. Congress refused to accept the more liberal of the two alternatives offered, which would have permitted the plan to go into effect only "if agreeable to the settlers."[72] The resolution finally adopted provided that any plan offered should be "consistent with the principles of the Confederation." It spoke of the plan not as one "for the temporary government of the inhabitants" but as one "for connecting [them] with the Union by a temporary government." And it embellished the promise of eventual statehood by speaking, in gratifyingly high-flown language, of welcoming the westerners "as citizens of a free, sovereign and independent State" to representation in the Union.[73]

This was the optimistic and liberal atmosphere that environed Jefferson and his committee when in early 1784 they drew up the report that would become the first great territorial ordinance of the new republic. Jefferson turned, of course, to the original congressional resolutions of October 1780. He interpreted them in accord with the new spirit that peace had brought, and he incorporated, as always, ideas that had been maturing in his own mind.

To create a system of fundamental law for territories in process of settlement raised problems of a sort never encountered in connection with the fundamental law of a well-established state. Principles were sought that would govern the process of development itself, not simply the operation of an already organized and balanced system. There were precedents, of course, for treating the governance of new territories as a problem of devising institutions appropriate to different stages of development. Almost always these were plans for colonial administration, however, not plans for constitutional self-government. Thus the Proclamation of 1763 made explicit use of the idea of two successive administrative stages.[74] By adding to this scheme a third stage, in which self-government would be complete and political equality recognized, the British plan of 1763 could be made acceptable to Americans after independence. This occurred, in fact, when Jefferson's Ordinance of 1784 was replaced in 1787 by the Northwest Ordinance, which prescribed a first stage of strictly appointive government, authorized in due course a second stage wherein an elective legislature would share power with officials appointed from outside, and promised a final advancement to fully self-governing statehood.

Though Jefferson in the Ordinance of 1784 employed the concept of progressive stages of government, he was not adopting the British formula of 1763 but profoundly altering it, and he was not laying down precedents that the Congress of 1787 would follow but precedents that it would repudiate. There was, to be sure, a superficial similarity between his plan and the earlier and later ones. Jefferson did provide for three successive chronological stages in the advance of the new areas to complete statehood. These stages represented, however, different degrees of elaborateness in governmental machinery, not different degrees or gradations in the right of self-government. The central feature of the Ordinance of 1784, both as Jefferson originally drafted it and as Congress finally adopted it, was its unhesitating grant of self-governing institutions to inhabitants of new lands from the very beginning.

At the initial stage of settlement, the inhabitants were not to draft a constitution of their own but were to adopt an existing state constitution.[75] This provision constituted in fact a built-in guarantee of self-government. The inhabitants of the new areas would be almost as completely self-governing at the beginning of the first stage as they would eventually become when full members of the Union. It was participation in the decisions of the latter, not management of their own affairs, that was deferred.[76]

The second stage would begin when population reached twenty thousand free persons, and would involve simply calling a convention which would draft a new constitution. It could add little to the already full measure of self-government enjoyed by the inhabitants. The third and final stage would be attained when the inhabitants became equal in number to those currently resident in the least populous of the original thirteen states. At this point the new political entity was entitled to take its place as an equal partner in deciding questions affecting the Union. The language of the clause was mandatory: "such state shall be admitted by its delegates into the Congress of the United States, on an equal footing with the said original states."[77] Admission could not be completely automatic, for the ordinance was incapable of overriding the requirement in the Articles that nine states give their assent. Nevertheless everything possible was done to make sure that progress from stage to stage, and ultimate admission to voting membership in the Union, would follow a timetable inexorably geared to predetermined and objectively measured standards of population growth.

The numbers required for advancement from one stage to the next were small, for the area of each new state was likewise intended to be small. Political philosophy dictated this decision about size. During the formative years of the nation, Americans were haunted by the dictum of Montesquieu: "It is natural to a republic to have only a small territory; otherwise it cannot long subsist."[78] The persistent belief that a wide extent of territory would prove incompatible with republicanism was to furnish, in 1787 and 1788, one of the most formidable arguments which advocates of the new Constitution were obliged to meet.[79] In the earlier years of the same decade, when policy toward the West began to take shape, Montesquieu's view was hardly even debatable; it stood as an unquestioned political axiom. In October 1780, for example, Joseph Jones, member of Congress from Virginia, was urging the legislature of his state to cede to the Union a substantial part of its western claims, explaining (in a letter to George Washington) that "We are already too large for the Energy of republican Government."[80] Jones had already moved that boundary lines in that region be so drawn "that no state be less than one hundred or more than one hundred and fifty miles square"[81]—a range of from 10,000 to 22,500 square miles. This became, for the early 1780s, the ideal standard.[82] Though eventually every state carved out of the American West greatly exceeded the maximum ordained in these original formulations,[83] the size that Joseph Jones proposed in 1780 was not in reality tiny by contemporaneous American standards. Six of the thirteen original states of the Union were smaller than the minimum of 10,000 square miles specified in the resolutions adopted on October 10, 1780.

In practice, the committee that drafted the Ordinance of 1784 and the Congress that adopted it made no attempt to lay out states of minimum size and were not quite able even to stay within the maximum limit. In the area north and west of the Ohio River—the only territory that had actually been ceded—the Ordinance of 1784 as finally adopted left the northernmost regions unorganized and laid out eight states in a well-defined area that can be estimated at two hundred thousand square miles, thus making the average size of each state some twenty-five thousand square miles.

One reason for delimiting with exactness the boundaries of future states was to make clear from the beginning the body politic in whose affairs the settlers would participate. Leaders of Congress were anxious to create communities in the West, not mere aggregations of people dispersed over wide and ill-defined areas. Because they expected an esprit de corps to develop, they were prepared to bestow not only immediate self-government but also the ultimate boon of membership in the Union upon populations which by modern standards seem tiny and therefore sparse.

In specific terms the Ordinance of 1784 gave each new state the right to draw up its own constitution when there were twenty thousand free inhabitants within its boundaries. Such a state would become a full voting member of the Union when its population came to equal the current population of the smallest state of the original thirteen.[84] In 1790, as the census was to show, this figure turned out to be just over fifty thousand persons.[85]

To make comparisons with the enormous populations of later times would be virtually meaningless. But it may be useful to look backward over the colonial period and to consider what levels of economic and social advancement these figures really signified to thoughtful contemporaries.

Taking the population standards of the ordinance as indices of this, one may say that the colonies of Virginia and Massachusetts had reached a level entitling them to write their own constitutions (i.e., a population of twenty thousand) by about the year 1660, and were prepared to assume the full responsibility of participating in intercolonial deliberations (having attained a population of fifty thousand) by about the time of the Glorious Revolution of 1688/89. By the middle of the eighteenth century all but four of the thirteen colonies would have attained the latter stage. For most of them the interval between the first and final stages would have been about thirty years.[86] If we consider what these individual colonies were like as self-conscious and self-governing political bodies, at these various dates, we can glimpse what was in the minds of the members of Congress in 1784 when they chose these figures to mark off the stages in the development of nascent political communities.

It is significant that in every version of the Ordinance of 1784 the political divisions for which governments were being provided were referred to as "states." The term was applied to them from the very moment of their creation, long before their admission to voting membership in the Union. In 1784 the word "territory" still possessed only its ancient meaning: "the land or country belonging to or under the dominion of a ruler or state."[87] The "Western territory" which figured in the title of the ordinance was simply the area in the West that was being ceded to the Union. This area or territory was to "be divided into distinct states."[88] And the inhabitants were never described as inhabitants of the territory, as if "territory" signified a definite civil division. Instead, Jefferson's draft spoke of "the settlers within any of the said states,"[89] and when this phrase was altered to read "the settlers in any territory so purchased and offered for sale,"[90] the new wording simply underscored the semantic fact that "territory" still meant an area of land not a unit of government.

Despite the essential radicalism of the plan presented by Jefferson and his committee, its main outlines underwent surprisingly little alteration in Congress. After debate, after some minor revision by the committee, and after a few amendments from the floor, the ordinance was adopted on April 23, 1784. Of the changes made, the most momentous in its ultimate consequences (though hardly in the minds of those who made the decision) was rejection by Congress of a provision that Jefferson had wished to include in the fundamental law of the territories. All governments there, whether temporary or permanent, would have been required to accept the principle "That after the year 1800 of the Christian aera, there shall neither be slavery nor involuntary servitude in any of the said states, otherwise than in punishment of crimes, whereof the party shall have been duly convicted to have been personally guilty."[91] This provision survived the first debates in Congress and retained its place in the revised draft of March 22, 1784.[92] Finally, however, it was challenged, and on April 19 it failed to win sufficient votes to secure its retention and was therefore deleted.[93] Eventually, of course, the provision was revived and incorporated in the Northwest Ordinance of 1787,[94] but its rejection in 1784 meant that it never attained the status of fundamental law, effective universally and uniformly throughout all new territories.

Though refusing to banish slavery from the territories, Congress was not averse to the idea of safeguarding certain natural rights by forming the provisions of the ordinance into a charter of compact and thus giving them the status of higher law. It was the more conservative implications of natural-law philosophy which especially interested the members. Congress widened the scope of Jefferson's proposed compact accordingly, and made it a vehicle for safeguarding property rights against confiscatory measures which radical territorial legislatures might be tempted to enact. As adopted by Congress the ordinance included three strongly worded clauses, not in the original draft, which forbade new governments to "interfere with the primary disposal of the soil by the United States," to impose any tax "on lands the property of the United States," or to tax "the lands of non resident proprietors" at a higher rate "than those of residents."[95]

For the rest, however, Congress in 1784 went along with most of the liberal features of Jefferson's plan, including its grant of virtually complete powers of self-government to western settlers at the very outset. But Congress insisted upon specifying more precisely the all-important moment when a government might legitimately be called into existence. Jefferson in earlier years had urged that western lands when once acquired by the United States should be given freely to actual settlers.[96] The actual taking up of land rather than the formality of purchase was to be the signal for establishment of a new government. Other members of Congress viewed ceded lands as an asset to be sold to shore up the shaky finances of the Union. Squatters not only defrauded the United States of expected revenues but also, through trespasses upon Indian lands, provoked reprisals and border warfare. Throughout the 1780s, therefore, Congress engaged in a succession of attempts to expel squatters from the Northwest.[97] Congress was hardly of a mind to permit the very persons who were illegally appropriating western land to take advantage of the privilege of unrestricted self-government which the Ordinance of 1784 proffered to *bona fide* settlers. Jefferson's original draft was thus modified so that forming a government could take place only after lands had actually been "offered for sale."[98] Congress, fearful of an initial period of anarchy, also insisted on spelling out its inherent power to preserve the peace prior to the time when land sale commenced and settlers set up adequate machinery of government.[99]

The alterations made by Congress constituted a serious inroad upon Jefferson's plan only to the extent that land sales were delayed. The amendments neither altered nor withdrew the right of inhabitants to establish their own government as soon as they wished, once they were in legal possession of their lands. In point of fact, of course, land sales *were* delayed—indeed, grossly delayed. Jefferson's ordinance, though formally adopted, became in the end a casualty of that delay. A committee under Jefferson presented to Congress a complementary measure for "establishing a land office for the United States" exactly one week after the adoption of the Ordinance of 1784,[100] but Congress argued for more than a year before so much as authorizing the surveys that were prerequisite to any sales of land. The measure that was finally enacted on May 20, 1785, moreover, was of a kind to delay, not to expedite, proceedings. It provided that sales would not commence until seven ranges had been platted.[101] And as late as April 1787 a committee of Congress reported that the surveyors were only halfway to this minimum objective.[102]

Under the circumstances, no effort was ever made to inaugurate the elaborate procedures that Jefferson had prescribed for converting the ordinance into a charter of compact. As time passed, disenchantment with the Ordinance of 1784 became apparent. Delegates in increasing numbers came to feel that Congress had unwisely proffered far too much power and control to future inhabitants of the western country. As early as 1785 the search was on for a territorial harness with tighter reins. By the spring of 1786 Congress was debating a plan which its sponsor, James Monroe, unabashedly described (and this in a letter to Jefferson himself!) as designed "in effect to be a colonial government similar to that which prevail'd in these States previous to the revolution, with this remarkable and important difference that when such districts shall contain the number of the least numerous of the '13. original States for the time being' they shall be admitted into the confederacy."[103]

This apparent repudiation of the constitutionalism that underlay the Ordinance of 1784 turned out to be neither final nor complete. In the summer of 1787 the pendulum swung back closer to its position in Jefferson's time. Though the Northwest Ordinance did not grant self-government to western settlers at the outset as Jefferson had proposed to do, it reiterated in language as impressive as his the promise that new states would receive, at a predetermined point in their cycle of growth, not only every privilege of republican self-government but also unqualified admission to the Union "on an equal footing with the original States, in all respects whatever."[104] Jefferson's idea of incorporating such guarantees in a solemn compact—an idea that Congress seemed ready to abandon in 1786—was revived, and not only revived but expanded.[105] Thanks to the skillful draftsmanship of Nathan Dane, the Articles of Compact of the Northwest Ordinance became a fully articulated bill of rights, comparable to those that prefaced most state constitutions and unlike anything that had as yet been drawn up as part of the fundamental law of the Confederation.

In the last analysis, there was no retreat from the consensus that had been painfully achieved in the years between 1754 and 1784. Constitutionalism—the idea that fundamental law could control even the process of expansion—remained somehow at the heart of the territorial system. Though appearances might often suggest that territorial regimes represented little else than the naked exercise of administrative authority by appointees of a largely indifferent central government, the long-run fact was otherwise. The promise that is constitutionalism was always there, and the promise was never in the end dishonored.

N O T E S

1. *Texas* v. *White,* 74 U.S. (7 Wall.) 700, at 725 (1869) (per Chief Justice Salmon P. Chase).
2. Memorial to Congress from the Legislative Council and House of Representatives of the Southwest Territory, September 18, 1794, printed in Clarence E. Carter and John Porter Bloom, eds., *The Territorial Papers of the United States* (Washington, D.C.: Government Printing Office, 1934–), 4:355, n. 21.
3. The Congress that met in 1774 as the First Continental Congress enjoyed, in effect, a continuous existence from that time until 1789, when it turned its authority over to the Congress established under the new Constitution. Until 1776 the proper designation of the body was unquestionably the Continental Congress. This term faded from use after the Declaration of Independence, which was made (according to its own words) by "The Representatives of the United States of America, in General Congress, Assembled." In writing out the first draft of the Articles of Confederation, John Dickinson originally used nearly the same phrase. Before submitting the document on July 12, 1776, however, Dickinson altered the phraseology to read simply "the United States assembled." In the course of the ensuing month and a half, Congress itself substituted the formula "the United States in Congress Assembled," and this became the official name in the Articles of Confederation. See the succession of drafts in *Journals of the Continental Congress, 1774–1789,* ed. Worthington C. Ford et al., 34 vols. (Library of Congress ed., Washington, D.C., 1904–37) [cited hereafter as *JCC*], 5:548 (Dickinson's manuscript draft, with emendations prior to presentation on July 12, 1776, arts. 11 and 12); 5:678 (printed draft of July 12, 1776, art. 12, and printed draft of August 20, 1776, art. 10); 9:910 (final version as adopted November 15, 1777, art. 5 et passim). After the ratification of the Articles in 1781 the designation Continental Congress is definitely incorrect. It is anachronistic, if nothing else, when applied to Congress after the Declaration of Independence. See "Biblio-

graphical Notes," *JCC,* 6:1117–28 (items 89, 98, 102, 109, 143, 144, and 145). Though little can be done now by way of correction, the nineteenth-century decision to apply the label "Papers of the Continental Congress" to the whole body of archives from 1774 to 1789, and the early twentieth-century decision to reprint the *Journal of the United States in Congress Assembled* under the title *Journals of the Continental Congress* seem definitely misguided. In the present paper I will refer simply to Congress, and will distinguish it (where necessary) from the Congress established under the Constitution by adopting the phrase commonly used in the early nineteenth century, "the old Congress."

4. The resolutions of October 10, 1780, are analyzed more fully in the latter part of this paper. They are printed in *JCC,* 18:915–16, but in a way that invites confusion.

5. Albany Plan of Union, July 10, 1754, printed (in definitive critical text) in the *Papers of Benjamin Franklin,* ed. Leonard W. Labaree et al. (New Haven: Yale University Press, 1959–), 5:374–92; the quotations are from p. 387 and pp. 389–90.

6. Royal Proclamation of October 7, 1863; in William Macdonald, ed., *Select Charters and Other Documents Illustrative of American History, 1606–1775* (New York: Macmillan Co., 1899), pp. 267–72, at 269. On the formulation of the policy embodied in the proclamation, see Jack M. Sosin, *Whitehall and the Wilderness: The Middle West in British Colonial Policy, 1760–1775* (Lincoln: University of Nebraska Press, 1961), chap. 3.

7. Macdonald, *Charters,* pp. 270–71.

8. Ibid., p. 271. The area which the king's proclamation would "reserve under our sovereignty, protection, and domination, for the use of the said Indians," is shown in Charles O. Paullin, *Atlas of the Historical Geography of the United States,* ed. John K. Wright (Washington, D.C.: Carnegie Institution of Washington and the American Geographical Society of New York, 1932), plate 41A. If the language of the proclamation with respect to watersheds is taken literally, then Georgia, alone among the states, was not affected by the proclamation line. Though Paullin so represents it, the intention was surely otherwise.

9. Proposed Articles of Confederation, submitted by Franklin, July 21, 1775, arts. 11 and 5, respectively; printed in *JCC,* 2:195–99, at 198 and 196. Franklin's original manuscript is in the National Archives Building, Washington, D.C., among the Papers of the Continental Congress, 1774–89, item 47 (Articles of Confederation, etc.), folios 1 et seq. This entire collection has been microfilmed as National Archives Microfilm Publication M247, and this particular document is on roll 61. The collection in the National Archives and the microfilm reproduction will be cited hereafter as Papers Cont. Cong. (M247), with the item number, folio number, and other information.

10. Draft of Articles of Confederation and Perpetual Union, as reported to Congress on July 12, 1776, art. 18; in *JCC,* 5:546–54. The original report, in the handwriting of John Dickinson, is in Papers Cont. Cong., item 47, fols. 9–20 (M247, roll 61). This first draft was printed as an eight-page pamphlet for the use of Congress, under stern injunctions of secrecy. A copy is in Papers Cont. Cong., item 47, fols. 21–28 (M247, roll 61), and the text of this printed version is reproduced in *JCC,* 5:674–89. One

important manuscript draft clause was not included in the printed version (see section [i] of note 11 below). Though the manuscript was delivered to the printers on July 13, the day after it was submitted (*JCC,* 6:1123), there may possibly have been some action in Congress before the actual printing began. Some support for this surmise may be found in the fact that the secretary of Congress, Charles Thomson, used Dickinson's original manuscript, instead of one of the printed copies of the first draft, to record in the form of marginal notations the changes voted in the course of the midsummer debates.

By contrast, when a second printing of the Articles was made, incorporating amendments adopted through August 20, Thomson used a copy of this six-page second printing to keep track of subsequent alterations. The copy in question, endorsed "Articles of Confederation belonging to the Secretary of Congress, corrected at the table," is in Papers Cont. Cong., item 47, fols. 69–75 (M247, roll 61); additional copies of the second printing, likewise with annotations, are found ibid., fols. 29–35 and 111–16. In this second printed version the provisions that had been marked "postponed" in the margin of the first manuscript draft were simply omitted.

11. Dickinson's manuscript draft contained at least three distinct provisions relating to the Indians, all of them borrowed from Franklin's proposal of 1775. Only one of these survived the debates of 1776, and it was hedged about with qualifications in the completed Articles as approved on November 15, 1777. Specifically: (i) Dickinson's manuscript draft required Congress "as soon as may be" to enter into treaties with the various Indian nations providing for "their limits to be ascertained, their Lands to be secured to them, and not encroached on." This was eliminated even before the draft was printed. See *JCC,* 5:549 (art. 14 and notes 2 and 3), and compare 679–80. (ii) All further purchases of land from the Indians by private persons or individual colonies (that is, states) were to be illegal and invalid until "the Limits of the Colonies are ascertained," and thereafter purchases outside those limits were to be made only by the federal government and "for the general benefit of all the United Colonies." *JCC,* 5:549, 679–80. When debate began, this was postponed until the provision for setting western limits to individual states could be considered. When the latter provision was defeated, the clause relating to purchases from the Indians died with it. *JCC,* 5:680, n. 2. (iii) Dickinson's draft gave Congress the power of "Regulating the Trade, and managing all Affairs with the Indians." During the earliest debates, this was amended to apply only to "Indians, not members of any of the States." *JCC,* 5:682 (art. 18 in version of July 12, 1776; art. 14 in version of Aug. 20). A further proviso was added later and appears in the completed Articles as follows: "provided that the legislative right of any State within its own limits be not infringed or violated." *JCC,* 9:919 (art. 9). (iv) Apart from these three specific provisions, one other point should be noted. In his proposal of 1775 Franklin included a stringent restriction which read as follows: "No Colony shall engage in an offensive War with any Nation of Indians without the Consent of the Congress, . . . who are first to consider the Justice and Necessity of such War." *JCC,* 2:197 (art. 10). Dickinson's draft included a watered-down equivalent, which first forbade any state to wage war of any sort without the consent of Congress, but then made exceptions. This provision

received the approval of Congress without apparent challenge and was included in the final version of the Articles. *JCC,* 5:549 (art. 13 of Dickinson draft); 9:912 (art. 6 of final version).

12. *JCC,* 5:550–51, 682 (art. 18).

13. *JCC,* 5:549, 680 (art. 15). When debate began, this article was postponed until the question of limiting the western claims of the states could be considered. When the decision went against setting western boundaries, this guarantee was dropped.

14. *JCC,* 5:551, n. 1.

15. John Adams, "Notes of Debates," July 25, 1776; reprinted in *JCC,* 6:1076–77.

16. Ibid., pp. 1082–83 (August 2, 1776).

17. *JCC,* 5:688, n. 1.

18. *JCC,* 5:682. Two related provisions (as mentioned in notes 11 and 13 above) were permanently dropped at the same time.

19. *JCC,* 9:806–7. New York, Pennsylvania, and Maryland favored the measure; Delaware (which presumably would have done so) had no representative present. On the continuing agitation of the question since midsummer debates of 1776, see the letters of October 24, November 21 and 24, 1776, February 10 [i.e., 16?] and August 25, 1777, printed in Edmund C. Burnett, ed., *Letters of Members of the Continental Congress,* 8 vols. (Washington, D.C.: Carnegie Institute of Washington, 1921–36), 2:140–41 (in note 3), 161, 162–63, 257, 468. In February 1777, Thomas Burke of North Carolina pointed to Pennsylvania, Maryland, and New Jersey as leaders of the movement for limitation, which Burke bitterly opposed. Ibid., p. 257.

20. *JCC,* 9:807–8. One of the two representatives from New Jersey followed the lead of the unanimous Maryland delegation, but the other states voted solidly against the motion. Seven months after submitting the Articles to the states, Congress devoted parts of three days in late June 1778 to a consideration of objections raised and changes proposed by the various legislatures, but all were voted down. *JCC,* 11:631–32 (Md., June 22), 639 (R.I., June 23), 649–50 (N.J., June 25).

21. In *The Federalist,* no. 43, James Madison commented that "The eventual establishment of *new States,* seems to have been overlooked by the compilers of that instrument [the Articles of Confederation]. We have seen the inconvenience of this omission, and the assumption of power into which Congress have been led by it." Jacob E. Cooke, ed., *The Federalist* (Middletown: Wesleyan University Press, 1961), p. 290. Madison assumed without question that the requisite power was unequivocally granted by the new Constitution of 1787 in the clause that read: "The Congress shall have Power to dispose of and make all needful Rules and Regulations respecting the Territory or other Property belonging to the United States." Art. 4, sec. 3, clause 2 (cited hereafter as the Territorial Clause). In the Constitutional Convention Madison had proposed a grant of power "To institute temporary Governments for New States arising" in "the unappropriated lands of the U. States." Max Farrand, ed., *The Records of the Federal Convention of 1787,* 4 vols. (New Haven: Yale University Press, 1911–37), 2:324 (August 18, 1787); hereafter cited as Farrand, *Records.* Madison was obviously satisfied that the Territorial Clause covered the matter, for he never

insisted upon his own phraseology after the Territorial Clause was adopted on August 30, 1787. Ibid., pp. 458–59, 466.

Chief Justice Roger B. Taney was to agree with Madison that the old Congress lacked power to legislate for the territories, but he rejected the view that the Territorial Clause cured the defect by bestowing the requisite power on the new Congress. The result was a highly ingenious argument, fully developed in Taney's opinion of 1857 deciding the *Dred Scott* case. After pointing out that the old Congress possessed no power under the Articles of Confederation to legislate on territorial matters, Taney proceeded to argue that in adopting the Northwest Ordinance Congress had exercised a quite different species of authority, essentially that of "a congress of ambassadors, authorized to represent separate nations." According to this view Congress had simply arranged a "compact or treaty" among the "sovereignities" who were ceding and accepting the territory in question, and who "had the right to exercise absolute dominion over it." Taney summed the argument up as follows: "It was by a Congress, representing the authority of these several and separate sovereignities, and acting under their authority and command (but not from any authority derived from the Articles of Confederation), that the instrument usually called the ordinance of 1787 was adopted." *Scott* v. *Sandford*, 60 U.S. (19 How). 393, at 430–31 (1857). On the basis of this line of reasoning, Taney was able to uphold the antislavery provision of the Northwest Ordinance as part of a treaty among sovereigns, while denying the validity of the similar antislavery provision of the Missouri Compromise. The latter was a mere legislative act, and it was not authorized by the Constitution, according to Taney, because the Territorial Clause did not apply to territory acquired after the adoption of the Constitution. *Scott* v. *Sandford*, at 432–33. The paradoxical (but intended) result of Taney's ingenious argument was that the ordinances of the old Congress, although admittedly ultra vires, had unquestionable legal validity, whereas a statute to the same effect by the new Congress, enacted under color of a seemingly relevant provision of the Constitution, was void.

22. Peter Force, ed., *American Archives*, 5th ser., vol. 3 (Washington, D.C., 1853), p. 178.

23. *JCC*, 5:688, n. 1. In a letter to the Secret Committee of Congress on December 1, 1776, Silas Deane made the shrewd proposal that a new state should "be entitled to a voice in Congress" as soon as it was ready to assume its due share "of the publick expenses of the continent, or United States." Force, *American Archives*, 5th ser., vol. 3, pp. 1020–21.

24. The most lucid account is by Merrill Jensen, *The Articles of Confederation: An Interpretation of the Social-Constitutional History of the American Revolution, 1774–1781* (3d printing; Madison: University of Wisconsin Press, 1959), pp. 120–24, 133–34, 150–60, 192–218, 225–38. Masses of detailed information are presented by Thomas P. Abernethy, *Western Lands and the American Revolution* (New York: Appleton-Century Co., for the Institute for Research in the Social Sciences, University of Virginia, 1937), especially chaps. 13, 17–20.

25. Declaration of Maryland, dated December 15, 1778, and presented to Congress on January 6, 1779; quoted in Jensen, *Articles*, p. 202. The declaration, mentioned but not printed in *JCC*, 13:29, is in Papers Cont. Cong.,

item 70 (Maryland and Delaware State Papers), fols. 293–99 (M247, roll 84).

26. George Mason of Virginia analyzed the effect of the clause with great shrewdness in a letter to Richard Henry Lee, dated April 12, 1779. Kate Mason Rowland, *The Life of George Mason, 1725–1792,* 2 vols. (New York: G. P. Putnam's Sons, 1892), 1:320–22.

27. Motion of Joseph Jones (Va.), seconded by James Madison (Va.), September 6, 1780. *JCC,* 17:808. A clause of this sort was designed, as Madison made clear in a later letter, to prevent the benefit of the grant from being "transferred from the public to a few landmongers." Madison to Jones, October 17, 1780, in Burnett, *Letters of Members,* 5:424; see also pp. 380–81, 399, 411–12, 417, 454.

28. See the present writer's argument to the same effect applied to a different situation, in "The American Civil War as a Constitutional Crisis," *American Historical Review* 69 (January 1964): 327–52, especially pp. 327–28.

29. *JCC,* 14:617–18. The instructions from the Virginia legislature, dated December 19, 1778, were presented to Congress on May 20, 1779.

30. Ibid., pp. 619–22. These instructions, adopted on December 15, 1778, and thus slightly antedating those of Virginia, accompanied the declaration that had been read to Congress on January 6, 1779 (see note 26 above). The instructions themselves had been held in reserve on that occasion, but on May 21, 1779, the day after Virginia proposed a confederation without Maryland, the delegates of the latter state laid their complete instructions before Congress, asking that they be spread upon the journals.

31. Letters of May 22, 1779; in Burnett, *Letters of Members,* 4:224–25, 226.

32. See Abernethy, *Western Lands,* pp. 224–25, 228–29.

33. Resolution adopted Oct. 30, 1779, after several amendments and roll calls. *JCC,* 15:1226–30. See also Burnett, *Letters of Members,* 4:500–513.

34. General Assembly of Virginia, Remonstrance to Congress, December 14, 1779; in Rowland, *Life of George Mason,* 1:342–43. Though the presentation of the remonstrance on April 28, 1780, is recorded in *JCC,* 16:398, the text is not printed there.

35. Members of the New York delegation in Congress began to urge such action as early as November 30, 1779. Two important and revealing letters of that date and of January 29, 1780, are in Burnett, *Letters of Members,* 4:530–31; 5:20–22. Opinion in Congress was growing more moderate. In November 1779 the North Carolina delegates observed that New Hampshire, Massachusetts, and Connecticut, "who formerly insisted strenuously on their claims to Lands Westerly, are indifferent about them." Ibid., 4:508.

36. *JCC,* 16:236. The text of the New York act, not printed in *JCC,* is in Papers Cont. Cong., item 67 (New York State Papers), vol. 2, fol. 250 (M247, roll 81). The terms of the original act were recited in the final deed of cession executed by New York on March 1, 1781. Carter and Bloom, *Territorial Papers,* 2:3–5.

37. *JCC,* 17:559–60.

38. Ibid., p. 580.

39. Ibid., pp. 806–7. Quotations are from the original report, which is printed in *JCC* under date of final adoption. Alterations made by Congress are indicated by lining out.

40. See Jones to Jefferson, June 30, and Jones to Washington, September 6, 1780; in Burnett, *Letters of Members*, 5:244–46, 363–65.
41. *JCC*, 17:806–7. In particular, the praise of New York was toned down, and the phrase quoted above was entirely stricken.
42. Ibid., p. 808. See also note 27 above.
43. See Jones to Madison, October 2, 1780, in Burnett, *Letters of Members*, 5:399.
44. *JCC*, 18:815–16. The committee reported on September 15, 1780, debate began on September 18, and the resolutions, as amended, were adopted on October 10. Ibid., pp. 828, 836, 915–16.
45. Jones's original motion to disallow private purchases from the Indians bristled with such peremptory phrases as "any private person . . . whatsoever" and "absolutely void." See note 27 above. According to the version that came finally before the House, no purchases from the Indians, unless "ratified by lawful authority," were to "be deemed valid or ratified by Congress." Even so, the modified clause failed to carry. *JCC*, 18:915–16 (October 10, 1780). The resolutions as reported by the committee on September 15, 1780 (in manuscript form, with subsequent deletions and interlineations), are in Papers Cont. Cong., item 20 (Reports of Committees), vol. 2, fols. 245–47 (M247, roll 29). The resolutions as adopted on October 10 are entered under their date in the manuscript journal, Papers Cont. Cong., item 1 (Rough Journals), vol. 29 (M247, roll 11), and were included in the contemporaneously published journal. See the reprint: *Journals of the American Congress: From 1774 to 1788*, 4 vols. (Washington, D.C.: Way & Gideon, 1823), 3:535. In *JCC* a single printing of the document is made to do double duty. The committee report is not printed under its date (September 15), but under the date of final adoption of the resolutions. *JCC*, 18:915–16. Typographical indications are supposed to enable the reader to arrive at the texts both of the report and of the final resolutions, but the result is ambiguous and potentially misleading.
46. An Ordinance for the Government of the Territory of the United States Northwest of the River Ohio, July 13, 1787; Articles of Compact, art. 4; in Carter and Bloom, *Territorial Papers*, 2:39–50, at 47.
47. Resolution of October 14, 1783. *JCC*, 25:678–79.
48. U.S., *Constitution*, Art. 4, sec. 4.
49. Thomas Jefferson, *Papers of Thomas Jefferson*, ed. Julian P. Boyd et al. (Princeton: Princeton University Press, 1950–), 1:363, 383.
50. See Thomas D. Clark, *A History of Kentucky* (New York: Prentice-Hall, 1937), chap. 6.
51. Octavius Pickering, *The Life of Timothy Pickering*, 2 vols. (Boston: Little, Brown, & Co., 1867), 1:548.
52. Ordinance of 1784 (in all its successive drafts). Jefferson, *Papers*, 6:603, 608, 614.
53. Thomas Paine, *Public Good: Being an Examination into the Claim of Virginia to the Vacant Western Territory, and of the Right of the United States to the Same: To Which Is Added, Proposals for Laying off a New State, to Be Applied as a Fund for . . . Redeeming the National Debt* (Philadelphia: John Dunlap, 1780); reprinted in *The Complete Writings of Thomas Paine*, ed. Philip S. Foner, 2 vols. (New York: Citadel Press, 1945), 2:303–33, at 332. The new state would be considered a part of the

Union from the beginning and would send a representative to Congress with a right to debate "but not to vote . . . till after the expiration of seven years."

54. U.S., *Constitution*, Art. 6, clause 2.

55. A three-man committee to "prepare a plan for temporary government of western territory" was appointed on February 3, 1784, consisting of Jefferson (of Va.) as chairman, and Jeremiah Townley Chase (Md.) and David Howell (R.I.) as members. Secretary of Congress, Journal of Committee Assignments, as cited by Boyd in Jefferson, *Papers,* 6:585. The committee filed its report on March 1, 1784, the manuscript written entirely in Jefferson's hand. The report was read on the third, debate began on the eighth, and the measure was recommitted on the seventeenth. A revised report was presented on the twenty-second and read on the twenty-fourth. After further amendment the document was adopted on April 23, 1784. All printed texts of the several versions of the Ordinance of 1784 are superseded and all references to the original manuscripts are rendered unnecessary by the definitive critical texts established by Julian P. Boyd in his edition of Jefferson, *Papers,* 6:581–617, which furnishes an elaborate historical introduction and notes all variant readings in the three successive versions; that is to say: (i) the original Report of Western Territory, March 1 (pp. 603–5); (ii) its Revised Report, March 22 (pp. 607–9); and (iii) the Ordinance of 1784 as enacted, April 23 (613–15).

56. Report, March 1, 1784; in Jefferson, *Papers,* 6:605.

57. Ordinance as enacted, April 23, 1784; in Jefferson, *Papers,* 6:615. The change was made in the course of debate after submission of the revised report. See ibid., pp. 609, 613, n. 27.

58. Northwest Ordinance, July 13, 1787; in Carter and Bloom, *Territorial Papers,* 2:46.

59. See notes 27 and 45 above.

60. Madison to Jones, October 17, 1780, in Burnett, *Letters of Members,* 5:424. In a letter of November 21 to the same correspondent, Madison remarked dryly: "I do not believe there is any serious design in Congress to gratify the avidity of land mongers, but the best security for their virtue . . . will be to keep it out of their power." Ibid., p. 454.

61. Condition 7 of the Virginia act of January 2, 1781, as quoted in the report upon it made by a committee of Congress, *JCC,* 25:561–62 (September 13, 1783).

62. Ibid., pp. 562–64.

63. Virginia, act of October 30, 1783, as recited in the state's deed of cession of March 1, 1784. Carter and Bloom, *Territorial Papers,* 2:6–9.

64. Ibid., pp. 12–18.

65. Stephen Higginson (Mass.) to Theophilus Parsons, April 1783, in Burnett, *Letters of Members,* 7:123. Color is given to this charge by a remark of Robert R. Livingston to the governor of New York recommending that in the face of efforts "to appropriate all the western lands to the use of the United States," their state should "contrive to make a sacrifice of part to secure the remainder." Livingston to George Clinton, November 30, 1779, ibid., 4:530.

66. *JCC,* 18:915; 25:562–64.

67. U.S., *Constitution,* Art. 4, sec. 3.

68. Preliminary articles of peace between the United States and Great Britain, containing precisely the terms that ultimately became final, were signed on November 30, 1782. The text reached Congress on March 12, 1783, and was discussed for four days in supposed secrecy, which, however, did not prevent publication of the peace terms in the newspapers. *JCC,* 25:924–26 (Madison's notes of debates; there were no entries in the official journal). In the final negotiations France and Spain had not been consulted, hence it was their deferred signing on January 20, 1783, that brought the preliminary treaty into effect and that led to a British proclamation of February 4 ending hostilities. News both of the signing and of the proclamation reached America on April 9 (Burnett, *Letters of Members,* 7:132, 134), though the documents themselves were not available to be read in Congress until the next day (ibid., pp. 134–35; *JCC,* 25:957). On April 11 Congress proclaimed the cessation of hostilities (*JCC,* 24:238–41), and on the fifteenth it ratified the preliminary articles (ibid., pp. 241–52). The final treaty (to be distinguished from the preliminary articles, though the terms were not altered) was signed in Paris on September 3.
69. *JCC,* 25:955–57 (Madison's notes of debates). The official journal does not record the motion and the ensuing debate.
70. *JCC,* 24:384–86.
71. *JCC,* 25:677–78.
72. Ibid., p. 679. This substitute was moved by David Howell (R.I.), who was to be one of the three members of the committee that drafted the Ordinance of 1784. Jefferson, chairman of that committee, was not yet in attendance, and the vote of Virginia was cast by Madison and Arthur Lee against the proposal, which received the favorable votes of only Rhode Island, Connecticut, and Maryland.
73. *JCC,* 25:678, 694. After the defeat of Howell's motion, this substitute was adopted without a roll call. Ibid., p. 680.
74. See note 6 above.
75. Ordinance of 1784; in Jefferson, *Papers,* 6:608, 614; and cf. p. 603.
76. The new states would not be hampered by their initial adoption of the statutes of an existing state, for the Ordinance of 1784 specifically provided "that such laws nevertheless shall be subject to alteration by their ordinary legislature." Ibid., pp. 603, 608, 614. Nor was participation completely denied, for the governments of new areas were entitled from the moment of their organization "to keep a member in Congress, with a right of debating, but not of voting." Ibid., p. 615; and cf. pp. 604, 609.
77. Ibid., p. 615; and cf. pp. 604, 608–9.
78. Montesquieu, *The Spirit of Laws,* trans. Thomas Nugent, 3d ed. (London, 1758), 1, 175 (book 8, chap. 16).
79. See, for example, George Clinton's statement, quoting Montesquieu, in "The Letters of Cato" (no. 3, October 25, 1787), reprinted in John D. Lewis, ed., *Anti-Federalists versus Federalists* (San Francisco: Chandler Publishing Co., 1967), p. 190; and Alexander Hamilton's answer in *The Federalist,* no. 9 (November 21, 1787), ibid., p. 262.
80. Jones to Washington, October 1780; in Burnett, *Letters of Members,* 5:396.
81. *JCC,* 17:808 (September 6, 1780).
82. Some three years later, on June 5, 1783, Theodorick Bland proposed that the ceded territory "be laid off in districts not exceeding two degrees of

Latitude and three degrees of Longitude." *JCC*, 24:385. In the region just north of the Ohio River, this would mean a rectangle of approximately one hundred and forty miles from north to south and one hundred and sixty miles from east to west, with an area of twenty-two thousand four hundred square miles. It is interesting to note that the documents relating to cessions by the states employed the formula proposed by Jones, whereas the Ordinance of 1784 followed the example set by Bland and fixed the boundaries and areas of the new states by parallels of latitude two degrees apart, together with meridians of longitude.

83. The smallest, Indiana, has an area of 36,000 square miles, ranking thirty-eighth among the fifty states.
84. See note 77 above.
85. Delaware in 1790 had a free population of 50,207, plus a slave population of 8,887 [U.S., Census Office, First Census (1790)], *Return of the Whole Number of Persons* (Washington, D.C.: W. Duane, 1802), p. 3.
86. These conclusions are based on an analysis of estimated populations of individual colonies from 1610 to 1780, as compiled by Stella H. Sutherland in U.S., Bureau of the Census, *Historical Statistics of the United States, Colonial Times to 1957* (Washington, D.C.: Government Printing Office, 1960), p. 756; see also pp. 743–44. The figures are for the white population; the free population would be somewhat larger.
87. *Oxford English Dictionary*, s.v. "territory," definition 1(b).
88. Ordinance, April 23, 1784; in Jefferson, *Papers*, 6:613. In his original draft Jefferson wrote "formed" instead of "divided" (ibid., p. 603), thus repeating the exact language of the resolution of October 10, 1780. *JCC*, 18:915.
89. Report, March 1, 1784; in Jefferson, *Papers*, 6:603.
90. Revised report, March 22, 1784, carried unchanged into the Ordinance as enacted April 23; in Jefferson, *Papers*, 6:606, n. 10, 608, 614.
91. Report, March 1, 1784; in Jefferson, *Papers*, 6:604. This was the last in the set of five provisos stating the principles which "both the temporary and permanent governments" were to accept "as their basis."
92. Revised report, March 22, 1784; in Jefferson, *Papers*, 6:608; the word "duly" was deleted.
93. *JCC*, 16:247. Actually, a majority of the states that voted (six out of eleven) and a majority of the delegates present (sixteen out of twenty-three) favored the provision, but the rules of Congress required an affirmative vote by a clear majority of all the thirteen states in the Union (i.e., seven states). Technically the vote was six states in favor, three opposed, and one divided, with one other state (N.J.) excluded from the count because no quorum of its delegates was present. (Its lone representative was in fact favorable.) Virginia stood among the states opposed, for Jefferson was outvoted in his own delegation. According to him, the vote of Virginia would have been divided "had not one of its delegates been sick in bed." Jefferson to Madison, April 25, 1784; in Jefferson, *Papers*, 7:118. But the presence of this delegate would not have altered the final result, for what was needed was a complete shift of Virginia from the negative to the affirmative column. More decisive would have been the attendance of the second delegate from New Jersey, John Beatty (likewise "sick in his chambers," according to Jefferson's report). Had he been present and had he voted for the antislavery clause (as Jefferson expected him to do), the

provision would have carried regardless of Virginia's adverse or divided vote. See the record of attendance in Burnett, *Letters of Members,* 7:lxx, lxxvii.

94. On March 16, 1785, eleven months after the rejection just discussed, a new antislavery clause was introduced by Rufus King (Mass.), seconded by William Ellery (R.I.), in the form of an amendment to the previous year's ordinance. *JCC,* 28:164. It was referred to a committee composed of the two movers, together with David Howell (also R.I.), who had been one of the drafters of the original ordinance. The committee added a clause for the rendition of fugitive slaves, thus providing a basis for compromise, and reported the amendment favorably on April 6, 1785. Ibid., p. 239. On May 1, William Grayson (Va.) wrote Madison that "Mr. King of Massachusetts has a resolution ready drawn which he reserves till the Ordinance is passed for preventing slavery in the new State. I expect Seven States may be found liberal enough to adopt it." Burnett, *Letters of Members,* 8:110. Further action on the proposal was, in fact, reserved until July 13, 1787, when the provision was adopted at the very last moment as an amendment to the Northwest Ordinance, proposed by Nathan Dane in King's absence. *JCC,* 32:343.

95. Ordinance as adopted April 23, 1784, provisos 3, 5, and 7; in Jefferson, *Papers,* 6:614–15; see also editor's notes, 609–13. For other amendments proposed and acted upon in Congress, see *JCC,* 26:257–59, 277.

96. When the Articles of Confederation were under discussion Jefferson proposed an amendment invalidating future purchases of land from Indians except by the United States, providing that such land "when purchased shall be given freely to those who may be permitted to seat them." *JCC,* 5:680, n.

97. On September 22, 1783, Congress by proclamation forbade "all persons from making settlements on lands inhabited or claimed by Indians" and "from purchasing or receiving any . . . cession of such lands . . . without the express authority . . . of . . . Congress." *JCC,* 25:602. Two years later, on June 15, 1785, it issued another proclamation against "such unwarrantable intrusions," warning squatters to depart "without loss of time." *JCC,* 28:462. Two years later still, on April 16, 1787, Secretary at War Henry Knox reported that there has been a "usurpation of the public lands by a body of armed men," and warned Congress that "if such audacious defiance of the power of the United States be suffered with impunity a precedent will be established, to wrest all the immense property of the western territory out of the hands of the public." *JCC,* 32:213. After passage of the Ordinance of 1787, yet another report to Congress urged stringent punishment of "lawless persons" committing "depredations" upon Indians. *JCC,* 33:410–11 (July 26, 1787).

98. Two changes were involved: (i) procedures were to be initiated, not (as Jefferson had phrased it) by "the settlers within any of the said states," but by "the settlers on any territory so . . . offered for sale" (see Jefferson, *Papers,* 6:603; 605, n. 2; 606, n. 10; 608; 610, n. 7; 614); and (ii) the compact would become unalterable only "from and after the sale of any part of the territory of such state" (ibid., pp. 613, n. 27; 615).

99. The interpolated provision read as follows in its final form: "That measures not inconsistent with the principles of the confederation, and neces-

sary for the preservation of peace and good order among the settlers in any
of the said new states, until they shall assume a temporary government as
aforesaid, may from time to time be taken by the United States in Congress assembled." Ordinance, April 23, 1784; in Jefferson, *Papers,* 6:615.
This represented a very great toning down of the language of the amendment first proposed on April 21 by Jacob Read (S.C.) and James McHenry
(Md.), which would have provided that prior to establishment of a temporary government "the said settlers shall be ruled by magistrates to be
appointed by . . . Congress . . . , and under such laws and regulations as . . .
Congress . . . shall direct." *JCC,* 26:259. The provision finally adopted was
moved (in slightly different language) by Elbridge Gerry (Mass.) and
seconded by Hugh Williamson (N.C.) on April 23. Ibid., p. 274.
100. Report of April 30, 1784; in Jefferson, *Papers,* 7:140–43; see also p. 118.
The committee had been appointed on March 2, the day after the filing of
the report that led to the Ordinance of 1784.
101. An Ordinance for Ascertaining the Mode of Disposing of Lands in the
Western Territory, May 20, 1785; in Carter and Bloom, *Territorial Papers,*
2:12–18.
102. Report of the Board of Treasury, April 4, 1787; in Carter and Bloom,
Territorial Papers, 2:24–25. See also the report of a committee which on
April 25 recommended a more rapid system of survey and sale. *JCC,*
32:238–41.
103. Monroe to Jefferson, May 11, 1786; in Jefferson, *Papers,* 9:511. Mild
though Jefferson's reply turned out to be, a rebuke of the newly revived
colonialism was surely implicit in his statement that any plan for the
government of western settlers should "treat them as fellow citizens" and,
by giving them "a just share in their own government," cause them to
"pride themselves in a union with us." Equally clear was Jefferson's warning that "to treat them as subjects" would cause them to "abhor us as
masters, and break from us in defiance." Jefferson to Monroe, Paris, July
9; ibid., 10:113.
104. An Ordinance for the Government of the Territory of the United States
Northwest of the River Ohio, July 13, 1787; in Carter and Bloom, *Territorial Papers,* 2:39–50, at 49 (fifth article of compact).
105. Ibid., pp. 46–49.

The Northwest Ordinance and the Principle of Territorial Evolution

ROBERT F. BERKHOFER, JR.

TO THE REVOLUTIONARY GENERATION, the thirteen states singly and in confederation were *"novus ordo saeclorum,"* as the Continental Congress proudly proclaimed on the Great Seal of the United States. What distinguished this "new order" from the old one in Europe, in the opinion of the era, were the enlightened ideals and, more significantly, practices of religious freedom, economic opportunity, relative social equality, and, most important, republican government. In short, Americans had established a way of life that men of the time termed "republican." They had achieved this way of life upon a scale never before seen in history, and they saw themselves as leaders on the path of progress. As a result, they believed their institutions ought to be consciously transformed in line with republican ideals. Thus they sought deliberate innovation in government, church-state relations, foreign policy, and society by means of constitutions, statutes, and treaties. In light of this general spirit of innovative idealism, the United States territorial system must be viewed as an attempt to do for colonial relations what had been done otherwise to bring forth a new nation upon new principles. The Northwest Ordinance was therefore the culmination of American thinking about the nature of a colonial system for a republican empire.[1]

The new colonial system provided for colonies to evolve from dependency to statehood equal in privileges and duties with those of the original thirteen. The innovative principle was equality with the mother country. But such equality was to be achieved only after a period of subordinate colonial status. Both the granting of full statehood and the provision for territorial evolution were consistent with republican ideals.

Research for the background of this article was made possible by summer grants from the University of Minnesota Graduate School (1964) and the American Philosophical Society (1968).

Any status less than eventual statehood would have been a betrayal of the very principle upon which Americans had fought the Revolution. After all, the issue between the colonies and England was representation. Americans claimed that their interests could only be maintained in Parliament by men from their own locale. Otherwise, they were being ruled without their consent in violation of basic English and natural rights and thus relieved of loyalty to the king and England, as they declared in independence. Therefore, in order to be consistent with their principles as well as to attract trans-Appalachian settlers who held the same opinions to the Confederation, western men would have to be represented in governments of their own choice confined to their own locale.

Americans from the beginning of the Revolution proposed that the "western territory" be laid off as a new state or states. As early as December 1776, Silas Deane proposed that a part of the territory be sold to a company of associates to help defray war expenses and that this portion constitute a "distinct state."[2] Thomas Paine published, in late 1780, similar ideas in a pamphlet whose long title indicated its contents: *Public Good: Being an Examination into the Claim of Virginia to the Vacant Western Territory, and of the Right of the United States to the Same: To Which Is Added, Proposals for Laying off a New State, to Be Applied as a Fund for Carrying on the War, or Redeeming the National Debt.*[3] By advocating the right of the Continental Congress to establish new states, Paine, at the behest of Maryland interests, had entered the prickly cession controversy of whether Virginia and certain other "landed" states should hold the West for their exclusive advantage or whether this land should benefit all the states fighting the war.[4] Delegates from all states, regardless of their position on cession, favored the creation of new states in the West. Maryland's representatives, in opposing Virginia's claims, urged always that the area be "parcelled out at proper times into convenient, free, and independent governments."[5] A Continental Congress Finance Committee in 1778 suggested "that it be convenanted with the states that the Lands set off shall be erected into separate and independent states, to be admitted into the Union, to have Representation in Congress, and to have free Governments."[6] Finally in September 1780 Congress recommended that the landed states cede their claims to the United States, and immediately the Virginia delegates proposed an amendment providing for the formation of new states from any ceded territory.[7] As the amendment was adopted on October 10, it read:

That the unappropriated lands that may be ceded or relinquished to the United States, by any particular states, . . . shall be disposed of for the common benefit of the United States and be settled and

formed into distinct republican states, which shall become members
of the federal union, and have the same rights of sovereignty,
freedom, and independence, as the other states . . . . [8]

By the end of the Revolution, the question was definitely settled; the army
officers' petition for western lands, George Washington's recommendations
for handling Indian affairs, and the congressional Indian Affairs Committee
all assumed that at least one new state would be formed in the West.[9]

Equally well agreed upon by the end of the Revolution, it seems, was
the principle that such statehood must evolve from a previous condition
of subordination. The pressure of army officers for pay and lands, the
plight of the United States Treasury, and the prospect of Virginia's cession
of her western territory north of the Ohio River caused Congress during
the summer and fall of 1783 to talk about a mode of government for possible western states during their "infancy," as one congressman significantly
phrased it.[10] From these conversations came the resolution of October 15,
which led eventually to Jefferson's proposals. It ordered a committee

to report a plan, consistent with the principles of the Confederation,
for connecting with the Union by a temporary government, the
purchasers and inhabitants of said district, until their number and
circumstances shall entitle them to form a permanent constitution
for themselves, and as citizens of a free, sovereign and independent
State, to be admitted to a representation in the Union; provided
always, that such constitution not be incompatible with republican
principles, which are the basis of the constitution of the
respective states of the Union.[11]

Implicit in this resolution was the requirement that the committee produce
a plan reconciling republican government with the necessity of evolution.
Otherwise why provide for "a temporary government"?

Jefferson's plan of 1784, like those of his successors, provided for such
evolution through a series of stages.[12] The first stage[13] began when the
settlers within one of his proposed states received congressional authority
to establish a "temporary government," to adopt the constitution and laws
of one of the original states, and to divide their state into counties and
towns for the election of legislators. The second stage commenced when
the population reached twenty thousand free inhabitants, at which time
they would receive congressional authority to call a convention of representatives to establish a "permanent constitution and government." During
this stage, the state was allowed a delegate in Congress with the right to
debate but not to vote. When the population grew to the size of the least

populous original state, then the people entered the third stage. After congressional vote, the state would be allowed full membership in the Confederation with vote as well as voice in the Continental Congress. Jefferson's sequence of stages resembled somewhat the history of the original states with its proposed colonial agent, taxation with representation, and eventual statehood. At the same time, the success of the republican experiment was to be assured during the period of temporary government by requiring the selection of a constitution and laws from one of the original states, which limited the choice of government and restricted voting rights among other things.

The resemblance to the colonial history of the states was heightened by doing away with local autonomy before the first stage. During the debate upon the report, an amendment to place the initial settlers under congressional regulations and congressionally appointed magistrates was supported by nineteen congressmen, including Jefferson, to five against.[14] The amendment was lost because of the system of voting by states, so a milder amendment, perhaps drafted by Jefferson,[15] was passed permitting Congress to take measures "necessary for the preservation of peace and good order" among the settlers of the new states until the first stage.[16]

To provide such measures, Monroe became head of a committee instructed "to consider and report forms of government to be instituted in the Western Territory of the United States by Congress prior to the institution of temporary government there . . . ."[17] When Monroe solicited the opinion of various officials, he phrased the issue thusly:

Shall it be upon Colonial principles, under a governor, council
and judges of the U.S. removable at a certain period of time and
then admitted to a vote in Congress with the common rights of other
states, or shall they be left to themselves until that event?[18]

From this committee came the basic pattern of territorial evolution: a first stage of arbitrary government by congressionally appointed officials, a second stage of elected assembly with nonvoting delegate in Congress, and a third stage of full statehood. Now the idea of dependency had been extended and specified more concretely than before in order to, in the words of the report, "protect the persons and rights of those who may settle within such districts in the infancy of their settlement."[19]

Successive debates in Congress concerned the exact structure of the governments during the stages, but the adoption of the Northwest Ordinance finally fixed the colonial governments. During the first stage, all of the area north and west of the Ohio River was to be governed as one territory by a congressionally appointed governor, secretary, and three judges. When the territory contained five thousand free males, Congress would grant the people authority to elect an assembly that would share governance with the congressionally appointed governor and five-man council. Property qualifications were specified for voting as well as for office holding, and the governor had absolute veto over acts passed by the legislature. The territory was allowed a delegate in Congress to debate. When the population reached sixty thousand free inhabitants, then the territory could adopt a permanent constitution and government and could have its representatives admitted to the Continental Congress. The council and the governor's absolute veto in the second stage completed the resemblance between that stage and the colonial governments of the original states.

An evolutionary sequence of some kind was demanded by republican conceptions of the nature of frontier society, which in turn was conditioned by the ideals of what the state ought to be. Republican government should be devoted to the welfare of all in the state as opposed to that of only one man as in monarchy or a few as in aristocracy. Since the end was res publica, private citizens were supposed to put the "public good" or the "public welfare" above their own selfish or private interest. While a monarchy or aristocracy depended upon governmental authority for coercing the obedience of people to the ends of the state, a republic rested only upon the voluntary obedience of the citizenry. Thus, for a republic to endure, the citizens had to have a high degree of public-spirited virtue; no one could place selfish interests above the public good. While the commonweal was but the happiness of all of the individuals in the state, such would be achieved only through individuals seeking common rather than private ends.[20]

Although the ideal of social equality was espoused, no true republican doubted that some social hierarchy did and ought to exist. Men were not equal in capacity or talent for government. The officials of the state should be the talented, or a natural aristocracy. It was also assumed that men economically independent of others through the ownership of property were more likely to be virtuous. As John Adams argued:

the only possible way then of preserving public virtue, is to
make the acquisition of land easy to every member of society;
to make the division of land into small quantities, so that the
multitudes may be possessed of landed estates.[21]

Most republicans believed the ideal occupation of the citizenry ought therefore to be farming. Jefferson's famed agrarianism rested upon just such premises.[22]

Thus the republican order rested upon foundations of class and implicit social hierarchy. To republicans, economic worth in addition to manhood determined full social and political equality. To this extent, republican theory presumed the coincidence of the social and political orders in the same sense as the traditional European conception of the organic society, in which the welfare of all was believed a unity from the top to bottom of the social ranks.

American republicans saw no contradiction between their espousal of equality and property-qualified participation in government, for they believed the ample lands of their country afforded opportunity for all to possess such a stake in society. As Ezra Stiles summarized the wonder of it all in his election sermon of 1783, "The United States Elevated to Glory and Honor": "But a *Democratical* polity for millions, standing upon a broad basis of the people at large, amply charged with property, has not hitherto been exhibited."[23]

These republican conceptions of virtue, public welfare, and social hierarchy formed the ideological screen through which American statesmen perceived frontier settlers. The early settlers beyond the Ohio were presumed to be either poor wretches or speculators. In either case, they were called "lawless," "banditti," or "adventurers,"[24] because they pursued selfish ends instead of the common good of all in the eyes of republicans. A government surveyor at the mouth of the Miami in 1785 phrased this belief very succinctly when he called these frontiersmen, "our own *white* Indians of no character who have their Private Views without Regard to public benefits to serve."[25]

The Indian-frontiersman comparison was a common one in the thinking of leading eighteenth-century Americans. As Benjamin Rush put it:

The *first* settler in the woods is generally a man who has outlived his credit or fortune in the cultivated parts of the state . . . . As he lives in the neighborhood of Indians, he soon acquires a strong tincture of their manners. His exertions, while they continue are violent, but they are succeeded by long intervals of rest. His pleasures consist chiefly in fishing and hunting . . . . In his intercourse with the world, he manifests all the arts which characterize the Indians of our country. . . . Above all, he revolts against the operation of laws. He cannot bear to surrender up a single natural right for all the benefits of government. . . . [26]

No wonder that, when Jefferson discussed government for these frontiersmen, he saw them as halfway between savages and "tractable people."[27]

Yet there was hope for the West, for Americans of that time were beginning to see a sequence of occupational stages marching westward.[28] To Crèvecoeur, the savage frontier whites preceded

by ten or twelve years the most respectable army of veterans who came after them . . . [who] will change in a few years that barbarous country into a fine fertile, well regulated district. Such is our progress, such is the march of the Europeans toward the interior parts of this continent.[29]

Rush talked more in terms of process:

From a review of the three different species of settler, it appears that there are certain regular stages which mark the progress from the savage to civilized life. The first settler is nearly related to an Indian in his manners. In the second, the Indian manners are more diluted. It is to the third species only that we behold civilization completed. It is to the third species only that it is proper to apply the term *farmers*.[30]

It was in this third stage that republican society was established on the frontier, for only then was the settler, as Rush describes him, "commonly a man of property and good character." He was an industrious agrarian who planted extensive fields, erected suitable buildings, and displayed economy and industry.

In proportion as he increases his wealth, he values the protection of laws. Hence he punctually pays his taxes toward the support of government. Schools and churches likewise, as the means of promoting order and happiness in society, derive due support from him; for benevolence and public spirit as to these objects are the natural offspring of affluence and independence.[31]

In this fashion, the West evolved into a republican society of hard-working farmers. Only the passage of years then seemed necessary for this desirable end.

Full-fledged republican government would come to the frontier by itself, but the Continental Congress wanted to assure its eventuality by prior tutelage through subordination as a colony. After all, not even the original thirteen states had achieved their present republican governments without a period of colonial growth under arbitrary governors. So why should the new western states not do the same, especially since they were presumed in addition to recapitulate the evolution of society as conceived then? Thus some system of territorial evolution from colony to statehood was deemed necessary. The length and circumstances of this period of dependence were disputable, but no republican denied some period of temporary government should exist.[32] An evolutionary governmental sequence was therefore incorporated into all versions of the ordinance from Jefferson's through Nathan Dane's.

At the same time as the selfish and savage frontiersmen were subjected to colonial subordination, they were promised eventual statehood in the strongest language possible at that time, a compact or convenant. They were subordinated to the older republics in order to prepare them for eventual equality in the confederation of those republics. The promise of full membership in the Continental Congress was offered as an inducement as well as a reward for remaining part of the United States of America. To achieve the ends of both new republican states and of a united republican empire, a new kind of colonial system was invented based upon the most enlightened ideals of the time. So successful were the legislators in devising such a system that terminology changed. In the United States, a "colony" became a "territory."[33]

The social philosophy that justified colonial dependency was at that very moment shifting in favor of a more modern set of ideals. With the rise of a democratic ideology, a man's political prerogatives were separated from the ownership of property, and (white) manhood became the sole criterion for his role in government. The pursuit of selfish ends became consistent with the common welfare of all. The hierarchy of social class was no longer considered necessary for the maintenance of social control and political authority.[34] As a result of these altered impressions of a man's worth and government's relation to society, America's image of the frontier also changed.[35] Democratic ideals and practices undermined the need for territorial evolution, property requirements for suffrage and office holding, and the arbitrary authority of the governor before statehood. In the end, however, the republican ideology that lay at the foundation of the territorial system was too deeply imbedded in the very nature of the system to erase some period of colonial dependency altogether.

NOTES

1. See the use of the word "empire" by Jedidiah Morse, *The American Geography* (Elizabethtown, N.J.: Shepard Kollock, 1789), p. 469. Compare Richard Koebner, *Empire* (Cambridge: At the University Press, 1961), pp. 85–219. On the political "newness" of the United States, see Bernard Bailyn, "Political Experience and Enlightenment Ideas in Eighteenth-Century America," *American Historical Review* 67 (January 1962): 339–51; and his *Ideological Origins of the American Revolution* (Cambridge: Harvard University Press, Belknap Press, 1967), pp. 160–319. For the new ideals in diplomacy and church-state relations, consult Felix Gilbert, *To the Farewell Address: Ideas of Early American Foreign Policy* (Princeton:

Princeton University Press, 1961); and Sidney E. Mead, *The Lively Experiment: The Shaping of Christianity in America* (New York: Harper & Row, 1963), pp. 16–71. French views of the early United States are analyzed by Durand Echeverria, *Mirage in the West: A History of the French Image of American Society to 1815* (Princeton: Princeton University Press, 1957).

2. Silas Deane to Secret Committee, December 1, 1776, in *American Archives*, ed. Peter Force, 5th ser., vol. 3 (Washington, D.C., 1853), p. 1021. Already on July 12, 1776, the first draft of the Articles of Confederation, article 18, proposed that there be new western "colonies, within which Forms of Government are to be established on the Principles of Liberty." In *Journals of the Continental Congress*, ed. W. C. Ford et al., 34 vols. (Library of Congress ed., Washington, D.C., 1904–37), 5:551. (Hereafter cited as *JCC*.)

3. Thomas Paine, *Public Good: Being an Examination into the Claim of Virginia to the Vacant Western Territory, and of the Right of the United States to the Same: To Which Is Added, Proposals for Laying off a New State, to Be Applied as a Fund for . . . Redeeming the National Debt* (Philadelphia: John Dunlap, 1780).

4. This controversy is the subject of Merrill Jensen, "The Cession of the Old Northwest," *Mississippi Valley Historical Review* 23 (June 1936): 27–48.

5. *Proceedings of the Convention of the Province of Maryland, Held at the City of Annapolis, on Wednesday the Fourteenth of August, 1776* (Annapolis: Frederick Green, 1776), p. 49. Compare *JCC*, 9:807 (October 15, 1777).

6. Ibid., 12:931–32 (September 19, 1778).

7. Ibid., 17:806–8 (September 6, 1780).

8. Ibid., 19:915 (October 10, 1780).

9. The petition is in William P. and Julia P. Cutler, *Life, Journals, and Correspondence of Rev. Manasseh Cutler, LL.D.*, 2 vols. (Cincinnati: R. Clarke & Co., 1888), 1:159–67; George Washington to James Duane, September 7, 1783, in George Washington, *The Writings of George Washington from the Original Manuscript Sources, 1745—1799*, ed. John C. Fitzpatrick, 39 vols. (Washington, D.C.: Government Printing Office, 1931–44), 27:133–40; committee report, *JCC*, 25:677–79 (October 15, 1783).

10. David Howell to Jonathan Arnold, February 21, 1784, in William R. Staples, ed., *Rhode Island in the Continental Congress, with the Journal of the Convention That Adopted the Constitution, 1765–1790* (Providence: Providence Press Co., 1870), p. 479. For a similar sentiment using the word "maturity" instead, see New Hampshire delegates to Meshech Weare, May 5, 1784, in *Letters of Members of the Continental Congress*, ed. Edmund C. Burnett, 8 vols. (Washington, D.C.: Carnegie Institution of Washington, 1921–36), 8:365.

11. *JCC*, 25:693–94 (October 15, 1783).

12. This plan plus its background is provided in Thomas Jefferson, *Papers of Thomas Jefferson*, ed. Julian P. Boyd et al. (Princeton: Princeton University Press, 1950–), 6:581–617. The evolution of the Northwest Ordinance may be found in two recent accounts: Jack E. Eblen, *The First and Second United States Empires: Governors and Territorial Government, 1784–1912* (Pittsburgh: University of Pittsburgh Press, 1968), pp. 17–51; Robert F. Berkhofer, Jr., "The Republican Origins of the American Territorial

54   ROBERT F. BERKHOFER, JR.

System," in Allan G. Bogue et al., eds., *The West of the American People* (Itasca, Ill.: F. E. Peacock Publishers, 1970).

13. In calling this the "first stage," I follow committee member David Howell in his letter cited in note 10 above. Compare Eblen, *United States Empires,* who speaks of four stages, p. 22.
14. *JCC,* 26:259–60 (April 21, 1784).
15. Jefferson, *Papers,* 7:612, n. 26.
16. *JCC,* 26:274–75 (April 23, 1784).
17. Ibid., 30:139, n. (March 27, 1786).
18. James Monroe to John Jay, April 20, 1786, in *Correspondence and Public Papers of John Jay,* ed. Henry P. Johnston, 4 vols. (New York: G. P. Putnam's Sons, 1890–93), 3:191.
19. *JCC,* 30:251–55 (May 10, 1786).
20. Besides Bailyn, *Ideological Origins,* the best works on the meaning of American republicanism are Gordon S. Wood, *The Creation of the American Republic, 1776–1787* (Chapel Hill: University of North Carolina Press, 1969), especially pp. 46–124, 413–25; and Jack R. Pole, *Political Representation in England and the Origins of the American Republic* (London and Melbourne: Macmillan & Co.; and New York: St. Martin's Press; 1966).
21. John Adams to James Sullivan, May 26, 1776, in *Works of John Adams,* ed. Charles F. Adams, 10 vols. (Boston: Little, Brown, & Co., 1850–56), 9:376–77.
22. An exposition of Jefferson's agrarianism is Alfred W. Griswold, *Farming and Democracy* (New York: Harcourt Brace, 1948), pp. 18–46.
23. In John W. Thornton, ed., *Pulpit of the American Revolution: Or, the Political Sermons of the Period of 1776* (Boston: Gould & Lincoln, 1860), p. 415.
24. For example, as used in: George Washington to Henry Knox, September 23, 1783, in Washington, *Writings,* 27:163–64; Virginia delegates to Benjamin Harrison, November 1, 1783, in Burnett, *Letters of Members,* 7:365; New York delegates to George Clinton, September 14, 1783, ibid., p. 301; Thomas Jefferson to Benjamin Harrison, March 3, 1784, in Jefferson, *Papers,* 7:4.
25. Samuel H. Parsons to William S. Johnson, November 26, 1785, in William S. Johnson Papers, Library of Congress, Washington, D.C.
26. Benjamin Rush to Thomas Percival, October 26, 1786, in Benjamin Rush, *Letters of Benjamin Rush,* ed. Lyman H. Butterfield, 2 vols. (Princeton and Philadelphia: Princeton University Press, 1951), 1:400–401. Compare St. John Crevecoeur, *Letters from an American Farmer* (London: T. Davies, 1783), pp. 55–57, 63–67.
27. Jefferson frequently viewed the problems of governing frontiersmen in this manner. For example, Jefferson to Madison, July 9, December 16, 1786, in Jefferson, *Papers,* 10:112–13, 603. On his reasoning from Indian society, see his *Notes on the State of Virginia,* ed. William Peden (Chapel Hill: University of North Carolina Press, 1955), p. 93.
28. That the frontier in the late eighteenth century was not conceived in the same manner as Turner's, however, may be seen from John T. Juricek, "American Usage of the Word 'Frontier' from Colonial Times to Frederick

Jackson Turner," *Proceedings of the American Philosophical Society* 110 (February 1966): 10–34.

29. Crevecoeur, *Letters,* p. 57. Compare G. K. Hogendorp's observations to his mother in Jefferson, *Papers,* 7:219.

30. Rush, *Letters,* p. 404.

31. Ibid., p. 403. Compare Crevecoeur's description of the middle settlements in Crevecoeur, *Letters,* pp. 54–55.

32. The one exception I find is the Timothy Pickering plan, in Octavius Pickering, *The Life of Timothy Pickering,* 2 vols. (Boston: Little, Brown, & Co., 1867), 1:546–49, but there was no need in his plan for a period of colonial dependency because rank and property were built into the proposed state from the beginning of settlement. Even radical Tom Paine thought some period of temporary government might be necessary for the new states. Paine, *Public Good,* p. 38.

33. This began during the debates over Monroe's plan, so it became the accepted usage in the Northwest Ordinance.

34. The best treatment of the ideological transition from republicanism to democracy is Yehoshua Arieli, *Individualism and Nationalism in American Ideology* (Cambridge: Harvard University Press, 1964).

35. The changing attitude may be traced in Rush Welter, "The Frontier West as Image of American Society: Conservative Attitudes Before the Civil War," *Mississippi Valley Historical Review* 46 (March 1960): 593–614; and Henry N. Smith, *Virgin Land: The American West as Symbol and Myth* (Cambridge: Harvard University Press, 1950).

Note: Relationships between the ordinances of 1784 and 1787 are explored further in Robert F. Berkhofer, Jr., "Jefferson, the Ordinance of 1784, and the Origins of the American Territorial System," *William and Mary Quarterly,* 3d ser. 29 (April 1972): 231–62.

Discussion of Sources

LEONARD RAPPORT

ON THE FIRST DAY of September 1774 a forty-five-year-old Irish-born Phila-delphian got married. Four days later the newlyweds went to pay their respects to the bride's aunt. The bridegroom tells what happened.

> Just as I alighted in Chestnut Street, the door-keeper of Congress
> (then first met) accosted me with a message from them, requesting
> my presence. Surprised at this, and not able to divine why I was
> wanted, I however bade my servant put up the horses, and followed
> the messenger myself to the Carpenter's Hall and entered Congress.
> Here was indeed an august assembly! and deep thought and
> solemn anxiety were observable on their countenances! I walked
> up the aisle, and standing opposite to the President, I bowed, and
> told him I waited his pleasure. He replied, "Congress desire the
> favor of you, Sir, to take their minutes." I bowed in acquiescence,
> and took my seat at the desk.[1]

Charles Thomson thereby entered into another alliance, one that lasted for fifteen years, from the Continental Congress's first day to its last.

As to how long the bride waited in Chestnut Street we have no record. Perhaps the honeymoon did not end quite as soon as it sounds. Though the groom implies that he immediately picked up the pen, the journal of the Congress for that first day, September 5, is in the hand of another. It is not until September 10, 1774, that it first appears in the handwriting that was to become so familiar, the hand of the man who created, received, collected, and maintained the body of records we call the Papers of the Continental Congress.

It is in the Papers of the Continental Congress that we find the official

56

version of the Ordinance of 1787; it is in these papers that we find the official record of the actions that led up to that ordinance.

We will not find in these papers, even approximately, the complete story of the origins of the Northwest Ordinance. To learn why what happened did happen, to learn how it happened, to learn sometimes, even, what happened, we have to look elsewhere. We have to look in other records in the National Archives, we have to look in the records of certain of the states, but mostly we have to look in the personal papers of the people involved in the evolution of this ordinance; in the papers of Thomas Jefferson, James Monroe, Nathan Dane; in the papers of other members of the Continental Congress; in the papers of certain nonmembers such as Manasseh Cutler; perhaps even in the papers of persons as remote as Edward Coles, who seventy years after the event mentioned almost parenthetically something of interest that Madison once told him.

But the official source, the primary source, has to be the Papers of the Continental Congress. If we are interested in the question of the comma that plagued the first governor of a territory, we have to turn not to the thirty-four volumes, published in this century, entitled *Journals of the Continental Congress, 1774–1789,*[2] but to the original records of that Congress. And even in that body of papers for a detail of punctuation we may have to go beyond the official printings of the ordinance to the ultimate records, the manuscript journal (for Clarence Carter found at least 140 differences in punctuation alone between the first official printing and the manuscript journal). "That the Journal itself may have been in error is not impossible," said Carter. "Nevertheless, the Journal is the final authority: we cannot go behind it."[3]

Clarence Carter did not mean we should not go beyond the official records. He was aware that historians and others would explore widely and would use the official and the unofficial records of the actions of the Continental Congress in ways we cannot anticipate. We have followed Professor Bestor's exploration of the implications of the Ordinance of 1787, using records created long after that date. At this moment, perhaps, someone somewhere is following a line of investigation that began with the Ordinance of 1787 and will, perhaps, end in the records of the Interstate Commerce Commission or of the Civil Aeronautics Board. We here in the National Archives cannot begin to guess the limits to which a free-ranging mind may soar or where it may finally touch down. We can only wait for it to land and then offer what assistance we can.

If you have ever used the papers of the Continental Congress in the original or on microfilm, you have, probably, eventually asked yourself: is the trouble with me or with these records? If so, do not worry. Edmund C. Burnett, when halfway through his eight-volume *Letters of Members of the Continental Congress,* wondered: "I have long been curious to know when, why, and by whom the present arrangement of the Papers and this system of numbers was originated, but thus far I have not succeeded in solving the mystery." "It is," he went on to say, "to a considerable extent haphazard and without logic."[4]

How Thomson could have operated with the papers in such order—or disorder—must have puzzled Burnett the rest of his life.

Several years after Burnett's death the papers were transferred from the Library of Congress to the National Archives; and several years after that the mystery was solved.

The late Carl Lokke, then head of the National Archives branch having custody of both the Papers of the Continental Congress and of the records of the Department of State, in the latter records found the story of what had happened.

In 1834, a clerk in the Department of State, William A. Weaver, took out of their original arrangement, rearranged, and mounted into volumes in an order apparently of his own devising, the thousands and thousands of loose papers created by or received by the Congress. Dr. Lokke set straight the report insofar as Thomson was concerned.

In fair weather and in foul [wrote Dr. Lokke], in war and in
peace, in sickness and in health, this devoted public servant
developed and carried out a system of creating and preserving
records that bears careful scrutiny. The fantastic examples of
disorder found among the Continental Congress Papers today
(and congealed in Weaver's numerical system) should be ascribed
to Posterity rather than him. Thomson was a man of order.[5]

Dr. Lokke was aware that Thomson, by applying the rule that "what Congress adopted, I committed to writing; with what they rejected I had nothing further to do,"[6] created session minutes that left much to be desired. But offsetting this was the care with which he preserved the records of the Congress. In 1827, said Lokke, Jared Sparks found the papers "much more full and perfect than he had imagined. We find them so today."

I have gone into these details of record-keeping history not only to rehabilitate any egos that may have been bruised in encounters with the Continental Congress Papers but also to call to the attention of prospective users Edmund Burnett's warning that "instances of documents found in unexpected places might be multiplied without number, and that the labels on the volumes sometimes don't give even a clue to the volumes' principal contents."[7]

Implicit in Burnett's warnings is the fact that the researcher who looks no further than the obvious volume labels is, in effect, entrusting the selection of his documents to the judgment of a clerk who lived a century and a third ago, and about whose original qualifications we know little more than that he had five children and a sick wife and needed the work.

Let us look at some of these volumes that are, for the Ordinance of 1787, of obvious interest. Certainly the volume labeled "Copies of Ordinances and Other Papers Relating to the Western Territory of the United States, 1787–88" is of prime interest. But did Weaver round up and mount in this volume *all* of the documents to which this label applies? Another volume is "Memorials of the Inhabitants of Illinois, Kaskaskia, and Kentucky, 1780–89." However, there are nineteen other volumes of memorials, petitions, remonstrances, and addresses to the Congress. Can we assume that from these Weaver extracted and mounted in the volumes just mentioned all the memorials of possible interest to us? I could read off the titles of a half-dozen other volumes and ask similar questions about each.

It is not too hard to find the obvious, as classified by William Weaver. But to go beyond the obvious is not always quick, simple, or easy.

At present the best general guide to the papers are the two accompanying pamphlets to the National Archives microfilm publication of the papers. Even more detailed than the texts of these pamphlets are the roll notes, filmed at the beginning of each roll of microfilm, which describe in detail what is on that particular roll.

I also call to your attention the card index that occupies the first three rolls of microfilm. This a name and subject index to 73 of the 196 major units of the papers, prepared under the direction of J. Franklin Jameson by Dorothy Eaton while the papers were at the Library of Congress. Mrs. Eaton's index tells us the nature of the document (particularly useful now that we see them only on microfilm); identifies the handwriting, including emendations; tells, if an enclosure, where the enclosing document is to be found (and vice versa); supplies for undated documents a probable date; and gives other helpful information about these papers that Mrs. Eaton knew so well.

Even with these aids the Papers of the Continental Congress are a tough collection. They are the most complicated, the hardest-to-find-your-way-around-in set of papers I know of anywhere. That is why, I believe, that even though they have for decades been open and available to researchers and have for the past seven or eight years been available, in toto, on microfilm, they are seldom used in original form by persons writing on the Northwest Ordinance (or on other subjects in the period of the Confederation. I base this on a quick run-through of what we have here in our own National Archives Library. If this is an unfair statement I will stand corrected).

I do not suggest that whenever a scholar has occasion to look up the text of the Ordinance of 1787 he go to the microfilm reader. I do suggest that when he quotes for publication from a document, the original of which is in the Papers of the Continental Congress, he consider using the original document as reproduced on our microfilm publication rather than from Peter Force's *American Archives* or the various other handy editions of documents of the Congress—particularly those editions done in the days before Farrand, Burnett, Carter, and our chairman, Julian Boyd. The trust placed in nineteenth-century documentary publications (and in a few of the poorer twentieth-century ones) is a continuing phenomenon. For example, scholars persist in quoting from Elliot's *Debates* in spite of the fact that whoever does so takes his life in his hands; and in spite of the fact that everything in Elliot is, I believe, with one exception, readily available in purer versions.

With the bicentennial of the American Revolution coming on, we in the National Archives anticipate a great increase of interest in the records of the government of the united colonies and of the United States in Congress Assembled, 1774–89. These records are, largely, the Papers of the Continental Congress. We have already started to do what we can to render as intelligible and as usable as possible this terribly confused group of papers. We will do it with words and, if necessary, with diagrams, with pictures—we will employ any media and any methods that will help open these records to those who have need to use them. If you have any ideas about this, please volunteer them.

I close by saying that I feel it to have been somewhat presumptuous to have talked about documentary sources of the eighteenth century and the Papers of the Continental Congress, when there is on this panel someone who could have told you more, and told it better; a person who knows the documentation of the period as no one else; a person who treats these documents with a knowledge, skill, and grace that we have not seen before, and may not, in our time, see again. As an example—one of many such—of what I am talking about, I refer you to the editorial note on the 1784 "Plan of Government of the Western Territory" in volume 6 of the *Papers of Thomas Jefferson,* by our chairman, Mr. Julian Boyd.

NOTES

1. Edmund C. Burnett, ed., *Letters of Members of the Continental Congress,* 8 vols. (Washington, D.C.: Carnegie Institution of Washington, 1921–36), 1:10, n. 2.
2. Worthington C. Ford et al., eds., 34 vols. (Library of Congress ed., Washington, D.C., 1904–37).
3. Clarence E. Carter and John Porter Bloom, eds., *The Territorial Papers of*

the United States (Washington, D.C.: Government Printing Office, 1934–), 2:42.

4. Edmund C. Burnett, "The Papers of the Continental Congress" (Address delivered in the Manuscript Division, Library of Congress, Washington, D.C., January 18, 1929. Typescript in the Manuscript Division), p. 5.

Herbert Friedenwald (according to Carl Lokke, "perhaps the best informed man in the country on the Continental Congress Papers") was blunter: " . . . their present arrangement is so confusing as to have made it possible for documents to escape the vigilant eye even of a Bancroft. . . . That method [a topical arrangement] was, to a certain extent, followed by the men who originally put the manuscripts in order for binding, but of its utter inadequacy and hopeless confusion all who have consulted them will sadly bear witness. And yet their present order was doubtless considered a good one in its day." (Herbert Friedenwald, "The Journals and Papers of the Continental Congress," *Annual Report of the American Historical Association* [1896], pp. 86 and 126; Carl L. Lokke, "The Continental Congress Papers: Their History, 1789–1952," *National Archives Accessions,* no. 51 [June 1954], p. 13).

5. Carl L. Lokke, "Early Methods of Record Keeping in the Federal Government," (1955. Typescript copy in National Archives Library, Washington, D.C.), pp. 9–10.

6. Burnett, *Letters of Members,* 1:10, n. 2. The account is ascribed to Thomson by an anonymous writer in the *American Quarterly Review* (1:30). Burnett believes it was probably drawn up from the writer's recollection. According to the account, after Thomson was seated as secretary the first speaker was Patrick Henry. Henry compared their situation to that of a man in trouble who calls together his friends, solicits their advice, accepts that which seems best, " 'and think[s] no more of the rejected schemes with which he would have nothing to do.' " "I thought," continued the venerable narrator, "that this was very good instruction to me, with respect to the taking the Minutes. What Congress adopted, I committed to writing; with what they rejected, I had nothing farther to do; and even this method led to some squabbles with the members who were desirous of having their speeches and resolutions, however put to rest by the majority, still preserved upon the Minutes."

7. Burnett, "The Papers of the Continental Congress," p. 8.

THE TERRITORIES

AND THE

CONGRESS

EDITOR'S NOTE

*The following two essays, with ensuing commentary
and discussion, constituted the second formal session of
the conference. The speakers were introduced and the
discussion period was conducted by Howard R. Lamar.
The purpose of the session was to focus attention upon
the most significant of the branches of the federal government during the early developmental period of the
American territorial system. The judicial branch was
clearly passive during this period, and the executive
branch generally did not seek opportunity to exert influence in territorial development except through the appointive power. The legislative branch was obviously
predominant in its major functions of creating territories
and states, establishing the legal framework for each
in turn (with the opportunity for annulling local actions
in detail), controlling the purse strings, and confirming
or refusing to confirm executive appointments. Study of
the operations of the legislative branch in early territorial history is therefore a requirement with a high
priority.*

Early Delegates in the House
of Representatives

JO TICE BLOOM

THOMAS JEFFERSON, in drafting the Ordinance of 1784, provided for a delegate to Congress to be elected during the period of temporary government, who would have the right to debate but not to vote in Congress. Ten years later, after the adoption of the Ordinance of 1787 and the Constitution, Dr. James White presented his credentials as delegate from the Territory Southwest of the River Ohio to the House of Representatives and requested seating as a member of the House. For the first time, the office was filled and James White began the task of representing the territories, which his successors from thirty-three territories continued until 1959.[1]

The territorial delegate occupied a unique position in territorial government, for he was the only elected official to have a designated role in the operation of the federal government. Amid the abundance of presidentially appointed territorial officials, the delegate had the unique function of representing the people of the territory at the seat of national government. Unlike his colleagues in Congress, however, he did not share his responsibility with others. He represented all the diverse economic, political, and personal interests of his constituency by himself. Nor had the role of the delegate in the legislative branch been established by tradition in the British Empire or the American Confederation. The men who filled the office and their colleagues in the House defined the role over years of working on the legislative problems of the new nation. The first twenty men who held the office were key men in creating the precedents and traditions which their successors would follow, although changes occurred as the years passed.

When the Ordinance of 1787 was passed, the authors did not list the duties, privileges and obligations of the delegate. As sons of the British Empire, the members of the Continental Congress knew the duties of the British colonial agents and were fully aware that the territorial delegate

65

was simply the traditional colonial agent with a new legal status. Arthur St. Clair, revolutionary war hero, president of the Continental Congress in 1787, and governor of the Northwest Territory, expressed the ideas of his peers in 1799 when he addressed the legislature of the Northwest Territory on the delegate's role:

This is, gentlemen, a right of no small consquence, for there are
many matters of considerable importance to the people that must
come before and be decided on by Congress, and can only
advantageously be brought forward and managed by their delegate,
who . . . although he will have no vote, will not be without
influence, and, for the information that may be necessary to the
members unacquainted with our circumstances, will naturally
be resorted to; and he will have an equal right with the members of
the States that compose the Union to propose for their consideration any law that may appear to be useful to the nation
or to the territory.[2]

Crucial decisions regarding this "right of no small consequence" were made in 1794, when the House debated the seating of Dr. James White. Some members suggested that the delegate should sit in both houses because the Ordinance of 1787 referred only to "Congress" at a time when Congress was unicameral and the 1789 adaptation of the ordinance did not make provision for the new bicameral Congress. Other members of the House questioned the propriety of White's sitting in the House when he had been elected in the manner of senators, by the territorial legislature, not by popular election. The majority voted to seat White in the House and accord him recognition as a nonvoting member of that body.[3]

With the question of White's seating settled, the House immediately faced the problems of his privileges and duties. James Madison asked if White should take the oath, arguing that since White would not be voting he did not need to take the oath. The majority of the House supported this view.[4] Within two weeks both houses of Congress passed a bill providing that White would have the same franking privileges and the same pay as members of the House of Representatives.[5]

When the second territorial delegate appeared in Congress five years later, the House automatically accepted his presence and extended franking and pay privileges to him. William Henry Harrison of the Northwest Territory took the oath without question and established the precedent that all future delegates would take the oath.[6]

Harrison, at twenty-six one of the youngest men to grace the halls of Congress, created quite a stir. His involvement in House business created an activist tradition for the delegates who desired such an active role. Immediately upon his seating, Harrison moved the formation of a committee to deal with problems of actual settlers on public lands. The Speaker of the House named Harrison chairman when he appointed the committee and Harrison ably led the committee's deliberations.[7] As the first delegate to chair a select committee of the House of Representatives, he began a practice best exemplified by George Poindexter of Mississippi Territory who chaired twenty-two select committees during his six years in the House. Poindexter's activity may be partially explained by his close friendship with Speaker of the House Henry Clay.

During the early period, delegates were never barred from serving on standing committees by any action of the House. They probably did not serve on these committees for the simple reason that a delegate was never appointed and therefore the tradition never began. Delegates apparently voted in the meetings of the select committees during most of the pre–Civil War period. Throughout the antebellum period, they took an active part in the actions of committees and the House, introducing bills, proposing resolutions, raising points of order, and making every kind of motion other than a motion to reconsider.[8]

One tradition frequently observed by delegates was the idea that delegates should speak only on matters directly concerning their territories. This attitude apparently stemmed from a proposed amendment in 1794, offered by William B. Giles of Virginia, that would have restricted delegates to debating only those questions "touching on the rights and interest of the people of the Territory."[9] Although most of the delegates kept their comments on the floor and their committee activities restricted to matters of immediate concern to their territories, others had no hesitation about speaking or acting on any matter which came before the House.

William Henry Harrison's work on public land laws was of national scope, although his immediate concern was the residents of his own territory. Efforts of Daniel Clark of Orleans Territory to discredit General James Wilkinson fall in the same category. Clark was primarily concerned with politics in his territory where the Burr conspiracy was causing major turmoil, but he was also motivated by the national implications of Wilkinson's corruption. He attempted to present information on the floor of the House of Representatives, and with the aid of John Randolph of Virginia, launched a congressional investigation of Wilkinson. Although denied the right to be a defense witness in the Burr trial, Clark continued his accusations through publications and was eventually proven correct by archival material in Havana.[10]

By tangling with a national personality on a touchy issue, George Poindexter also gained national publicity. During the 1811 debate on the enabling act of Orleans Territory, Josiah Quincy of Massachusetts led the opposition. Voicing classic arguments against admitting western states, Quincy felt "compelled to declare it as my deliberate opinion, that if this bill passes, the bonds of this Union are virtually dissolved."[11] Poindexter leapt to his feet and, raising a point of order, asked the Speaker of the House "Whether it be competent in any member of the House to invite any portion of the people to insurrection, and, of course, to a dissolution on the Union?"[12] Although the Speaker ruled in favor of Quincy, Poindexter did not let Quincy's comments pass and answered the New Englander in a lengthy address the next day.[13] The Mississippi delegate's speech was widely reprinted throughout the country.

Poindexter also took part in debates over rechartering the Bank of the United States in 1811 and on problems of national defense in 1812. His comments on national problems were not confined to the House floor. His most notable quotation comes from his correspondence with Cowles Meade, long-time secretary of Mississippi Territory. Poindexter wrote in reference to the Non-Intercourse Act of 1809 that "We shall have Non-intercourse until the nation will be overrun with Old maids and witches."[14]

Among those delegates who became involved in national problems, John Scott of Missouri took part in a great American crisis. Actively involved in the controversy over the Missouri enabling and admission acts, Scott worked closely with a former territorial delegate and judge, Jesse B. Thomas, now senator from Illinois. Scott consistently and adamantly promoted the Missouri argument for the preservation of slavery within its boundaries and for the right of each state to decide the slavery issue for itself. Scott's name is prominent in any history of the controversy, and he remains the most notable of the antebellum delegates for his activities as a delegate.[15]

The delegates' most important work in Congress was to attend to territorial matters. They regularly received instructions from their legislatures with information on the needs and desires of their constituents. For example, in 1801 the legislature of the Northwest Territory instructed Delegate Paul Fearing to secure title to school lands due from Judge John Cleves Symmes as well as to those school lands due from the federal government. In addition to having commissioners appointed to settle land claims in Wayne County (Detroit), he was to secure legislation to modify the governor's veto and to widen suffrage in the territory. Most important of all, the legislature wanted congressional approval of a recent territorial act dividing the territory along the Scioto River, and an enabling act with this boundary.[16] Fearing was notably unsuccessful in securing any legislation fulfilling his instructions.

Not only did territorial legislatures send instructions, but they also sent special petitions and memorials to Congress. Usually the delegate presented these petitions. If the delegate and the legislative majority represented different political factions, the legislature would often send the peititions to another member of Congress for presentation. John Crowell of Alabama Territory was a delegate not thoroughly trusted by either the legislature or the governor. Despite his close ties to the Georgians who administered government in the territory, Crowell had little to do in Congress. Most petitions from the legislature were sent to Speaker of the House Henry Clay, Representative Thomas W. Cobb of Georgia, or Senator Charles Tait of Georgia.[17]

Some delegates also presented petitions from areas which had not yet achieved territorial status or from territories which needed additional help. George Poindexter of Mississippi regularly presented petitions and memorials from Orleans Territory because Julien Poydras, the Orleans delegate, was notably reticent. While Rufus Easton was contesting John Scott's election from Missouri Territory, Nathaniel Pope of Illinois introduced resolutions and presented petitions from Missouri Territory. The favors were usually returned in unobtrusive ways. Former delegates were also helpful to territories and their legislatures in putting material before the House, the most outstanding examples being William Henry Harrison and George Poindexter, who both served in Congress for many years after their work as delegates had ended.

Petitions sent to Nathaniel Pope of Illinois Territory exemplify requests delegates received. Problems of the Indian trade disturbed the residents of Illinois and Missouri territories, and the Illinois legislature asked Pope to seek solutions. Pope succeeded in placing the problem before both the Committee on Indian Affairs and the Committee on Foreign Relations for consideration.[18] A petition from the legislature seeking compensation for settlers who suffered enemy depredations during the War of 1812 was referred to the Committee on Claims.[19] The Missouri legislature also petitioned for full pay for rangers who served during the War of 1812, for more post roads, and for extension of preemption privileges to those settlers who lost property along the frontier.[20] Pope presented the petition from the Illinois legislature requesting statehood and then chaired the select committee which drew up the enabling act.[21]

Petitions from individuals and local groups to be presented and referred to committees for action also occupied time. Jonathan Jennings of Indiana Territory was very conscientious about his constituents' problems and handled such matters expeditiously. He received petitions which were typical of those which came from most territories. Knox County, Indiana Territory, asked that commissioners be appointed to examine and settle disputes over land titles.[22] Citizens of the territory asked that the suffrage be extended.[23] Jennings chaired a committee which considered a petition of Indiana inhabitants who requested a road from Jeffersonville to Detroit.[24] People of the territory, involved in local politics and aware of their colonial status, often requested an improvement in political conditions; Indianans requested a law which would prohibit United States officials from interfering in local elections and a law to permit popular election of the delegate.[25] Other petitions included requests from officers and soldiers asking for their pay, from citizens complaining about arbitrary conduct of the governor, and from inhabitants asking for statehood.[26] The purchase of public lands was a matter of constant concern to settlers in all territories, and settlers in Indiana constantly sent petitions to Jennings seeking relief from land problems, which were usually referred to the Committee on Public Lands. They asked for more time on their payments, for preemption privileges on land they had already settled, and for donation lands in areas where settlers served as a barrier against Indians.[27] There were also petitions for pensions and individual claims which required congressional action, but these were few and usually went to the Committee on Claims without presentation to the House or mention in the *Annals of Congress* or the *House Journal.*

Legislation to benefit their territories was of prime importance to all delegates. Congress extended beneficial legislation territory by territory. A good example of such piecemeal legislation is the delegate's election. Under the Ordinance of 1787, the territorial council and the House of Representatives, meeting in joint session, elected the delegate. George Poindexter of Mississippi Territory first suggested popular election to the House and on January 9, 1808, voters of Mississippi Territory received the privilege of choosing their delegates to Congress at the same time they chose representatives to the territorial House.[28] Congress granted the same privilege to the voters in Indiana Territory in 1809.[29] The 1812 act granting second stage government to Illinois Territory included the right of popular election of the delegate.[30] At the same time Congress passed the act for Illinois, an organizing act for the territory of Missouri was under discussion. Despite the fact that the territory of Louisiana had been operating since 1804 without difficulty and needed only a new name as a result of the admission of the state of Louisiana (formerly the territory of Orleans), Congress insisted on passing a complete organizing act for the renamed territory—Missouri. This act, passed in June 1812, provided for popular election of the delegate to Congress.[31] Thus, all delegates who served between 1813 and March 1817 were popularly elected. In March 1817 the organizing act for the territory of Alabama provided that the General Assembly, meeting in joint session, should elect the delegate.[32] In contrast, Congress granted voters of Michigan Territory the right to elect their delegate, but made no provision at this time for the election of a legislature in 1819.[33] The organizing act of 1819 for Arkansas Territory stated that when the people elected their first House of Representatives, they could also elect their first delegate.[34] This slow process of treating each territory separately increased the work of the delegates and slowed the process of providing beneficial legislation.

The delegates successfully sought legislation broadening the suffrage and providing for popular election of sheriffs, attorneys general, and council members in their territories. Attempts to restrict the governor's veto were unsuccessful. The boundaries of territories and states became issues for debate with each organizing or enabling act, and the delegates in Congress worked hard to insure the best possible boundaries for their territories or states-to-be. The work of Nathaniel Pope of Illinois was particularly notable, since he moved the boundary far enough north to include the site of Chicago within the boundaries of the new state of Illinois. Residents of the frontier constantly demanded legislation on the disposal of public lands beneficial to their interests. These demands provided constant labor for delegates and the Committee on Public Lands. Settlement of divergent claims from previous periods of occupation by other nations, especially in Orleans, Mississippi, and Missouri territories, were of vital importance to residents and to reelection for delegates. William Lattimore and George Poindexter worked for years to settle the Yazoo claims in Mississippi, for example, finally succeeding after several reelections for each.

A few delegates left an image of little activity in surviving records. Senior statesman Julien Poydras of the territory of Orleans did little committee work and rarely spoke on the House floor. At sixty-three years of age he did not have the energy of his younger colleague, George Poindexter, and evidently let Poindexter do much of the hard work. Thomas Marston Green of Mississippi Territory and John Crowell of Alabama Territory did some committee work, but they never spoke for the record. Benjamin Stephenson of Illinois Territory did not serve on any committees and never spoke, but extant correspondence indicates that he did accomplish some legislation and appointments for his territory. Narsworthy Hunter of Mississippi Territory was a complete contrast to his successors George Poindexter and William Lattimore, both extremely active politicians. Hunter took his seat in Congress on December 21, 1801. On March 12, 1802, the House was informed that Hunter had died the previous evening. He was accorded the full formalities of Congress and was buried in the congressional cemetery. There is no record he did anything else as delegate.

Men like Edward Hempstead of Missouri Territory, James White of the Southwest Territory, William McMillan of the Northwest Territory, Daniel Clark of Orleans and Shadrach Bond of Illinois worked quietly and diligently in corridors and committee rooms and on the floor of the House.

They secured legislation and appointments, were often reelected, and made small splashes in the history of Congress and the nation. They contrast strongly with the flamboyant personalities or extreme politicking of such men as Jonathan Jennings of Indiana and George Poindexter or William Lattimore, both of Mississippi.

For all of the delegates but one, the biggest challenge was to secure the enabling act for their territory. Many of the men knew that statehood was not possible during their terms of office, but petitions were presented and select committees often established. Such pressure and agitation may easily have hastened statehood; certainly it did little harm. Other delegates lobbied hard for statehood, served on committees, and lost their jobs when the struggle for statehood was successful. Four statehood campaigns turned into more than routine admission problems. These four, the Southwest Territory, the territory of Orleans, Missouri Territory, and the Northwest Territory will be discussed in some detail, for the delegates played significant roles in these campaigns.

Dr. James White of the Southwest Territory helped set the pattern for the future quite by accident. The territory and its leaders were quite anxious for admission to the Union, and White discovered that Congress was not particularly ready to admit a territory to statehood. Kentucky and Vermont had been admitted to the Union shortly after the creation of the Southwest Territory, and Congress appeared to be in no hurry to admit more states. White, through discussions with members of Congress and the administration in Philadelphia, conceived a plan which he thought might force admission. The plan, as outlined in a letter to Governor William Blount, called for the governor to take a census, for the governor and the legislature to call a convention to write a constitution, and then for voters to elect new state officials, presenting Congress with a fait accompli. Governor Blount promptly put the plan into action. In February 1796, White presented the constitution for the new state of Tennessee to Congress, and very quickly received the working support of the new state's representatives to Congress. House debate over the admission of Tennessee became a discussion of proper procedures to be followed for admission, and the procedure enunciated by William L. Smith of South Carolina became routine procedure for almost all future states. Smith called for Congress to retain complete control over admission of new states, and, through an enabling act, to make provision for a census, for a constitutional convention to meet, and for state elections to be held. If and when Congress approved the proposed constitution, the new senators and representatives would be seated. Thus, as a result of White's work, but in a complete reversal of his proposal, statehood procedures were established.

The Senate passed an enabling act for Orleans Territory early in 1810, but the bill died in the House. A new bill was introduced into the House in December 1810 and in January was bitterly debated. Josiah Quincy of Massachusetts objected to the admission of any more western states, much less states created from territory which had not been part of the United States in 1783. Other congressmen questioned the loyalty of the French Creole population and wondered if such people could properly preserve the American heritage. Enough members of both Houses objected to the possibility of serving in Congress with men of color that persons of mixed blood were denied the franchise in the enabling act. Unlike those for other territories, the enabling act stipulated that the state's constitution "shall contain the fundamental principles of civil and religious liberty; that it shall secure to the citizen the trial by jury in all criminal cases, and the privilege of the writ of habeas corpus." All records of the state government and all laws and written proceedings were to be conducted and recorded in English. Finally, the constitutional convention had to "declare its assent, in behalf of the people of the said territory, to the adoption of the constitution of the United States."[35] The stringent requirements reveal American fears about the "foreign" population residing in the future state of Louisiana. Both Julien Poydras and George Poindexter worked long and hard hours to secure admission for the state. In an unusual situation, neither delegate served on the select committee which drafted the bill. Poydras hardly spoke in debate, probably because of the strain and because his French accent would not win friends. Poindexter spoke often and was one of the leaders to secure statehood for Louisiana.

The story of the admission of Missouri is familiar to all students of American history and represents one of the few times that the admission of a new state precipitated a national crisis. The work of John Scott to secure both enabling and admission acts has been discussed earlier. The storm which arose over Missouri's statehood illustrates the importance of slavery in the West, a problem that would create future national crises.

The Northwest Territory attained statehood by a relatively calm, normal procedure, similar to that of most other territories, except for one not-so-small item: the last delegate from the Northwest Territory fought against statehood! Opposing groups of land speculators created the political parties. The speculators of the Virginia Military Tract were closely allied to the Virginia Jeffersonian Republicans. Land speculators of Cincinnati and Marietta became Federalists partly from natural inclination and partly from the need to have party support in Congress. When Paul Fearing was seated as delegate in the House, the territorial Federalist party, which included both governor and legislative majority, was represented by a leading land speculator and long-time Marietta resident. The Republican majority in the House received information and encouragement from territorial Republicans in the nation's capital. The debate over statehood lasted three months in 1802, and only Fearing and Roger Griswold of Connecticut spoke in opposition. Fearing opposed statehood because the enabling bill proposed boundaries for the new state of Ohio which would logically put the new state capital in the heart of the Republican countryside and leave the Federalist strongholds on opposite sides of the state. The Federalists' misgivings were realized when statehood came, despite the efforts of Fearing to maintain territorial status and Federalist control.

Between the seating of James White in 1794 and the admission of Missouri in 1821, a quarter century elapsed and twenty men held the office of territorial delegate. What then was the new official? Was he important to Congress or to his territory? What was his significance in the eyes of those who worked in politics in that quarter century? To William L. Smith of South Carolina the delegate of 1794 was "no more than an Envoy to Congress."[36] In 1817 John Randolph of Virginia questioned "the propriety of considering the Delegates in any other light than as mere agents of the Territories, without any title to the privileges of the members."[37]

To the people of the territories the delegate was an important official and they pleaded long and hard for second-stage government, which entitled them to a delegate. A citizen of Indiana, arguing in 1804 for a delegate as opposed to an agent, pointed out that a delegate's "remonstrances will be entitled to respect and attention; they will have weight."[38] Abraham Baldwin of Georgia, supporting the seating of James White, argued that a delegate's position "was infinitely higher than that of strangers in the gallery."[39] Governor Ninian Edwards of Illinois Territory wrote that the delegate "stands precisely in the same relation to the people of a territory that any representative in congress does to the people of his district."[40] Perhaps Congressman Thomas Robertson of Louisana, who worked closely with delegates for many years, came closest to the true significance of the territorial delegate in the United States when he said in 1817:

The people of the frontier country had rights as well as the
people of the states, of which distance ought not to deprive them:
their Delegates (or Representatives) had duties to perform here
as important to their constituents, as essential to the rights of any
citizen, as any member of this House.[41]

NOTES

1. Unless otherwise noted, all material is taken from Nancy Jo Tice, "The Territorial Delegate, 1794–1820" (Ph.D. diss., University of Wisconsin, 1967).
2. William H. Smith, ed., *The St. Clair Papers,* 2 vols. (Cincinnati: R. Clarke & Co., 1882), 2:445–56.
3. U.S., Congress, House, *Annals of Congress,* 3d Cong., 2d sess., 1794, pp. 884–90.
4. Ibid., p. 889.
5. Ibid., pp. 891, 906, 914, 1485.
6. Ibid., 6th Cong., 1st sess., 1799, pp. 187, 197, 199, 200, 201.
7. Ibid., 1799–1800, pp. 209, 527, 651 ff., 661, 691.
8. U.S., Congress, House Report 10, 27th Cong., 1st sess., Serial 393, p. 5.
9. *Annals of Congress,* 3d Cong., 2d sess., 1794, pp. 886–87.
10. Thomas P. Abernethy, *The Burr Conspiracy* (New York: Oxford University Press, 1954); Nolan B. Harmon, Jr., *The Famous Case of Myra Clark Gaines* (Baton Rouge: Louisiana State University Press, 1946); Walter F. McCaleb, *The Aaron Burr Conspiracy* (New York: Wilson-Erickson, 1936).
11. *Annals of Congress,* 11th Cong., 3d sess., 1811, p. 525.
12. Ibid., p. 526.
13. Ibid., pp. 555–70.
14. Poindexter to Cowles Meade, November 11, 1811, J. F. H. Claiborne Collection, Department of Archives and History, State of Mississippi, Jackson, Miss.
15. *Annals of Congress,* 16th Cong., 1st sess., 1820, pp. 1405–1552; Glover Moore, *The Missouri Controversy, 1819–1821* (Lexington: University of Kentucky Press, 1953).
16. Smith, *St. Clair Papers,* 2:454–57.
17. Thomas P. Abernethy, *The Formative Period in Alabama, 1815–1828,* 2d ed. (University: University of Alabama Press, 1965), p. 42; *Annals of Congress,* 15th Cong., 1st sess., 1817–18, pp. 462, 591, 1451; ibid., 2d sess., 1818–19, pp. 244, 370.
18. *Annals of Congress,* 14th Cong., 2d sess., 1816, pp. 336–37.
19. Ibid., 1817, p. 715.
20. Ibid., p. 1024.
21. Ibid., 15th Cong., 1st sess., 1818, pp. 782, 814.
22. Ibid., 10th Cong., 2d sess., 1809, p. 935.
23. Ibid., 11th Cong., 2d sess., 1810, p. 1224.
24. Ibid., 3d sess., 1811, p. 830.
25. Ibid., 1st sess., 1811, p. 455.
26. Ibid., 12th Cong., 1st sess., 1812, pp. 823, 846; ibid., 13th Cong., 3d sess., 1815, p. 1116.
27. Ibid., 12th Cong., 1 sess., 1812, p. 1493; ibid., 2d sess., 1813, p. 710; ibid., 13th Cong., 2d sess., 1814, pp. 855, 1696.
28. *Laws of Congress,* 10th Cong., 1st sess., pp. 14–16.
29. Ibid., 2d sess., p. 235.
30. Ibid., 12th Cong., 1st sess., p 435.

31. Ibid., pp. 438–42.
32. Ibid., 14th Cong., 2d sess., pp. 242–44.
33. Ibid., 15th Cong., 2d sess., p. 14.
34. Ibid., pp. 44–46.
35. Ibid., 11th Cong., 3d sess., pp. 322–25.
36. *Annals of Congress,* 3d Cong., 2d sess., 1794, p. 889.
37. Ibid., 14th Cong., 2d sess., 1817, p. 415.
38. *Indiana Gazette,* Vincennes, August 28, 1804.
39. *Annals of Congress,* 3d Cong., 2d sess., 1794, p. 897.
40. Ninian Edwards to Richard M. Johnson, Elvirade, Illinois Territory, March 14, 1812, quoted in Clarence E. Carter and John Porter Bloom, eds., *The Territorial Papers of the United States* (Washington, D.C.: Government Printing Office, 1934–), 16:199–200.
41. *Annals of Congress,* 14th Cong., 2d sess., 1817, pp. 415–16.

Stephen A. Douglas and the
Territories in the Senate

ROBERT W. JOHANNSEN

ON MARCH 14, 1844, Senator Arthur P. Bagby of Alabama, responding to the urgent appeal of the delegates representing the nation's three territories, introduced a resolution in the Senate calling for the appointment of an additional standing committee, the Committee on Territories. The resolution apparently excited little debate, although several senators voiced their opposition to its passage. George Evans, senator from Maine and chairman of the Senate Finance Committee, for example, regarded the new committee as unnecessary "on the ground that the business of the Territories was as well attended to now as it could be." Bills relating to appropriations and the disposition of the public lands in the territories would, he argued, still be referred to other committees. An attempt to lay Bagby's resolution on the table, supported by the chairmen of fourteen of the Senate's twenty-four standing committees, failed, and on March 25 it was adopted.[1]

The territories of the United States had long been represented in the House of Representatives by nonvoting delegates, and since 1825 the lower house had also channeled territorial business through a standing committee. The territories, Bagby pointed out in defense of his resolution, had no immediate representative in the Senate to forward their business; the new committee, he hoped, would "give greater facility and security" to the transaction of matters relating to the territories.[2] A more precise definition of the committee's jurisdiction, however, was not forthcoming, while the opposition to its creation indicated that it was regarded as a potential threat to the power of other Senate committees. These problems, present at its birth, dogged the committee and its members during the next decade and a half. They were sharpened by the rapidly expanding importance of the committee and by the strength and prestige of its chairman during most of those years.

77

Few in 1844 could have foreseen the significance which the Senate Committee on Territories would assume within a short period of time. The three territories whose delegates had urged the committee's creation were all admitted as states within four years—Florida in 1845, Iowa in 1846, and Wisconsin in 1848. But when the committee was formed in 1844, the United States stood on the threshold of its most dramatic expansion. Texas, annexed in 1845, bypassed the territorial stage of government, but the settlement of the Oregon boundary dispute and the termination of the Mexican War brought vast new lands into the United States for which territorial government seemed appropriate. The nation's boundary was pushed westward from the Rocky Mountains to the Pacific Ocean thus forcing a reappraisal of federal policy toward what had now, with an unexpected suddenness, become the national heartland. Caravans of covered wagons carried settlers to the far reaches of the continent, and the cry was raised for the extension of organized government to the new lands. The trails westward crisscrossed the prairies and plains; what had been regarded as a permanent Indian frontier now lay athwart the main routes of transportation. Pressures mounted for the opening of settlement and the organization of government in an area that only a short time before was regarded as a barren and uninhabitable desert. As population grew both on the Pacific Coast and in the intervening country, the needs of the new frontier communities multiplied, and it was to Congress that the settlers naturally looked for their satisfaction.

Finally, national expansion brought the question of slavery to its most critical juncture. The slavery issue, in a most dangerous and explosive form, became intertwined with questions of territorial policy, and it fell to the Senate committee to unravel the threads and to find a solution that would satisfy the protagonists. These circumstances—national expansion and the slavery agitation—combined to make the Senate Committee on Territories one of the most powerful groups in the national legislature. It became the focus for political intrigue and maneuver as well as the source of sectional compromise. The story of the territories in Congress and the development of territorial policy through legislation during the fifties cannot be understood without a thorough understanding of the decade's political struggles, for the territories became pawns in a conflict that far transcended the needs and desires of the nation's frontier communities. Sectional politics dictated the course of territorial policy; in the periods of political crisis that shook the nation in the 1850s—the conflict over the organization of the Mexican Cession, the Compromise of 1850, the bitter controversy over the Kansas-Nebraska Act, and the struggle over Kansas's Lecompton Constitution—the Committee on Territories assumed an importance that was denied to the Senate's other committees.

A committee of such key importance required leadership that was commensurate with its role. That leadership was provided by Stephen A. Douglas, senator from Illinois, who held the chairman's post from 1847, when he first entered the Senate, until he was removed by a party caucus for political reasons in the last days of 1858. Douglas brought to his responsibilities an almost obsessive commitment to the development of the West and considerable experience in dealing with its problems. A fervent expansionist, he regarded the establishment of government on the nation's frontiers as partial fulfillment of a destiny that was peculiarly American. The West, to Douglas, played a large and significant role in the unfolding American mission. It was the most national area of the country—"the heart and soul of the nation and the continent"—the seat of progress and the source of strength. It was, he insisted, "the hope of this nation—the resting-place of the power that is not only to control, but to save, the Union." As a westerner, Douglas once declared, "I belong to no section."[3]

Ten years following his arrival in Illinois, at which time he had announced that he had "become a *Western* man" with "Western feelings, principles and interests,"[4] Douglas was elected to a seat in the House of Representatives. Shortly afterward he formulated a program for the West that suggested his deep concern for national growth. The establishment of territorial governments in Oregon and Nebraska, he urged in 1845, would consolidate America's hold on the Pacific shore; the construction of a Pacific railroad would bind the West to the nation and, together with a free land policy, would promote its settlement.[5] While he continued to do battle for the latter measures, it was the extension of governmental institutions to the frontier that virtually monopolized his attention and consumed most of his energies. In December 1845, Douglas was appointed chairman of the Committee on Territories in the House of Representatives, and when he entered the Senate two years later it seemed logical that he should be selected for a comparable post.

Douglas undertook the tasks of his chairmanship with a breadth of vision and a wholehearted devotion that had been unmatched by his predecessors in the committee's brief history. "From early youth I have indulged an enthusiasm, which seemed to others wild and romantic," he told a group of Californians in 1851, "in regard to the growth, expansion, and destiny of this republic." He had studied the country between the Mississippi and the Pacific until he felt he knew it quite as accurately as the older states of the Union. He familiarized himself with the history and development of territorial government in the United States, and the ease with which he cited precedents and quoted passages from earlier territorial legislation frequently astounded his colleagues. The steps by which a territory moved into statehood attracted his attention and he spent much time in a close study of the state-making process. "The preparation of the various bills necessary to give government to the people of the territories, and prepare them for admission into the Union as states," he stated, "required labor and investigation." It was, he added, a labor of love—"a labor in which duty and inclination ran in the same channel."[6]

Douglas's deep concern for the territories often subjected him to ridicule and criticism in the Senate. Senators from eastern states were not always willing to accept his persistent arguments for the necessity of territorial organization in the West. In 1854, a Connecticut senator insisted that too many territories had already been organized and that the Treasury would not be able to support them. Urging that the creation of new territories was contrary to the interest of the older states, he alluded to Douglas's "remarkable fecundity in the line of Territories." Others echoed these sentiments. The Union, it was said, would be wrecked by the constant tendency to expansion, for by increasing the number of states the chances of resistance to the national government were multiplied. During the debates over the Kansas-Nebraska Act, another senator, turning to Douglas, declared, "I think for a long time he has had a passion, amounting to a sort of mania, for the organization of new Territories, and the founding of new States."[7]

In the absence of direct territorial representation in the Senate, Douglas came to regard himself as an informal delegate for all the territories. During his tenure as chairman of the territorial committee, he wrote, modified, and sponsored bills for the organization of seven territories—Oregon, Minnesota, Utah, New Mexico, Washington, Kansas, and Nebraska. He proposed several more which were never approved by Congress. The establishment of territorial government, he repeatedly pointed out, was a national necessity, essential to American expansion and to the settlement and development of the West. "All the Territories of the Confederacy," one former territorial governor told the senator, "bear the impress of your Statesmanship." Douglas insisted that it was his responsibility to take the interests of the territories under his special care. "Inasmuch as there was no delegate to represent them in the Senate of the United States, I have acted as a delegate for these seven Territories."[8]

Douglas's view of the scope and responsibilities of the Senate Committee on Territories was in keeping with his own personal interests. Everything, he maintained, that pertained to the territories came under the purview of his committee, a position that frequently brought him into conflict with the chairmen of older established standing committees. While still a member of the House of Representatives, Douglas defended the wide-ranging responsibilities of the committee and as senator he reiterated his conviction many times. The committee on Territories, he declared, had been constituted "to take charge of the Territorial business . . . and its province included military affairs, judicial affairs, post office affairs, and everything else which related to the Territories." He conceded that there were other committees which had concurrent jurisdiction but maintained that "if the Committee on Territories had not the right to take cognizance of all laws necessary to the organization of Territories, and to the protection of our citizens there, they had no rights."[9] He reminded his colleagues that the Senate, "by a unanimous vote, appointed me chairman of the territorial committee, and associated five intelligent and patriotic Senators with me, and thus made it our duty to take charge of all territorial business."[10] During most of the period, however, the committee members played minor roles compared with that of the chairman. Douglas was often careless about calling meetings of his committee, and committee members, unable to match the extent of his knowledge concerning the territories, frequently absented themselves from its deliberations. Committee reports emanated from Douglas's pen virtually without consultation, and charges were often made that committee members had not even seen some of the reports before their submission to the Senate. His exercise of near-absolute power over territorial matters concerned some senators, especially as the territories became more involved in political and sectional controversy. When, late in 1853, the size of the committee was increased from five to six members, it was as much an attempt to curb the power of the chairman as it was an effort to provide equal representation to the free and slave states.

The Senate committee was still new when Douglas assumed its chairmanship; the first chairman to be thoroughly identified with the West, he was anxious that the committee's authority be clearly established and accepted. In some cases this meant a reversal of previous Senate procedure. During the discussions that eventually led to the Compromise of 1850, Douglas insisted that all bills admitting new states properly belonged to the Territorial Committee. He was immediately challenged by several Southern senators who pointed out that the Judiciary Committee had traditionally considered such bills. The bill in question provided for the admission of California (one of several introduced) and the politics of the slavery question had much to do with the challenge. Douglas seized upon the incident to plead the case of his committee and to register strong objections to the manner in which the committee had been treated in the reference of other bills. The experience was not new to him. Earlier, in the House, he had charged that "there seemed to be a game playing . . . to say to the Committee on Territories, You have reported on subjects which you ought not to have reported on."[11] The time had arrived, he told the Senate in 1850, to settle the question once and for all.

The California bill, he protested, legitimately belonged to the Territorial Committee rather than the Committee on the Judiciary, which was considered "safer" by proslave Southern senators. If it did not, he asked, why was the Territorial Committee organized in the first place? "What is the object of a Territorial Committee? What are its duties, and what subjects were intended to be referred to it? If a bill forming a new State out of the Territories, or a bill creating territorial governments is not to go to that committee, what, then, is there left to be sent to it?" His patience grew thin—a bill for a land office in a territory goes to the Committee on Public Lands; legislation relating to Indians in a territory is referred to the Committee on Indian Affairs; bills relating to federal district courts in the territories go to the Judiciary Committee. All of these subjects, he emphasized, were properly the concern, and only the concern, of the Committee on Territories. He hoped that a test question could be made on the California bill and suggested that if the Senate disagreed with his position he would willingly relinquish all his duties on the committee to someone more attuned to the Senate's wishes.[12] The Senate did not rise to the bait. The bill that finally admitted California was matured in Douglas's committee, but the scope of the committee's authority was never precisely defined. Douglas continued to face the problem throughout the fifties, although in one sense a victory had been won, for future bills admitting new states did become the responsibility of the Territorial Committee. Douglas, convinced that statehood was an integral part of territorial policy, approached this aspect of his task with the same thoroughness that characterized his attention to territorial matters. "When it becomes my duty, as chairman of a committee of this body," he once revealed, "to report a bill for the admission of a new State, I review the precedents under our own Constitution. I examine the practice in other cases, and trace the history of our legislation upon the subject from the formation of the Government. I look into the action of all the departments of the Government, and examine the decisions of the courts."[13]

Not all of the business of the territorial committee was as spectacular or as controversial as it proved to be during the debates over the Compromise of 1850, the Kansas-Nebraska Act, and the Lecompton Constitution. Much of it was routine but it was a routine to which Douglas religiously applied himself. A sampling of legislation reported by Douglas from his committee indicates bills for the relief of territorial officers who were out of pocket for some of the expenses of administration, appropriations for public buildings, the construction of roads and the sinking of wells, the protection of school lands in the territories, the definition and surveying of boundaries, the reimbursement of settlers for expenses incurred in Indian wars, and the regulation of the salaries of officials. He fought for placing the territories on an equality with the states in a number of different instances, for example, providing equal mileage for Oregon's territorial delegate with the senators and representatives from California. But while the Senate proved willing to consider such routine matters when they applied to states, there was often a reluctance to bring them up when they related to the territories. The territories, sparsely populated, far distant and represented in the Senate only by Douglas, were no match for the attention which the states could generate on the Senate floor.

One of Douglas's persistent complaints against his colleagues was the neglect to which routine territorial business was subjected. His constant reminders that territorial bills were pending and his repeated efforts to set aside special days for the consideration of territorial business often succeeded only in branding him as a nuisance. In 1852, Douglas reminded the Senate that he had struggled without success for five months to obtain a single day for the consideration of territorial legislation; the following year, he complained that "I have given way now for two sessions, and the Senate has not touched a territorial bill of any importance during this Congress." On the last day of the session in March 1853, Douglas observed that "the members of the body are in very good humor, all having got what they wanted except the Territories. I hope we shall do something for them." Again he was unsuccessful. Early in 1854, he gloomily concluded, "I find it generally to be the case with my territorial bills, that if I do not get them acted on early in the session they are crowded over by other business at the end of the session, and are always postponed for want of time."[14] Indeed, the neglect of the territories by Congress played a small role in Douglas's commitment to popular sovereignty, or territorial self-government. "I propose to organize the Territories," he declared in 1854, "and allow the people to do for themselves what you have so often refused to do for them."[15]

Douglas discovered that neglect of the territories could result not only from inaction but also from the interjection of what he considered extraneous issues into the discussion of territorial bills. As the territories became the focus of political and sectional disagreement on questions that transcended the needs and desires of the frontier, his impatience and anger mounted. One of these was the slavery question. This is not the appropriate occasion for a discussion of Douglas's views on slavery;[16] suffice it to say that he considered slavery to be a local, domestic institution and hence one to be decided by the states and territories involved with it. The need for organized government on the frontier was acute, and he rankled at the interminable delays occasioned by debate over questions which had little to do with satisfying this need. The people of California, he protested in 1849, were suffering "for the want of a government" while Congress discussed the slavery issue. "I have tried to get up State bills, territorial bills, and all kinds of bills, in all shapes, in the hope that some bill, in some shape, would satisfy the Senate," he declared. "But thus far, I have found their taste in relation to this matter too fastidious for my humble efforts." While he fought hard for certain basic principles to which he was devoted, he frequently indicated a willingness to compromise his views in the interest of achieving his larger goals. It was often expedient, he once said, to "yield a little that one might desire" rather than to insist "upon his own peculiar views" and thereby "hazard the whole, and lose the object he had in view." With reference to California, he explained, "all I ask is, that we give the people there some safe government; all I ask is action."[17] When the fate of the people in Kansas became involved in bitter and lengthy debate, most of which had little bearing on their need for sound and orderly government, he suspected a deliberate delaying tactic at the expense of the territories.[18]

Douglas not only attempted to end the neglect which the territories frequently suffered at the hands of Congress but also to separate the question of the organization of new territories and the admission of new states from politics, a task of formidable proportions which he soon discovered. He sought a uniformity in territorial legislation that would terminate the kind of ad hoc or patchwork policy which had come to characterize national policy and that would make the organization of territories and the admission of states an almost automatic process. Innovations introduced in one territory, he thought, should be made applicable to all territories. Stimulated by the sectional disagreement over slavery's relationship to the frontier and strongly influenced by agitation from the territories themselves, Douglas developed his famous doctrine of popular sovereignty. Popular sovereignty, by extending the limits of self-government in the territories, would allow the people of the territories to assume control over matters which had heretofore been handled by Congress. The fact that popular sovereignty, by removing the question of slavery in the territories from Congress, would also serve as a sectional compromise necessary to the preservation of the Union only enhanced its value in Douglas's thinking.

In his early contacts with territorial organization as a member of the House of Representatives, Douglas had indicated support for the traditional role of Congress toward the territories. Congress and the territories, he stated then, were like father and son; just as "the father may bind the son during his minority" so must Congress exercise jurisdiction and control over the territories "during their infancy."[19] In reporting his bill for the creation of Oregon Territory in 1846, he alluded to the fact that all previous territories had been organized "on the same principles, and had the same general provisions running throughout their charters." The pattern had undergone some modification "as experience had indicated necessary;" of all of them he regarded the most recent, that of the territory of Iowa, as the most perfect. Hence, Oregon's government was to be based closely upon that of Iowa.[20] At the same time, the Oregon bill contained a germ of the popular sovereignty which Douglas would soon develop, for Oregon's settlers had already formed a provisional government and the area was, for all practical purposes, already self-governing. In drafting his bill, Douglas was careful to recognize this fact by allowing the laws of the provisional government to continue undisturbed, provided they were consistent with the Constitution.

Under the stress of the debates over the Wilmot Proviso and the threat that territorial legislation might become hopelessly entangled with the politics of the slavery question, Douglas moved rapidly toward the formulation of a new policy. He based his arguments on moral right. "I do not speak of constitutional rights," he declared. "I do not choose to go into abstractions and metaphysical reasoning, but I speak of those moral rights which are violated when we go to dictating forms of government to a people who are about ready to assume the position of an independent State."[21] But, he pointed out, it was not just interference with a territory as it moved into statehood that concerned him. The territories, as territories, also must be free of congressional dictation. "Have the people of the territories of the United States no rights?" he asked. All men, he insisted, "have certain inherent and inalienable rights; and I have yet to learn upon what grounds the people of the territories are to be excluded from the benefit of this principle."[22] He did not deny the power of Congress to legislate for the territories but he did insist that the right of self-government must be conceded to them. Besides, he maintained in an 1850 version of what later became known as the Freeport Doctrine, laws passed by Congress for the territories would "always remain practically a dead letter" if they were in opposition to the wishes and interests of the people to be affected by them.[23] From these beginnings, Douglas gradually evolved and matured his belief in popular sovereignty. No longer was it simply a matter of moral right; it became a constitutional right as well. No longer was he willing to concede an absolute power of Congress over the territories; the territories assumed a status that was in some ways analogous to that of the states. The people of an organized territory possessed the power and the right, "under the Constitution and laws of the United States, to govern themselves in respect to their own internal policy and domestic affairs."[24]

Popular sovereignty was written into the bills creating Utah and New Mexico Territories and Douglas hailed the passage of these bills in 1850 as establishing a new basis for territorial policy. The bills, he later wrote, "were intended to have a far more comprehensive and enduring effect than the mere adjustment of the difficulties arising out of the recent acquisition of Mexican territory."[25] Acting on this conviction, Douglas gave his doctrine its fullest expression in the Kansas-Nebraska Act four years later. Not only were the people of the two territories to be left "perfectly free to form and regulate their domestic institutions in their own way," but Douglas also altered the traditional pattern of territorial organization in other ways. Restrictions on territorial legislation that had characterized earlier acts were dropped, the provision for congressional veto or disallowance was struck out, and a modification of the governor's veto power was proposed whereby the legislature could reenact any bill with a two-thirds majority. In 1861, he carried popular sovereignty to an ultimate stage when he urged, unsuccessfully, that the people of a territory be allowed to elect all of their own officials. "I desire to deprive this Government," he stated at the time, "of the power of having any Federal policy in regard to the politics of the Territories."[26] Kansas and Nebraska were the last territories to be organized under Douglas's leadership but the discussion of territorial policy raged on as popular sovereignty became the focus of bitter political and sectional attack. Douglas, at the center of the controversy, found himself forced to defend, develop and clarify his position.

The authority of Congress to organize territorial governments, Douglas maintained, did not derive from the controversial clause of the Constitution which empowered Congress to pass all rules and regulations dealing with the territory or other property of the United States. Instead, it was embodied in the power to admit new states. The organization of a territory was a necessary and proper step in the establishment of state governments. Inasmuch as the equality of all the states was a "fundamental principle in our federative system" and the "basis upon which the American Union rests," the organic act of a territory must contain no provision or restriction that would impair the equality of the proposed or future state with the original states. Nothing in the organic act must inhibit in any way the sovereignty of the state to be formed out of the territory. In other words, Douglas wrote in an 1856 report, "the organic act of the Territory . . . must leave the people entirely free to form and regulate their domestic institutions and internal concerns in their own way."[27] In seeking acceptance of popular sovereignty, Douglas compared the condition of the territories with that of the thirteen colonies before the American Revolution. To make "laws for a distant people, regulating their domestic concerns, and affecting their rights of property, without giving them a representation" was to violate one of the principles of the Revolution. "I am asserting," he proclaimed, "on behalf of the people of the Territories, just those rights which our fathers demanded for themselves against the claim of Great Britain."[28]

A territory, however, was not itself a sovereign power. Its sovereignty was "in abeyance, suspended in the United States in trust for the people when they become a State." Douglas did not deny the role of Congress in prescribing the limits of territorial authority, but he did assert that Congress was bound to grant to the territory all the power that could be given under the Constitution with the understanding that Congress would not interfere with whatever legislation the territory might enact. The people of a territory must be vested "with all the rights and privileges of self-government, on all rightful subjects of legislation," or, put another way, they should be given "all the powers of legislation on all questions of a local and domestic character."[29] "There seems to be a strange impression abroad that this Government, which has but a few specified powers, so far as the States are concerned," Douglas asserted in 1861, "is omnipotent in the Territories of the United States. I deny the omnipotence of the Federal power either in States or Territories."[30]

Douglas elaborated on the role of Congress in admitting new states in answer to those who supported Kansas's proslave Lecompton Constitution. Southerners insisted that Kansas be admitted as a state under conditions which were denied to such free territories as Minnesota and Oregon. When the English bill was proposed as a compromise of the Lecompton controversy, Douglas objected to its unfairness to the other territories. For political reasons, Kansas was to be given special treatment. Douglas seized the opportunity to urge a general consideration of the state-making process, a good example of the degree to which the political controversies of the fifties dictated territorial policy.

The United States, Douglas declared, holding the sovereignty of a territory as trustee, could not be divested of that sovereignty nor the territory invested with the right to assume and exercise it without the consent of Congress. In other words, no territory could assume the powers of a state without Congress's approval (as the members of the Lecompton convention were apparently trying to do). Douglas insisted that the distracting questions of slavery and sectional equilibrium be circumvented by applying certain general rules that would make the admission of new states virtually an automatic process. No territory, he urged, should form a state government without the passage by Congress of an enabling act. Congress's consent should not be given unless the territory had population enough for one member of Congress according to the existing ratio, and in all cases the proposed state constitution should be submitted to the people for their ratification or rejection. Population was the crucial factor in determining the point at which a territory could become a state. Once the sufficient population had been attained, admission into the Union, to Douglas, was a "matter of right." A territory was justified in moving on its own, without an enabling act, only if there "has been long, protracted, and vexatious delay after they have population enough for a member of Congress."[31]

If Douglas had thought that popular sovereignty, as a new basis on which territories could be organized, would end territorial neglect and remove questions relating to the territories from politics, he was of course doomed to bitter disappointment. The territories had become the center of political conflict and so enmeshed in the growing debate over slavery that all considerations of practical territorial policy became lost in growing abstraction and bitterness. Douglas's own arguments grew out of the political challenges of the decade and were to a large degree responses to crisis rather than the calm, rational development of a line of thought. For this reason, his attempts to justify popular sovereignty were frequently fuzzy, obtuse, and even contradictory. Basic to all, however, was his deep concern for the territories and their sound, orderly development and his conviction that frontier dwellers, the inhabitants of the territories, had a right to self-government. Douglas may not have succeeded in his attempt to separate the territories from the turbulent politics of the decade but he was eminently successful in striking a responsive and sympathetic chord in the territories themselves. Popular sovereignty was good frontier doctrine and westerners were not slow to appreciate Douglas's efforts on their behalf.

"No man in the country," commented one territorial newspaper, "wields so potent an influence as Mr. Douglas, on all things pertaining to the Territories. He is familiar with their history, geography, climate and wants; and even from his bitterest revilers, his suggestions on matters of territorial policy command respect and attention."[32] Douglas regarded himself as the delegate in the Senate for the seven territories that were placed under his wing; there is ample evidence that the people in those territories thought of him in the same light. He was the recipient of a multitude of petitions, memorials and appeals from the territories, and his correspondence is filled with letters from territorials who sought his advice, expressing, as one frontiersman wrote, "full confidence in your knowledge of the wants of a people situated as we are."[33] One gets the impression that Douglas's contacts with the territories were frequently closer than those of the delegates who sat in the House of Representatives. His power extended beyond his responsibilities as chairman of the territorial committee and he exercised considerable influence over the internal political development of the various territories. "Your wishes . . . have been more consulted than all things else," wrote one Kansas officeholder of the attempt to form a Democratic party in 1857.[34] Douglas's familiarity with territorial matters and his close relations with the people of the territories made him a key figure in the distribution of the territorial patronage. Presidents and cabinet members consulted him, his recommendations were accorded considerable weight, and many territorial officeholders owed their positions to Douglas's endorsement.

Douglas's espousal of popular sovereignty, more than anything else, won him praise and support in the western territories. Since its inception in the late eighteenth century, the American territorial system had been under attack from those most affected by it, the people in the territories. The fairly rigid federal control exercised over the frontier, the imposition of "foreign" appointees on the territories, the restrictions on self-rule all provided sources of irritation and complaint to territorial settlers. Demands had been raised for the easing of territorial restrictions and the broadening of self-government but Congress's moves in this direction had too often been halfhearted and ineffective. Douglas, of course, was aware of this tradition of frontier discontent and his doctrine of popular sovereignty was in part designed to meet it. During the fifties, as territorial populations grew rapidly in size, the significance of popular sovereignty to this long agitation was quickly grasped. Douglas's new basis for territorial organization was celebrated as a great "democratic step forward, enlarging the rights of American citizens in the Territories." The passage of the Kansas-Nebraska Act, with its popular sovereignty, represented a "returning sense of justice in the policy of the government towards the Territories of the Union."[35] Some in the territories even appealed to Douglas to extend the terms of the Kansas-Nebraska Act to their own governments that they might enjoy the increased measure of self-government it provided.[36] For his persistent efforts on behalf of the territories, Douglas was enthusiastically praised "as the champion of the pioneer population of our happy country." The people of Oregon, wrote one westerner, "look upon you as their best friend in Congress," and a Nebraskan hailed Douglas as "the friend of the Territories and the Champion of the people's rights."[37] The evidence could be multiplied many times. The only discordant note was struck in Mormon Utah. While they had strong praise for his popular sovereignty, the Mormons dealt harshly with Douglas and for good reason. Long a friend of the Mormons in Congress, Douglas, in the mid-fifties, joined the hue and cry against the denomination. Denouncing the Salt Lake Mormons as "alien enemies" and "outlaws," he went so far as to propose the abolition of Utah's territorial government in order to deprive its population of the self-government they enjoyed.[38]

For all his concern for the territories and his persistent struggles on behalf of territorial legislation in the Senate, Douglas ultimately became the victim of the very politics he sought to remove from territorial policy. His efforts were not judged in terms of their impact on the needs and desires of the territories, except by the people in the territories; rather they were appraised in terms of their relation to the power struggle between North and South and to the issue of slavery. Despite Douglas's intentions, the territories continued to be but pawns in a larger political controversy. By the latter years of the decade, it became obvious to many of the Senate's leaders that Douglas's program for the territories held out little hope for the South's "peculiar institution." He was, by that time, the only remaining chairman of a major Senate committee from a free state, a fact that became unacceptable to Southern leadership. In December 1857, the membership of the Committee on Territories was reconstituted so as to place Douglas in the minority, a further step to reduce his power. Final action came a year later. Douglas's stand against Kansas's proslave Lecompton Constitution, his defiance of Southern leadership, and his enunciation during the debates with Abraham Lincoln of what became known as the Freeport Doctrine were the last straw. When Congress met in December 1858, Douglas was removed from the committee chairmanship by a Southern-dominated caucus. The action was a hard blow for the territories and left Douglas bitter and disappointed. "For eleven years," he observed in 1860, "my opinions were no disqualification for service at the head of the Territorial Committee, and if they were not for eleven years, why should they be for the twelfth year?"[39]

The story of the territories in the United States Senate during the crucial decade following the war with Mexico is Douglas's story. His removal from the Senate Committee on Territories not only closed an era in his career but it also terminated a period in which the territories were able to look to their most ardent champion in Congress. His concern for the territories, his interest in their development, and his efforts to secure fair and just treatment for their inhabitants remained undiminished. Douglas throughout his career revealed a passionate devotion to the future greatness and destiny of the American Union and this devotion continued even stronger than before. The West, the territories, to Douglas, always played the dominant role in the pursuit of the nation's inevitable destiny. His look was ever westward; his vision as unlimited as the West's trackless expanse. National expansion, the extension of government to the frontier through the organization of territories, and the preparation of the territories for admission to statehood were primary goals for the Illinois senator. The territories organized and the states admitted under his watchful eye remained as monuments to the devotion with which he pursued these goals.

NOTES

1. U.S., Congress, Senate, *Congressional Globe,* 28th Cong., 1st sess., 1843–44. pp. 392, 404, 438.
2. Ibid., pp. 739, 404.
3. Ibid., 31st Cong., 1st sess., 1849–50, app., p. 365; ibid., 33d Cong., 1st sess., 1853–54, app., p. 788.
4. Douglas to Julius N. Granger, December 15, 1833, in Stephen A. Douglas, *Letters of Stephen A. Douglas,* ed. Robert W. Johannsen (Urbana: University of Illinois Press, 1961), p. 3.
5. *Congressional Globe,* 28th Cong., 2d sess., 1844–45, p. 226; Douglas to Asa Whitney, October 15, 1845, Douglas, *Letters,* pp. 131–32.

6. *Illinois Daily Register* (Springfield), April 8, 1851.
7. *Congressional Globe,* 33d Cong., 1st sess., 1853–54, app., pp. 169–70, 393, 409.
8. *Chicago Times,* August 21, 1857. See also *Congressional Globe,* 34th Cong., 3d sess., 1856–57, p. 854.
9. *Congressional Globe,* 29th Cong., 1st sess., p. 126.
10. Ibid., 33d Cong., 1st sess., 1853–54, app., p. 326.
11. Ibid., 30th Cong., 2d sess., 1848–49, pp. 46–47; ibid., 31st Cong., 1st sess., 1849–50, pp. 86–87; ibid., 29th Cong., 1st sess., 1845–46, p. 125.
12. Ibid., 31st Cong., 1st sess., 1849–50, p. 211.
13. Ibid., app., p. 851.
14. Ibid., 32d Cong., 1st sess., 1851–52, p. 2251; ibid., 2d sess., 1852–53, pp. 934, 1117; ibid., 33d Cong., 1st sess., 1853–54, p. 239.
15. Ibid., 33d Cong., 1st sess., 1853–54, app., p. 326.
16. For a brief discussion of Douglas's views on slavery, see Robert W. Johannsen, "Stephen A. Douglas and the South," *Journal of Southern History* 33 (February 1967): 26–50.
17. *Congressional Globe,* 30th Cong., 2d sess., 1848–49, pp. 668, 551; ibid., 29th Cong., 1st sess., 1845–46, p. 686.
18. Ibid., 34th Cong., 1st sess., 1855–56, pp. 1100, 1253.
19. Ibid., 28th Cong., 2d sess., 1844–45, p. 284.
20. Ibid., 29th Cong., 1st sess., 1845–46, p. 1203.
21. Ibid., 30th Cong., 2d sess., 1844–49, p. 208.
22. Ibid., 31st Cong., 1st sess., 1849–50, app., p. 374.
23. Ibid., p. 1116; app., pp. 369–70.
24. J. Madison Cutts, *A Brief Treatise upon Constitutional and Party Questions, and the History of Political Parties, As I Received It Orally from the Late Senator Stephen A. Douglas, of Illinois* (New York: D. Appleton & Co., 1866), p. 124. See also Robert W. Johannsen, "Stephen A. Douglas: Popular Sovereignty and the Territories," *Historian* 22 (August 1960): 378–95.
25. U.S., Congress, Senate Report 15, 33d Cong., 1st sess., 1859–60, p. 1.
26. *Congressional Globe,* 36th Cong., 2d sess., 1860–61, pp. 764–65.
27. Senate Report 34, 34th Cong., 1st sess., 1855–56, pp. 2–4.
28. *Congressional Globe,* 35th Cong., 2d sess., 1858–59, p. 1246; Douglas, "The Dividing Line between Federal and Local Authority: Popular Sovereignty in the Territories," *Harper's Magazine* 29 (September 1859): 519–37. For a discussion of this article, see Robert W. Johannsen, "Stephen A. Douglas, 'Harper's Magazine,' and Popular Sovereignty," *Mississippi Valley Historical Review* 45 (March 1959): 606–31.
29. Senate Report 82 (Minority Report), 35th Cong., 1st sess., 1857–58, pp. 52–53; *Congressional Globe,* 35th Cong., 2d sess., 1858–59, p. 1246.
30. *Congressional Globe,* 36th Cong., 2d sess., 1860–61, p. 430.
31. Senate Report 82 (Minority Report), 35th Cong., 1st sess., 1857–58, p. 53; *Congressional Globe,* 35th Cong., 1st sess., 1857–58, p. 504; ibid., 34th Cong., 3d sess., 1856–57, p. 851.
32. St. Paul *Pioneer and Democrat,* January 14, 1857.
33. William M. Ormsby to Douglas, February 12, 1858, Stephen A. Douglas Papers, University of Chicago Library, Chicago, Ill.
34. John Calhoun to Douglas, January 26, 1857, Douglas Papers.

35. *Oregon Statesman* (Salem), April 4, 1854; Santa Fe *Weekly Gazette,* April 19, 1856.
36. For example, David Newsom to Douglas, April 18, 1858, Douglas Papers.
37. Justin Chenoweth to Douglas, November 20, 1858, owned by Martin F. Douglas; Jesse M. Shepherd to Douglas, September 1, 1858, and Mills Reeves to Douglas, January 3, 1859, Douglas Papers.
38. *Kansas, Utah, and the Dred Scott Decision: Remarks of the Hon. S. A. Douglas, Delivered in the State House at Springfield, Ill., on the Twelfth of June, 1857* (n.p., n.d.), 6–8.
39. *Congressional Globe,* 36th Cong., 1st sess., 1859–60, p. 425.

Discussion of Sources

CHARLES E. SOUTH

To BEGIN THIS DISCUSSION of the sources for territorial history before 1860 in the records of Congress in the National Archives, I should like first to make an essential distinction. Congressional archives preserved in this institution are those records which were maintained either by congressional committees or by the chief administrative officers of the two houses—the clerk of the House and the secretary of the Senate—and therefore do not include extensive amounts of anything that could be called private papers of members of Congress. It is true that committee records will often contain letters to the chairmen from executive agencies, other members, and the public in regard to bills, appropriations, and so forth, which were kept in the committee files rather than in the chairman's personal office files (there is sometimes a hazy distinction between the two categories). There is no guarantee, however, of even this much being found, especially for the nineteenth century.

To turn in a more positive way to what is present, a substantial part of the records of Congress in the National Archives consists of the manuscript originals of documents that were printed and are available in such sources as the *American State Papers,* the *Annals of Congress* and its successors, and, after 1817, the myriad volumes of the Congressional Serial Set, which are sent today to libraries that are depositories for United States government publications. These published documents are generally of two types: communications of various kinds to Congress from the president and other executive officials, and reports of congressional committees to the two houses.

Some of the communications from the executive branch are those submitted regularly to Congress, such as the president's annual message, which was formerly accompanied by several departmental reports; and other reports required by law on, for example, contracts let by the War Department.

Other executive communications were sent in response to congressional requests for information.

The other main series of congressional archives that are in large part published consists of the committee reports—reports on specific subjects, bills, or petitions referred to the congressional committees for consideration. For example, a House select committee was appointed to consider a message of President Jefferson of December 23, 1805, which transmitted a communication from the newly arrived governor of the territory of Michigan. The House committee reported on it in March 1806. Jefferson's message, Governor William Hull's communication, and the House committee report are all in the *American State Papers*. The House committee also proposed a bill with its report, however, which is not included with the other published documents. This bill, H.R. 116, "to provide for the adjustment of land titles [town of Detroit] in the Territory of Michigan," provides a good introduction to a discussion of the congressional records in the National Archives that are not published, since original bills, which were printed only in a limited quantity, represent one major category of such records.

What we have in the National Archives, then, that has not been published, can for the most part be grouped in three categories: (1) original House and Senate bills and resolutions, often with proposed amendments; (2) records, other than printed reports, created and collected by congressional committees; and (3) petitions and memorials.

(1) Original bills are of value in tracing the history of legislation, since enacted laws may differ greatly from the form in which they were introduced. Bills are sometimes printed in the *Annals of Congress* and its successors, but this is not common. The House bill referred to previously, concerning land titles in Michigan, is found in the records of the Senate in the form passed by the House, consisting of twelve sections. As such it provided a general scheme for settling all disputed land titles and claims in the territory. The *Senate Journal* and the *Annals* note that the bill was amended by the Senate, but do not indicate how. A comparison of the original bill with the enacted law in the *Statutes at Large* reveals that the Senate knocked out ten sections so that the law provided only for the settlement of land titles in Detroit, especially for those owning land there when the town burned in 1805.

The series of original Senate bills in the National Archives is fairly complete from the First Congress; the Senate records also contain a substantial file of House bills that passed the House, from the First Congress. The records of the House are rather fragmentary for the very early period, due in part to the war damage in Washington in 1814, and there are very few original House bills until 1811.

(2) The second category of unpublished legislative archives involves the committee records proper, referred to simply as "Committee Papers." It is difficult, and I must emphasize this, to make many generalizations about the quantity or types of these committee papers, especially for the pre-1860 period. Many of these have been lost. In 1840 the clerk of the House wrote that a certain committee had not returned its papers to his office at the end of the session, as was supposed to be the rule; what had become of them he did not know, since "we have no charge, or jurisdiction over papers while in the possession . . . of a Committee." The bulk of the committee papers series is taken up by the original manuscripts of printed committee reports, but much else is included also—some unpublished reports and, especially, correspondence and other papers accompanying or relating to specific bills, as well as some general correspondence not on specific bills. Almost never, for the antebellum period, do these committee records include committee hearings or any other records which directly describe the internal proceedings of the committees. Hearings were not published in any very consistent way until near the end of the nineteenth century, except at times for testimony heard by select investigative committees, often printed as part of the committee report. An example of this is the House Special Committee to Investigate the Troubles in the Territory of Kansas in the Thirty-fourth Congress (1855–57). The printed report of this committee contains over one thousand pages of hearings. The original transcript of these hearings is in the National Archives with the original report; however, transcripts of hearings that were not published, if they exist for the antebellum period, are almost never found in the National Archives. Most of those committee records that would be of interest to you will be the papers accompanying specific bills and resolutions. Unfortunately, the papers of the two committees on the territories, which might be our point of greatest interest, are very limited in quantity. The House Territories Committee was created in 1825, the Senate body in 1844; the total records for both committees before 1860, excluding petitions, amount to perhaps some five linear feet. They consist mostly of the originals of committee reports, many of which are printed in the Serial Set or the *Territorial Papers* volumes. There are some committee reports which do not appear to have been printed; and there are some letters from territorial officials and delegates, generally in support of such requests as an increase in the legislative council of Florida, or payment of the claim of three New Mexico citizens who had loaned the new territory the money to hold its first legislature.

Other committees of course considered matters relating to the territories, to Senator Stephen A. Douglas's annoyance as Dr. Johannsen has pointed out, and their records are likely to be more voluminous. The records of the House Committees on Military Affairs and Indian Affairs for the Thirty-third Congress (1853–55) both contain letters from New Mexico officials and the delegate relating to the governor's calling out of the militia against the Apaches in 1854 and his request for money to pay for it. Additional papers from the Military Affairs Committee concern road and bridge construction in the same territory. Financial needs of the territories are also often reflected in the letters accompanying Treasury estimates sent to the Committee on Ways and Means.

The bulk of these unpublished committee records consists of papers relating to the various kinds of private claim and relief bills. These claims papers are found in nearly all committee records (especially the Committees on Claims, Private Land Claims, and Public Lands) and, while their interest to a genealogist or local historian is obvious, they also may be of use on a wider front. Sizable bill files are especially likely to be produced by disputed land claims. A prominent example of this kind of thing in Wisconsin Territory is a Senate bill of the Twenty-sixth Congress (1839–41) to confirm the title of three claimants, Francis Laventure et al., to land which was part of Milwaukee. The land had been divided and sold so that over one hundred people were involved when the General Land Office decided that the government had not had the authority to sell the land when it did so (because an Indian treaty had not technically been ratified). Disturbances broke out when people who had contracted to buy the land refused to pay, now seeing a way to get it for nothing. The documents on this case in the records of the Senate Public Lands Committee include maps, resolutions of the territorial legislature, and numerous protests and denunciations from the affected settlers.

Claims arose for many reasons besides land. You may remember the 1806 law to settle land claims in Detroit; more than twenty-five years later the Senate Judiciary Committee was considering a bill arising from a claim by two Michigan territorial judges for compensation for their services as commissioners under this act, services performed in addition to their judicial duties. A number of letters from the judges, Governor Lewis Cass, and the Michigan delegate supported the claim; and one letter from a judge to Delegate Lucius Lyon gave him specific orders on handling the matter in Congress. The judges had to wait another ten years, however, before an act was passed for their relief.

(3) The third major group of unpublished congressional archives consists of petitions and memorials—documents expressing opinions on public issues or asking Congress to take some specific action, sent in by legislatures, other organized groups, or individuals. Dr. Bloom has provided several good examples of the content of these petitions, and the *Territorial Papers* volumes have reprinted a great many of them from our records, so that further illustrations should not be necessary. It should be noted, how-

ever, that petitions comprise a larger and more consistently present file than the other committee records in the National Archives. (There are practically no House petitions until the Sixth Congress—1799–1801.) Petitions may sometimes be almost the only manuscript documentation on major issues in Congressional archives. There are nearly one thousand petitions in the records of the House and Senate for the Thirty-third Congress (1853–55) concerning the Kansas-Nebraska bill and the general issue of territorial slavery extension. The only additional records on this measure are the original bills, S. 22 and H.R. 236, with proposed amendments. For any session of any Congress a multitude of petitions from territories or on territorial subjects can be found. The index of the *House Journal* for the Twenty-eighth Congress, first session (1839–40), indicates that the Florida legislature alone sent thirty-eight petitions, many of which were requests for public buildings and internal improvements. In addition to serving as a guide to public sentiment, to some extent, petitions may sometimes contain accompanying papers on bills introduced in response to them, as is the case with two resolutions of the Iowa state legislature found in the petition file of the Senate Territories Committee for 1856–57. They asked that Iowa's northern boundary be extended west to the Missouri River at the expense of Minnesota Territory. With the petitions are drafts of a bill by an Iowa senator to do this, letters from the senator and the Minnesota delegate, letters from the General Land Office giving statistics on the land, and two maps, one of them manuscript.

That concludes the description of the three major types of unpublished records to be found in the records of both houses, but there is an additional series of Senate records which should be noted. This series consists of records accumulated by the Senate in connection with its consideration of presidential appointees requiring Senate confirmation. These papers consist mainly of letters of recommendation or opposition from private citizens and members of Congress, and sometimes letters from executive departments. Such papers are not present for all nominees, since many appointments stirred no controversy. For the antebellum period nomination papers are present, in varying quantity, for some seventy territorial nominees. These papers tend to be vigorous in tone. Arthur St. Clair's reappointment as governor of the Northwest Territory in 1800 produced many identically worded protests from Ohioans, accusing him of "using his prerogatives as an engine of deception and extortion" and observing that to state all their complaints would require a recital of all of St. Clair's official acts. One William Lynde, named by Polk to be United States attorney for Wisconsin Territory, was accused by his enemies of being an abolitionist and a drunkard; a Yale classmate wrote to defend Lynde of the former charge by recalling how the nominee, while at Yale, had joined in "expelling from the church with eggs and sticks a very offensive and abusive [abolitionist] lecturer." More than one of these nomination files indicate that the chief opponent of territorial governors up for reappointment was the territorial delegate (for example, White and DuVal in Florida and Poindexter and Williams in Mississippi). Light may also be shed on quarrels between factions within the territorial governments. The 1808 reappointment file of Governor Hull of Michigan contains many papers relating to his quarrel with Secretary Stanley Griswold, including several letters from both officials. One Hull supporter said that Griswold had "collected to his banners a few of the most restless and contemptible inhabitants . . . and formed a dis-organizing Junto." Curiously enough, this writer, Hull's son-in-law, was appointed in the next Congress as collector of the district of Michilimackinac.

I would like to close with a comment on accessiblity of legislative archives. The records of the Senate for the nineteenth century are generally open for research without restriction, while authorization to use any House records of any period not previously published must be obtained from the office of the clerk of the House. This authorization is generally requested through the researcher's congressman. Although this procedure may cause slight delay, the authorization has always been given, I believe, and should not discourage serious inquiries.

Comment on the Bloom and
Johannsen Papers

J. W. SMURR

I DO NOT THINK that Mrs. Bloom fully exposes the significance of what she is looking at. It would be tempting and certainly more gracious to criticize her paper from the standpoint of intent, as some of you are perhaps inclined to do, thinking that she tried to cover too wide a field and thus left an unfortunate and undeserved impression of superficiality. The soft option is not open to me, because I believe that her approach to territorial matters, a common one in use today, is self-defeating, and will remain so until writers stop regarding constitutional history and constitutional law as arcane disciplines which only a handful of resident wizards at a few leading universities should be expected to know anything about.

The actions of Congress in dealing with territorial problems will always seem vague, capricious, or even mysterious, so long as one fails to see the underlying if sometimes unexpressed assumptions which were decisive in most of these cases; and I mean assumptions about the Constitution of the United States.

One very good reason for delegates not serving on standing committees in Mrs. Bloom's era was doubt of their legal entitlement to do so. Nor could they lawfully offer motions to reconsider, because (unless I recollect House rules wrongly), only one who had participated in the final floor vote previously held was authorized to make such a motion, and as nonvoting members of Congress the delegates simply did not qualify. Mrs. Bloom senses an inconsistency at this point, for "delegates apparently voted" as members of select committees. I have room here only for a general observation, even if it must look like the splitting of hairs. Properly speaking, committees do not "vote"; they merely recommend. It is the full House that "votes," meeting on the floor as representatives from the states. Territories were not states. The ordinance said so, federal statutes said so, all the courts said so, and even Calhoun did not deny it. The "superficiality" I mention in Mrs. Bloom's paper, therefore, is in reality a failure to make constitutional connections between constitutional events. In the absence of this binding tie, even the most expert paper is likely to seem no more than a random collection of data. Imprecision of thought sometimes creeps in, another hazard. It is not correct, for example, that the enabling act for Orleans Territory denied the franchise to persons of mixed blood. What Congress did was to leave the matter up to Orleans; knowing what Orleans would do, to be sure, but refusing to do the dirty work itself. Here again, I see constitutional scruples at work.

Mr. Johannsen's paper is defaced by the same flaw. If Douglas is to be accepted as an eponymous hero who gave his name to a whole territorial age, his performance must be measured against the constitutional traditions in which he worked. Otherwise the result is to exaggerate his achievement. Consider his role in the Oregon business. Oregon was a de facto government in international law, and as such its own laws would automatically continue in force until a new sovereign displaced them by formal act. Douglas knew this. He also knew that there had always been trouble before when Congress failed to continue the laws of older territories once it decided to create new territories from among them. Validating the laws of Provisional Oregon can be explained without looking for germs of popular sovereignty in the chairman's mind. Congressmen who had no particular commitment to territorial reform were also interested in seeing Oregon left with sufficient laws to carry it over the hump. Was popular sovereignty "written into the bills creating Utah and New Mexico . . ."? Not so long as Congress retained the disapproval power and continued the irreversible gubernatorial veto. The "fullest expression" of the doctrine appears in the Nebraska-Kansas Act, we are told, yet here appeal to the United States Supreme Court was not only allowed (as formerly), but the Court was positively encouraged to play a leading role, not only by the terms of the act itself but by the express wish of a powerful group in Congress who hoped the Court would settle the slavery controversy and, necessarily, the fate of popular sovereignty with it. The debates are full of this kind of thinking. Should the Court elect to continue with the doctrines of Marshall, the doctrines of Douglas would not count for very much. Nor did they. It is to the Judiciary Committee that one must look for the decisive actions of the Douglas era. That is what farsighted Southerners wanted, and they got their reward in the *Dred Scott* case.

Johannsen concedes that Douglas's concept of popular sovereignty evolved from actual events and was never very well thought out. "Fuzzy, obtuse, and even contradictory," are some of the words used to describe Douglas. Allan Nevins, be it noted, also used the word obtuse: Douglas was "morally obtuse." I am less charitable. Douglas's impatience with constitutional "metaphysics" was sometimes a cover for his own doubts. How else could the great advocate of local self-government in good conscience propose to strip the people of Utah of every vestige of it? This was Douglas at his worst. I am well persuaded that had he survived the war he would have taken the same road as another such liberal, Matthew Deady, and adjusted his views to a more nationalistic climate, especially if there were an office in it for him.

But this is a side issue with me, and I offer a final consideration of a constitutional sort. The best judges, I believe, agree that the great breakthrough in territorial democracy was the Wisconsin Act of 1836, and I think they would also agree that none of Douglas's innovations altered that system fundamentally. Of course, Douglas would have gone further, but, personal ambition aside, he was defeated by the legal complexities of the task. Like everyone else, he had failed to make a study of the emerging constitutional plight of the territories until it was too late to change it. The theoretical underpinnings of the system had become lost in the penumbra of more glamorous and—need I add?—more politically rewarding things. I think that historical scholarship has shared in this blindness and indifference.

But I take heart from recent developments. Territorial students are beginning to pay more heed to the pioneer works of this difficult branch of knowledge. If my own study of territorial public law fails to make the grade, I expect there are others who will do better. With only his summary before me, I am nevertheless quite confident that Mr. Bestor's paper, scheduled for delivery this morning, will have done much to lighten the gloom; and I look forward with keen anticipation to the papers of Guice and Knecht, both very much in point. This conference may succeed in giving specialists and general scholars what they have long needed: an appreciation of the fundamental rules of the territorial game: the law of the Constitution.

DISCUSSION NOTE

In the general discussion at the conclusion of the session one of the points raised was Douglas's motivation on popular sovereignty—whether he adopted this position as a great proponent of democracy or merely as an expedient for defusing the slavery issue. The questioner pointed out that Douglas opposed certain changes in territorial government which would have promoted democratic selfgovernment, and particularly that he was an active patronage-monger in perpetuating the system of outside appointees while territories were pleading for their residents to have a greater share in their rule. Johannsen replied that Douglas was certainly an enigma in many ways—inconsistent, contradictory, *human*—and that he did not want to seem to be engaged in special pleading for Douglas. But he reported that a student's recent research into President Buchanan's patronage policies showed that Douglas carried more weight with Buchanan in the matter of patronage than has been believed previously, and that most of the appointments to territorial office supported by Douglas were from within the territories.

Jo Bloom, responding to Smurr's criticism, emphasized her disagreement with his preoccupation of interpreting the Constitution in studying territories. Her intent was to find out what actually happened in Congress, not merely what the Constitution provided should take place: "It isn't constitutional law, it isn't necessarily law, it is the study of men and exactly what they did." A general discussion ensued on whether or not the present resident commissioner from Puerto Rico should be considered a delegate, apparently resolved by the understanding that here was a distinction in title without a difference in function.

TERRITORIAL COURTS

OF THE

FAR WEST

EDITOR'S NOTE

The following two essays, with ensuing commentary and discussion, constituted the third session of the conference. Earl Pomeroy introduced the speakers and conducted the discussion period. In preliminary remarks he pointed out that "The stream of American constitutional historiography as a whole has been narrow in that, generally speaking, it has featured those developments associated with national political crises and with decisions by the United States Supreme Court, to the exclusion of other developments." Constitutional historians abroad, he felt, have exhibited broader concerns than have their counterparts in this country: "Historians and politicians stress the importance of state government in the federal system, but historians have not been much interested in writing about it . . . ." He recollected that in 1915 Elihu Root had urged delegates at the New York state constitutional convention to "study the history of changes in the governments of other states, only to find that such a history did not exist . . . ." The volume by James O. Dealey, then commissioned by Root, "despite its shortcomings remains standard fifty-four years later." Welcoming the present session, Pomeroy urged that not only historians but also lawyers should write of "public administration and the development of public law in the territories, of the courts as institutions, [and] of the judges as institution-bearers."

The Role of the Territorial Supreme Courts: The Historian's View

J O H N   D .   W .   G U I C E

IN REFERENCE to Arizona's pioneer politicians, Howard Lamar warned that "villains of yesterday's texts have a way of becoming the heroes of today's books."[1] It may behoove historians of the 1970s to be mindful of Lamar's admonition, for close examination of the supreme courts of Colorado, Montana, and Wyoming Territories reveals that their justices are indeed candidates for such a transformation.[2] Few scholars have seen fit to study their role, and those who have often did so from a moralistic rather than from a functional view.[3]

The carpetbagger theme dominates most accounts, which also tend to classify the courts as the weakest branch of a territorial administration abounding in corruption and incompetence.[4] However, when the activities of the territorial supreme courts of Colorado, Montana, and Wyoming are reassessed critically, the villains are less prevalent and more builders are discovered, a finding which well may be verified by subsequent study of other areas. In addition to fulfilling vital juridical responsibilities, a surprising number of judges contributed substantially to the political, economic, and social development of the territories. Equally significant, however, is the light which activities of the judiciary shed on federal-local relationships and eastern influences in territorial history.

Rejection of the simplistic carpetbagger characterization of territorial justices is appropriate in view of recent calls for a fresh examination of Reconstruction politicians. Richard N. Current admonishes that the carpetbagger stereotype cannot be uncritically accepted,[5] and he questions whether or not so-called carpetbag officials differed in decency and ability from other politicians of the same time and place.[6] In like manner, the validity of applying the carpetbagger label so frequently to territorial supreme court justices of the Reconstruction as well as later periods must be challenged.

One effective approach to the history of the courts is to accept it as a history of their judges. Such was the advice of Wilbur Fisk Stone, pioneer Colorado justice and historian. "Every court takes its quality and complexion from the judge," counselled Stone, "and its influence and effects are measured by the structure of the man and not the machine."[7] In adopting this recommendation, temptations of condemnation and exculpation must be rejected in favor of an assessment of positive contributions of the court.

The role of the jurist in the lawmaking process is not to be neglected, but it must be emphasized that supreme court justices were also in the midst of the often unglamorous process of territorial operation and development. Since territorial history will remain incomplete until the functions of all officials in the growth of the territories have been determined, accounts stressing merely the pejorative aspects of the judiciary offer a restricted view. Perhaps chroniclers have been distracted by the glaring inadequacies of the judicial systems imposed on the territories.

Isolation of the territories has perhaps been more scholastically confining than either the carpetbagger fixation or the accent on moralistic criticism. However, appeals for a reorientation of western history have received a positive response.[8] Provincialism, antiquarianism, and popularization are being abandoned noticeably and, at the same time, scholarship is being extricated from a local framework that, according to Earl Pomeroy, has "slighted similarities, antecedents, and outside influences generally."[9]

Though the history of the territorial supreme courts has yet to take its proper place within the new scholarship of the West, during the approaching decade studies of the judiciary should effect fresh interpretations. The supreme court justices, for example, were similar in many respects to William H. Goetzmann's explorers who were "programmed" for the extension of their cultures.[10] By training and tradition, lawyers tend to be more highly "programmed," to borrow Goetzmann's computer-oriented terminology, than most settlers or even explorers. Of all the heritages transplanted from England, and thence to the West, perhaps none was more deeply rooted than the common law. Strained and even broken on occasion by the demands of mountains and plains, the common law nevertheless was as fundamental a component of the "program" as any institution. It was so much a part of the American heritage, in fact, that its carriers failed to attract the attention due them. In short, parallels definitely may be drawn between the activities of the explorers and those of the judiciary.[11]

Other recent interpretations are strengthened by a study of the courts. In *Wyoming: A Political History, 1868–1896*, Lewis L. Gould examined the role of the federal government and national parties in the political and economic development of Wyoming's territorial and early statehood periods, and he established that a considerable degree of national-local interplay existed. Gould's thesis is supported strongly by the history of the courts under examination here whose activities are clearly illustrative of federal and eastern influence in the territories.

Considering the trend of recent publications, therefore, it is appropriate to suggest that studies of territorial supreme courts will be incorporated into the mainstream of interpretation. Nevertheless, environmental and local themes still clearly dominate the scant bibliography of the courts, and rather than dealing with functional and operational achievements of the bench, most accounts are biographical and reminiscent in scope. Consequently, the semilegendary Roy Bean concept of Western justice has been perpetuated despite the role of the bench in the processes of acculturation and innovation.

Though excitement and danger were not strange to pioneer judges, their duties were, in the main, laborious and far from romantic.[12] Territorial judges, usually from the East and as often unpopular, carried with them, as did members of the early bar, familiar codes and texts from the states. Close supervision of the territorial supreme courts by the United States attorney general as well as the subordination of the territorial bench to the United States Supreme Court were additional factors which intensified the federalizing or nationalizing effects of supreme court justices.

The significance of the courts as institutional vehicles must not be emphasized to the point of obscuring their roles as innovators. Decisions of territorial jurists stand as strong testimony to the modifications imposed on a people's heritage by their environment. The prose of Walter Prescott Webb provided an indelible commentary on the strain and rupture of institutions, including the law, west of the Mississippi.[13] In retrospect, it is surprising that Webb's observations did not provoke a more detailed evaluation of the innovative aspects of trans-Mississippi territorial courts.

Additional knowledge of the social and economic conditions of the litigants is a valuable by-product of the search for judicial contributions. Court records, often tedious and forbidding, have been described as virtual "mines of social history,"[14] and Justice Department files, strange as it may seem, offer an interesting view of economic conditions of Rocky Mountain territories.[15]

A system of laws to protect newly discovered treasures and to restore and maintain social order was one of the strongest demands of settlers of trans-Mississippi territories. Complaints against the congressionally designed territorial system are often emphasized, while urgent appeals for judicial organization are generally overlooked.[16] Newspaper columns and correspondence files reflect the eagerness with which establishment of the courts was anticipated. Denver's *Rocky Mountain News* deemed the presence of Colorado's first chief justice "necessary before the wheels of Government could fairly be set in motion,"[17] and the paper covered the court's activities in minute detail.[18] Territorial officials estimated that damage to industry caused by delay in judicial organization ran into the millions of dollars, and citizens echoed these sentiments as they petitioned for the establishment of courts which were expected to maintain "security to life and property."[19]

The judicial structure formed by Congress placed the justices in an awkward if not untenable situation and its imperfections, ignored by their designers, were the basis of many criticisms leveled at the justices. The possession by supreme court members of both original and appellate jurisdiction in the same causes was perhaps the most serious and frequently cited objection to the structure. Considering the improvisation of codes, practices, and facilities required of the judges, the organic acts, because of their general scope, must have appeared to the early judges as "hardly more than a right to exist."[20] Under prevailing conditions, establishment of law and order and transition from one system of jurisprudence to another was no mean task.[21]

Of all the impediments facing the judiciary, none could have been as distressing as financial hardship stemming from inadequate appropriations. Because Congress could have substantially remedied it, this malady was particularly irritating.[22] Meager compensation, poor facilities, and insufficient operating expenses severely impeded the territorial supreme courts, and their achievements are magnified in view of these circumstances.

In relation to the total picture of territorial operations, the Civil War appears as a peripheral issue. However, in Colorado, the war significantly increased the opportunity of the justices to affect development of the territory, and in Montana and Wyoming the political climate within which the court operated was dramatically influenced by the aftermath of the conflict. The intensity of pro-Southern sentiment in all three territories is sometimes overlooked. Colorado's first chief justice, Benjamin F. Hall, was widely praised by Union sympathizers for his role in saving that territory from infiltration by Confederate agents. The most highly publicized incident involved Hall's denial of the writ of habeas corpus to Capt. Joel McKee who was arrested for allegedly recruiting an army of Confederate sympathizers.[23] The Civil War compounded the already adverse financial and political conditions under which supreme courts functioned in several territories, a fact which must be recalled when an assessment of these institutions is offered.

It appears that Congress intentionally patterned territorial supreme courts as political entities. Appointed by the president for four-year terms, and having no assurance of tenure even for that period of time, the justices depended on their political acumen for both appointment and security of office. As Jack Ericson Eblen observed recently in reference to the governors, this "tells nothing about the worth of the men appointed."[24] But it does reveal still another handicap under which they labored. Caught between national and local political forces, justices often were the victims of attacks, blatantly political in origin, which could come from any quarter.[25] Forces created by the collision of national and local pressures crushed weaker men and forged justices of stature from those of more substance. This aspect of judicial history is ground for additional investigation of the extent of national influence in territorial development.

The surprising feature of the Colorado, Montana, and Wyoming territorial supreme courts is the number of capable justices who served despite inadequate recompense, insufficient operating funds, vast districts, and political intrigue in addition to the general adversities of the frontier. If the entire span of each territorial history is considered, two observations are apparent. One, the combined administration experienced a higher rate of turnover than did the judiciary alone.[26] Two, the character of the judiciary in the later territorial periods improved considerably over that of the Civil War and immediate postwar eras.

Each of these territorial supreme courts was stabilized by the lengthy tenure of one or more judges. Chief Justice Moses Hallett set the style of Colorado's bench at a high level through ten of the court's fourteen years. Montana's two most distinguished jurists, Hiram Knowles and Decius S. Wade, between the two, served some twenty-seven years, and in Wyoming Jacob B. Blair completed three terms.

A denial of the malfeasance of some jurists has no place in a reevaluation of the constructive role of the territorial supreme courts. The presence on the bench of a number of judicial derelicts is a matter of record, and accounts of their antics are, indeed, entertaining.[27] However, their careers, while they do not add to the image of the bench, do not detract from the achievements of the judiciary as a body. It would be equally futile to undertake an assessment of the motivations of each individual, even if it were possible, for it would tell us nothing of his abilities and contributions.

Environmentalists, sometimes gleefully, point to the breakdown of the common law in the Rocky Mountains and high plains. Indeed, it is in the adaptation of the law to the peculiar needs of the region that the supreme court justices proved to be particularly innovative. Men with previous experience in the Rockies, though it may have been of only a few years' duration, as a rule performed with greater distinction and made their presence felt in more lasting fashion than their counterparts appointed directly from the East. Youth appears to have been a catalyst in the innovating process, for a number of the outstanding jurists, if not young when they stepped up to the bench, were claimants to the resilience of youth when they arrived in the West.

Though innumerable problems challenged the initiative and ingenuity of the judges during the transitional periods while the legislatures were enacting territorial codes, the decisions of most consequence regarded mining and water law.[28] Mining involved an abundance of litigation in which speedy settlement was imperative, and the property in dispute was generally of inordinate value. Therefore, in Colorado and Montana, vociferous demands immediately arose for replacement of less gifted jurists and appointment of men capable of dealing with mining problems.[29] Opinions of Chief Justice Hallett gave legitimacy to regulations and procedures of mining districts, the validation of which departed from the common law.[30] During four decades, one as a territorial justice and three as a United States district judge, Hallett earned a preeminent national reputation for his mining opinions.[31] Montana Territory, in Hiram Knowles, Decius S. Wade, and William J. Galbraith, was also favored by the appointment of men capable of dealing with mining litigation.

The most abrupt departure from the common law in the trans-Mississippi territories may have been in the area of water law. The doctrine of riparian rights was replaced by that of prior appropriation. Though this concept had its origins in California, it was refined in Colorado and extended clearly to apply to irrigation as well as mining. Hallett, in a landmark opinion in 1872, explicitly stated that the right to pass over lands of other ownership to obtain a water supply existed "not by grant, but by operation of law."[32] With this heritage, it was natural for the state of Colorado later to assume leadership in development of an administrative system of water control, influencing the codes of over a third of the other states.[33]

Considering the overall scope of their activities, the role of territorial supreme courts was definitely ambivalent. On the one hand they represented the power and direction of the federal government and national political parties, and on the other the same men reflected local needs and the impact of environment. As such they illustrate clearly to the historian the fallacy of generalization and serve as a strong argument for multiplicity of interpretation, a concept which invalidates isolation of the territories in historical analysis. That some of the appointees were scoundrels cannot be denied, but the carpetbagger stereotype is no longer acceptable in reference to the majority of the group. The functional view vindicates the role of the justices as a body for they were civilizers, builders, and makers of laws who contributed substantially to the development of the territories.

In their determination to accent federal, national or eastern influences on territorial development, scholars must not overreact as did some of Frederick Jackson Turner's disciples. Future analysis of the significance of territorial supreme courts may have a moderating effect on historians as they seek to place the territories in their proper perspective.

With supreme courts in mind, Gov. Benjamin F. Potts of Montana wrote in 1870 that "an able Judge has more power for good here than all the Federal officers put together."[34] A century later this may become, if not "The Historian's View," at least a subject of his serious consideration.

NOTES

1. Howard R. Lamar, "Carpetbaggers Full of Dreams: A Functional View of the Arizona Pioneer Politician," *Arizona and the West* 7 (Autumn 1965): 188.
2. *The Rocky Mountain Bench: The Territorial Supreme Courts of Colorado, Montana, and Wyoming, 1861–1890* (New Haven: Yale University Press, 1972).
3. Lamar, "Carpetbaggers," p. 188. William M. Neil, "The American Territorial System since the Civil War: A Summary Analysis," *Indiana Magazine of History* 60 (September 1964): 219–40.
4. The carpetbagger theme is stressed in T. Alfred Larson, "Exiling a Wyoming Judge," *Wyoming Law Journal* 10 (Fall 1955): 171–79. Still the most helpful explanation of trans-Mississippi territorial government is Earl S. Pomeroy, *The Territories and the United States, 1861–1890: Studies in Colonial Administration* (Philadelphia: University of Pennsylvania Press, 1947). Contributions of the territorial supreme courts to jurisprudence are recognized in Gordon M. Bakken, "The English Common Law in the Rocky Mountain West," *Arizona and the West* 11 (Summer 1969): 109–28.
5. Richard N. Current, "Carpetbaggers Reconsidered," in *A Festschrift for Frederick B. Artz,* ed. David H. Pinkney and Theodore Ropp (Durham, N.C.: Duke University Press, 1964), pp. 156–57.
6. Richard N. Current, *Three Carpetbag Governors* (Baton Rouge: Louisiana State University Press, 1967), p. xi.
7. Wilbur F. Stone, "History of the Appellate Courts of Colorado," An Address before the Denver Bar Association, April 5, 1905, 34 *Colorado Reports*, xxiv.
8. Earl S. Pomeroy, "Toward a Reorientation of Western History: Continuity and Environment," *Mississippi Valley Historical Review* 41 (March 1955): 579–600. Ray A. Billington, "Introduction," *The American West: An Appraisal*, ed. Robert G. Ferris (Santa Fe: Museum of New Mexico Press, 1963), pp. 8–12.
9. Pomeroy, "Toward a Reorientation," p. 583.
10. William H. Goetzmann, *Exploration and Empire* (New York: Alfred A. Knopf, 1966), p. xi.
11. Ibid.
12. General Records of the Department of Justice, Record Group 60, National Archives Building, Washington, D.C., abound in letters referring to routine problems of maintaining the courts. While many are found in the Source-Chronological Files, pertinent references are also in Appointment Papers,

Attorney General's Instruction Books, Attorney General's Letterbooks, Attorney General's Papers, and Judges and Clerks Letters Sent. (Hereafter records in the National Archives Building are indicated by the symbol NA. The symbol RG is used for record group.)

13. Walter Prescott Webb, *The Great Plains* (Boston: Ginn & Co., 1931).

14. Richard B. Morris, "The Courts, the Law and Social History," *Essays in Legal History in Honor of Felix Frankfurter,* ed. Morris D. Forkosch (New York: Bobbs-Merrill Co., 1966), p. 409.

15. Attorney General's Papers and the Source-Chronological Files contain many letters on financial matters. Typical is Hiram Knowles, justice, to Charles Devens, attorney general, February 15, 1878, Source-Chronological Files, Montana, RG 60, NA.

16. Federal statutes creating the various territorial supreme courts are compiled in *Organic Acts for the Territories of the United States with Notes Thereon, Compiled from Statutes at Large of the United States,* 51st Cong., 1st sess., Senate Document 148, 1900, Serial 3852.

17. *Rocky Mountain News,* July 8, 1861.

18. Ibid., July 9–10, 12–13, 15–16, 23–27, 1861. It was common for territorial newspapers to follow closely court proceedings.

19. William Gilpin, governor, to Edward Bates, attorney general, October 8, 1861, Attorney General's Papers, Colorado, RG 60, NA. Petition to President Andrew Johnson submitted by A. A. Paddock, July 21, 1868, State Department Territorial Papers, Wyoming, General Records of the Department of State, Record Group 59, NA. Petition from Pueblo City, no date, Appointment Papers, Colorado, RG 60, NA.

20. *Contributions to the Historical Society of Montana,* Biographical Sketch of Hezekiah L. Hosmer, vol. 3 (1900), p. 291.

21. Examples of transitional difficulties are in John D. W. Guice, "Colorado's Territorial Courts," *Colorado Magazine* 45 (Summer 1968): 204–24.

22. Territorial finances are summarized in Pomeroy, *The Territories and the United States,* pp. 28–50. Particular problems of the Colorado, Montana, and Wyoming Territorial Supreme Courts are in Guice, "The Territorial Supreme Courts," pp. 63–80.

23. State Department Territorial Papers, Colorado, RG 59, NA; Attorney General's Papers, Colorado, RG 60, NA; Denver *Weekly Commonwealth and Republican,* August 20, 1863.

24. Jack Ericson Eblen, *The First and Second United States Empires: Governors and Territorial Government, 1784–1912* (Pittsburgh: University of Pittsburgh Press, 1968), p. 274.

25. Appointment Papers, RG 60, NA, contain literally thousands of references to political pressures. A classic statement of adversities faced by the justices is the letter from Montana Justice Hiram Knowles to Attorney General E. R. Hoar, March 6, 1870, Appointment Papers, Montana, RG 60, NA.

26. Pomeroy, *The Territories and the United States,* app. 1. Guice, *The Rocky Mountain Bench,* p. 62.

27. The incidence of incompetence and corruption dropped with the maturity of the territories, a natural phenomenon, perhaps, or a reflection of the national political atmosphere, or, possibly a combination of these factors.

28. Supreme courts also provided leadership in effecting needed improvements in operations of lower territorial courts. Some such changes are acknowl-

edged in Clark Spence, "The Territorial Bench in Montana: 1864–1889,"
Montana: The Magazine of Western History 13 (January 1963): 61.
29. Petitions for the removal of Benjamin F. Hall and Charles Lee Armour,
July 14, 1863, Appointment Papers, Colorado, RG 60, NA. Henry M.
Teller to George H. Williams, attorney general, April 27, 1874, Source-
Chronological Files, Colorado, RG 60, NA. *Laws of the Territory of Mon-
tana Passed at the Third Session of the Legislature* (Virginia City, Montana
Territory: J. P. Bruce, Public Printer, Montana Territory, 1866), p. 94.
30. Charles Howard Shinn, *Mining Camps: A Study in American Frontier
Government* (New York: Charles Scribner's Sons, 1885), pp. 27–28, 280.
31. *Colorado Bar Association Report* 16 (1913): 311; 116 U.S. Report, 529;
William A. Riner, "Honorable Moses Hallett," *Wyoming Law Journal* 4
(Fall 1949): 86–95.
32. *Yunker* v. *Nichols*, 1 *Colorado*, 553.
33. William J. Burke, "Western Water Law," *Wyoming Law Journal* 10 (Spring
1960): 180; idem., "The Origin, Growth, and Function of the Law of
Water Use," *Wyoming Law Journal* 9 (Winter 1956): 97. The influence
of the Colorado system has actually extended east of the Mississippi. William M. Champion, "Prior Appropriation in Mississippi: A Statutory Analysis," *Mississippi Law Journal* 39 (December 1967): 1–38.
34. Potts to President Ulysses S. Grant, November 25, 1870, Appointment
Papers, Montana, RG 60, NA.

The Federal Judges of the Utah Territory from a Lawyer's Point of View

WILLIAM LEE KNECHT

IT MUST BE INEVITABLE when a practicing lawyer looks at a judiciary that he puts himself across the bar from them, and wonders what it would have been like to practice before that court. Only a historian can fully appreciate, I suppose, the changes that have occurred in our society since 1850, but a lawyer would find both less and more change than the average person. I say that because lawyers revel in precedents and are comfortable when surrounded by the established way of doing things. It has been interesting to me to find, as I rummaged about in old territorial files, the same kinds of entry books and the same headings on papers that I am familiar with in my daily practice. It brings one up short, however, to find those pleadings scratched out on tiny fragments of leftover paper, obviously salvaged from some other and primary use. This sort of shock makes real the austerity of day-to-day living on the frontier a hundred years ago.

There was a camaraderie among members of the bar that would have been useful, had I been a practicing attorney in Utah Territory, for generally speaking the first and unavoidable conclusion of anyone doing research on Utah history is the discovery of the gulf that separated the courts from the people that they were supposed to serve. This sort of gulf existed in other territories, too,[1] but was most pronounced in Utah. There the judges not only suffered from all the estrangements that beset the judiciary everywhere, but there the separation was emphasized in the context of a power struggle between the church and the central government.[2]

It may well be that some of the problems that developed between the Mormons and the federal officers resulted from the fact that by the time the central government got around to granting territorial status in 1851,

114

Utah was, by comparison to most territories, already well-structured, and that quite rigidly. A strong, homogeneous group of people, already self-disciplined, with executive, legislative, and judicial systems, the Mormons were not in a posture easily to accept imposed institutions, much less imposed personalities. All the more so, when the people had strong feelings already about the central government's lack of sympathy and concern for their problems.[3]

In 1850 there were already in Utah county courts and a supreme court.[4] Their identity and jurisdiction are blurred and fuzzy now, for the persons as well as the offices often paralleled similar positions in the ecclesiastical hierarchy of the Mormon church. They were there and functioning, however, when Washington sent the first appointees to the territory.

What I say hereafter must be accepted as generalizations. When I divide the population of the territory into good guys and bad, I am generalizing, and we all should know it. When I talk about federal officers, for instance, I portray a uniformity that did not really exist. Judge John Cradlebaugh[5] fought like a tiger with his United States attorney, Alexander Wilson.[6] Chief Justice Michael Schaeffer was disliked by "everyone" in the territory.[7] Judge George P. Stiles[8] was a Mormon, but was excommunicated by the Mormons. With this acknowledgement of the defect in our nomenclature, let us examine some of the problems that arose in the territory of Utah.

The first court illustrates many of those problems. We do not know anything about Chief Justice Lemuel G. Brandenbury,[9] but Perry Brocchus[10] gained notoriety in New Mexico as well as in Utah. Zerubbabel Snow, the first Mormon appointee and the only one of the Mormon appointees (in 35 years) who stayed long in the territory, had quite a rewarding as well as an interesting career.[11] Since he remained in the valley to practice law after his term on the bench expired, we might take note of some of his experiences with successor judges as a vehicle to observe and comment upon the "Supreme Court of the United States, in and for the Territory of Utah."[12] (See the appendix to this paper for a list of appointees.)

Judge Snow arrived in the territory in 1851 and, according to an account given later, asked President Brigham Young for a place to stay.[13] Young reported that he offered Snow the same quarters that Young had had when he first came to the territory. He said Snow could have the mountains for walls and the sky for a ceiling and the ground for a bed, but that he had not time to go about hunting up a house for a judge.

When his brethren on the bench ran away late in 1851, Snow was left with the task of conducting court in the districts of all three judges. This was no great task in 1851, of course, because of two elements: there wasn't much "judging" to do, and most of what was to be done was easily handled by the probate courts. In Utah, as in some of the other territories, county or probate courts that had a very broad jurisdiction were established early.[14] In Utah that jurisdiction was universal. The judges were local men, appointed by the legislature. They were usually Mormon bishops or stake presidents, ecclesiastical authorities who were accustomed to being judges. In the church structure, the bishop was a judge by virtue of his office, and members of his congregation were supposed to bring their disputes to him for settlement before seeking redress in the law courts. Thus it was no strange thing for the residents of a county to seek out the bishop when matters could not be settled between themselves.

When the runaway officers had been deposed and friendlier judges appointed,[15] there were still two elements leading the indigenous population to seek out first the county or probate courts. First, there was the continuity in office of the appointee, and second, the functionaries attached to the court got pay in proportion to the fees that were paid into the court for filing papers and serving process. If the money was paid into the federal courts, it went out of the territory. If paid into the county or probate courts, it stayed in the hands of the Mormons. There was a side element of this arrangement that contributed in great measure, I believe, to the quarrels over the jurisdiction of the probate courts. I have no doubt that much of the opposition of the indigenous population to the federal courts developed because someone was being deprived of fees at the probate court level. And when a federal court judge could appoint, and did appoint, brothers and sons as clerks,[16] that judge may have been biased in his outlook on the matter of the jurisdiction of a competing clerk and his court.

Judges (and lawyers, for that matter) had other problems in the territory. The government did not pay much money,[17] and clients did not have much money, and in Utah the money problem was especially severe because of the accelerated growth rate imposed by the artificially stimulated immigration rate.

But, as I said, the job was not worth much. It cost more to get to the territory than the post paid in a year, and when rent for a house also exceeded the salary attached to the post,[18] it is not hard to comprehend why so few competent, successful men would even consider accepting an appointment. Fewer did accept.[19]

Thus, Judge Snow turned to his old trade as a merchant to supplement his income. It took him more than a year to get drafts for his salary,[20] and he had a family to support. I hope that he had a vegetable garden in his backyard. And when the Utah legislature made it impossible for an attorney to collect a fee from his client, the attorneys as well as the judges were in a bind.[21]

Judge John Fitch Kinney, appointed chief justice in 1853 and again in 1860, was a merchant and real estate promoter.[22] Judge William W. Drummond was, among other and more untoward things, a gambler, usurer, and horse trader.[23] Chief Justice David P. Lowe came to the territory and left after a few months—there were no opportunities out there, he was reported to have said on leaving.[24] Judge James A. Miner in the 1880s was a real estate speculator who got rich out of the growth in Ogden.[25] Of course, his decisions in a few cases involving water rights of certain real property owned by his wife, his daughter, or his son-in-law did nothing to hurt the family's finances.[26]

Judge Robert P. Flenniken[27] begged President Lincoln to clear up the dispute between John Cradlebaugh and himself as to who rightfully held the judgeship in the Second District (Carson) because, Flenniken claimed, "Here in Carson with my family I could have done well. In any other place, unless I became a Mormon, I could have neither peace nor prosperity."[28]

Some of the judges were even accused of speculating in gold mines so that they could achieve great gain by making favorable decisions when their own companies became subject to them in court.[29]

Despite what we have said about the unrewarding position of judge in Utah, Judge Obed F. Strickland[30] thought that the post of associate justice was worth so much that he "bought" it from the tired and aging Judge Thomas J. Drake,[31] offering a promissory note in payment thereof. (When the note was presented for payment, Judge Strickland argued that such an agreement to sell a public office was contrary to public policy and that hence the courts should not enforce the note. And the court agreed.[32])

For the first thirty years or so, it is safe to say that the men appointed to the supreme court in Utah were political hacks who had worn out their welcome at home and were appointed out West to get rid of them, and thus stop their pleas for help. The appointment files in the National Archives reveal how some letter writers felt about the applicants: "Now in the name of the Democracy of the district, we protest. . . . Out of compassion for his circumstances, we did get Col. Polk to appoint him to Denmark—we knew that there was nothing to do there and the relations between the Government and ours required no ability to attend to them—Mr. Flenniken is a man of not much education or ability and we think he has had more than he ought already. . . ."[33]

There were some exceptions to the rule I just stated, of course, and Judge Delana Eckels and Judge James B. McKean may be examples. But Judge Eckels came out of oblivion and retired into oblivion. Judge McKean always used to say that he had not asked for the job, but since President Grant needed a faithful servant to enforce the laws, he accepted the assignment to Utah. The Archives records show that McKean flooded the chief executive with pleas over a period of years for appointment.[34] It could be to the Banana Republics, to anywhere—but somewhere, because the faithful ex-soldier could not earn his living at "lawing." It is thus true that Judge McKean did not ask for the job in Utah. That was only half the story. The other half lay buried in the Archives for almost a century.

We do not know much about Judge Leonidas Shaver.[35] I found the probate file for him. He had several large unpaid bills for opium, and among other claims on file was one for his salary which had been assigned by him prior to his leaving for Utah.[36] He probably had a mastoid infection and must have been in constant pain and unable to give the law very much attention. It is probably well that the law did not need much attention. He must have been a sorry specimen, no matter how viewed.

Then, added to all the other problems that territorial judges had, was the extraordinary struggle between federal officers and the leadership of the Mormon church. More than one judge stubbed his toe on that struggle. Brocchus was the first; he lasted in his job only as long as it took Daniel Webster to order him back to his post and to note the refusal.[37] Kinney suffered during his first term, for he was districted out of a job,[38] and then found Brigham Young urging his people to refuse jury duty.[39] Kinney quit in disgust, but when he came back the second time, he was, as the kids say, "in like Flynn."[40] Eckels brought (or came with) the army, but he and Cradlebaugh lost out to the executive power when Attorney General J. S. Black ordered the army to respond only to the governor's orders, not to the requests and demands of the judiciary.[41]

Thomas Jefferson Drake and Charles Burlingame Waite thought that they could cure the relic of polygamy, but they both failed. Drake retired, old and broke, and Waite returned home, with a wife full of gossip for a best-selling book that put her into the publishing business for years to come.[42] McKean was a crusader—probably of impeccable character, but of poor judgment and discretion. Surrounded by avaricious and hard-drinking bullies and aspiring anti-Mormons, he finally made the error of awarding alimony to Mrs. Brigham Young Number 19 or 27.[43] When Washington realized what he had done, he found himself surrounded by jubilant anti-Mormons, but out of a job. He died not long afterwards, perhaps of a broken heart.[44]

Illustrative of the problems that the president faced is the appointment record for the post of chief justice. Starting in 1875 there were eight appointments within a period of four and a half years.[45] Isaac Parker asked to be excused within one day of his appointment.[46] Judge Lowe tried it for a few months and returned to Kansas City where he knew who his enemies were, at least.[47] Alexander White tried it, but not for long.[48] John Coghlan would not have it.[49] Michael Schaeffer stayed a couple of years, but neither Mormon nor Gentile could stand him, and petitions for his removal were endorsed by both sides.[50] David Corbin, a carpetbagger from South Carolina, was appointed but could not get confirmation because of irregularities connected with an election down there.[51] Finally John Hunter came along and got and held the job for a respectable period of time.[52] By 1879–80 matters had been resolved on several fronts, and from that point on the judiciary became much more "judgelike" but much less "interesting."

I have said nothing about the specifics of the quarrel between the federal and the local inhabitants of the territory, as expressed in the intricacies of the two-headed court system with a "territorial" side and a "federal" side. It is worth exploring and is interesting, but it was an issue only until the power to appoint territorial court officers was taken away from the territorial legislature.

Let us take a brief look at the "judging" part of the judges in Utah. No great Holmes or Cardoza, no innovators, no explorers in the world of law: the judges there were, at best and worst, human beings. Too often ill suited to the situation they were put into, they found themselves pawns in struggle and turmoil over which they had no control or influence. Undoubtedly justice suffered when matters such as the autonomy of local government were never really settled (Titus sustained, McKean denied[53]). The jurisdiction of the probate courts was off-again, on-again,[54] until Congress entered the picture and legislated them almost out of existence.[55] The practicing lawyer and his client often had no redress from a judge's errors. A district judge had only to convert one of his two brothers on the bench when a matter was appealed to the higher court, in order to sustain his own ruling made below, and so reversals were few and far between. Appeal to Washington was limited, too, much more so than is the case today.

There are several interesting areas of speculation for the lawyer-historian, in analyzing the federal judges in Utah Territory. One might try and restructure the territory and its progress toward statehood, applying the rules of modern constitutional law. What would the "Warren" court, for instance, have said about the Anti-Polygamy Act of 1862 or the Edmunds-Tucker Act? Since I have the floor, I can speculate that they would have rejected both acts as unconstitutional. I am sure that they would have rejected some of the practices of the federal judges—for instance the practice of requiring a wife to testify against her husband, and of using military posses to serve process in purely civil matters.

A second and perhaps more fruitful area for analysis is the question of whether the system as it existed was suited to conditions as they existed. I think we must conclude that it was not as good a system as the times could have provided. I don't think that there is any evidence that carpetbaggers ever did very much for *any* territory. Whether the fault of the system or merely its application, appointees generally had little long-term interest in the area to which they were appointed. It took a protracted struggle to get judges who knew anything about mining law when mining was the prime area of litigation in the West. I think even the most dispassionate analysis would show that less than half of the judges appointed to the bench in Utah were in any way exceptional. I think it could be put even stronger: less than half of the judges appointed to the bench in Utah had the least understanding of the people they were appointed to serve, and less than half of them were of average competence, even considering the time and the place.

But who wanted to go to Utah in the first instance? The adventurer? The footloose? The unemployed? Once the War Between the States was over, much of the nation's indignation and self-righteousness was centered in Utah. Where delicate discretion was required to avoid total involvement on one side or the other, the appointees were very poor choices. And the results suggest as much. It is then fair to ask: "Could any other appointees have done better?" Some did. The assumption follows that others could have.

How could the system have been changed? Considering the time and the general appeal of the patronage practice, I doubt that much change could have or should have been expected. There was hardly a president, and probably fewer advisors to presidents, who would have been agreeable to raising pay to the point that the best lawyers would have found the bench an attractive appointment. There were few in power positions, if any, who would have agreed to the abolition of patronage privileges in the territories.

One last note: May I observe that I don't see anything from the research that I have done that supports the proposal advanced by one writer, at least, that the judges were good guys, just misunderstood?[56] The worst of the judges were probably as bad as their enemies report. The best may have been as good as their friends believed. Most of them were neither as good nor as bad as their partisans or detractors would have us believe.

My posture is this: Some may think we can make fair analysis of events and of decisions by restricting examination to (as the lawyers say) the four corners of the contract. I respectfully disagree. Until we know the heritage that a judge, for instance, or a territorial delegate brought to bear on an event or a decision, we have put little of life's excitement into the balance scale. It is the presence of that excitement that distinguishes the discipline of history from those of geology or metallurgy. Although I admit that all have their place, I for one prefer history to the others.

NOTES

1. New Mexico—see Arie W. Poldervaart, *Black-Robed Justice,* Publications in History, vol. 13 (Santa Fe: Historical Society of New Mexico, 1948); Montana—see Clark C. Spence, "Territorial Bench in Montana: 1864–1889," *Montana: The Magazine of Western History* 13, no. 1 (January 1963): 25–32. Of immense value and often overlooked is Carleton W. Kenyon's "Legal Lore of the Wild West: A Bibliographical Essay," *California Law Review* 56 (Berkeley: School of Law, University of California, May 1968): 681.

2. There are many sources for accounts of Utah and the conflict. Basic material is in General Records of the Department of State, Record Group 59; Records of the United States Senate, Record Group 46, National Archives Microfilm Publication M200; Records of the Office of the Secretary of the Interior, Record Group 48, M428; and General Records of the Department of Justice, Record Group 60, M680. These records are in the National Archives Building, Washington, D.C., and are hereafter indicated by the record group (RG) number, the microfilm publication (M) number, where appropriate, and the symbol NA.

   The "Journal History," Church Historian's Office, Salt Lake City, is an invaluable resource. Peter Crawley and I published a limited edition of a transcript of the "Manuscript History of Brigham Young," kept by his secretaries and extracted for H. H. Bancroft. See W. L. Knecht and P. L. Crawley, eds., *History of Brigham Young, 1847–1867* (Berkeley: Mass-Cal Associates, 1964). It was while working on that project that I realized how little anyone knew about the judges, their personalities, and the conflicts that developed. Thomas G. Alexander, "The Utah Federal Courts and the Areas of Conflict, 1850–1896" (Master's thesis, Utah State University, 1961), and Clair T. Kitts, "A History of the Federal and Territorial Court Conflict in Utah, 1851–1874" (Master's thesis, Brigham Young University, 1959), typify the work at that level. Leland H. Gentry, "The Brocchus-Young Speech Controversy of 1851" (Master's thesis, University of Utah, 1858), for the speech department, is about two speeches, one of which was never even reported. Leonard J. Arrington, "Crusade against Theocracy: The Reminiscences of Judge Jacob Smith Boreman of Utah, 1872–1877," *Huntington Library Quarterly* 24, no. 1 (1960): 1–45, is an excellent contribution. Other works which must be read include the following: R. N. Baskin, *Reminiscences of Early Utah* (Salt Lake City: Tribune-Reporter Printing Co., 1914); N. F. Furniss, *The Mormon Conflict, 1850–1859* (New Haven: Yale University Press, 1960); C. C. Goodwin, *History of the Bench and Bar of Utah* (Salt Lake City: Interstate Press Association, 1913); T. B. H. Stenhouse, *The Rocky Mountain Saints . . . of the Territory of Utah* (New York: D. Appleton & Co., 1873); O. F. Whitney, *History of Utah . . . and Development of the Territory,* 4 vols. (Salt Lake City: G. Q. Cannon & Sons Co., 1892–1904).

3. Hosea Stout, *On the Mormon Frontier: The Diary of Hosea Stout, 1844–1861,* ed. Juanita Brooks (Salt Lake City: University of Utah Press, Utah State Historical Society, 1964). This classic basic source should be high on everyone's reading list, for Stout was an insider of Mormon Church coun-

cils and seems to have been trusted by the federal appointees as well.

4. Stout, *Diary,* pp. 366–67.

5. Cradlebaugh was from Ohio. Appointed by President Buchanan, he arrived in Utah in November 1858, cold and frostbitten. Apparently friendly to the Mormons on his arrival ("Journal History," Church Historian's Office, Salt Lake City, 1858), he soon turned into a bitter and imaginative foe. He made the mistake of taking the army with him to hold court in Provo, and was removed by President Lincoln in 1860.

6. Wilson was United States attorney to the court composed of Chief Justice Eckels and Associate Justices Cradlebaugh and Sinclair; the latter were known affectionately as "one-eyed John" and "drunken Charley," respectively, by the Mormons. Wilson sided with Governor Cumming and Brigham Young against the incumbent judges. He reportedly received an appointment in 1860 to the bench, but never was confirmed, nor did he ever serve.

7. Schaeffer was a large, passive "Dutchman" often accused of sleeping when he should have been listening. Appointed chief justice in 1876, from Illinois, he continued on the bench until 1879 despite heroic efforts by parties of every complexion to remove him.

8. Stiles was an early convert to Mormonism. He blamed it on his parents. See Stiles to Jeremiah Black, United States attorney general, February 26, 1858, Buchanan's Administration, 1857–61, RG 60, M680, roll 1, NA. He had served as counsel for the Nauvoo (Ill.) City Council when it ordered the ill-timed destruction of the press of the newspaper, the *Expositor,* which probably set off the spark that led to the murder of the Mormon leaders, Joseph and Hyrum Smith. Dallin Oaks, "The Suppression of the Nauvoo Expositor," *Utah Law Review* 9 (1965): 862. Stiles was appointed in 1854 to succeed Zerubbabel Snow, the first Mormon appointee to the bench. Stiles alienated church leaders by his personal conduct, although his judicial decisions were generally favorable to their cause. They excommunicated him in 1856, and he became a confirmed enemy of the church. B. H. Roberts, *A Comprehensive History of the Church of Jesus Christ of Latter-Day Saints, Century I,* 6 vols. (Salt Lake City: Deseret News Press, 1930), 4:199.

9. Brandenbury is a real enigma for the researcher. Aside from the fact that he made a speech on the courthouse steps of Carlisle, Pennsylvania, in 1845, and that he was appointed chief justice of the first court to assemble in the territory, we do not know anything about him.

10. In addition to Poldervaart's book see *Minutes of the New Mexico Bar Association* (Santa Fe, 1895), pp. 19–23.

11. Snow was the first Mormon appointed to the court (1851). A schoolteacher and merchant turned lawyer, he had practiced in Ohio. He had known the founders of Mormonism, believed them, and persevered in his belief despite serious attacks by Brigham Young. His cursing by Young is reported in the *Journal of Discourses* (Salt Lake City, 1854 et seq.), 3:236 et seq. See also note 13 below.

12. This style, "The Supreme Court of the United States, in and for the Territory of Utah," was the cause of much ridicule. See T. J. Drake, Appointment Files, RG 60, M680, roll 1, NA. By 1875, at least, appointments were being made to the "Supreme Court of Utah Territory." President

Grant to D. P. Lowe, March 19, 1875, vol. 2, p. 368, Commissions of Federal Judges, 1837–88, RG 59, NA.

13. Brigham Young, "Address to the Saints in the South," *Deseret News,* June 27, 1858.

14. February 4, 1852, *Laws of Utah* (1852), published as *Acts, Resolutions and Memorials* (Salt Lake City: Joseph Cain, Public Printer, 1855), pp. 120–28; Earl S. Pomeroy, *The Territories and the United States, 1861–1890: Studies in Colonial Administration* (Philadelphia: University of Pennsylvania Press, 1947), pp. 58–60.

15. Lazarus H. Read of New York (1852–53) and Leonidas Shaver of West Virginia and Missouri (1852–53) were warmly liked by the Mormons.

16. H. H. Henderson, A. C. Emerson, and John M. Zane were a few of the nepotistic appointments that come quickly to mind.

17. Salaries were set at $1,800 at first. They reached a high point in 1870 of $3,500. Pomeroy, in *The Territories and the United States,* discusses the issue of judges' salaries. His little work is an essential element in any review of any phase of territorial administration.

18. "Judge Kinney pays $2,000 per annum for a house for his Family to live in." Kinney, Drummond, et al. to C. Cushing, United States attorney general, August 30, 1855, Pierce's Administration, 1853–57, RG 60, M680, roll 1, NA.

19. The president apparently signed commissions to sixty men. Five of these appointees never even started for their post in the territory. See the appendix to this paper for a list of appointees.

20. "Journal History," April 29, 1852.

21. Brigham Young ventured the opinion that no one should be paid for his services to either the church or the state. The legislature then enacted an ordinance placing restrictions on the payment of lawyers' fees. Stout, *Diary,* February 10, 1851, p. 392. Then in 1852 the legislature passed an ordinance which said "No person . . . shall be compelled by any process of law to pay the counsel so employed, for any services rendered as counsel, before or after or during the process of trial. . . ." *Acts, Resolutions and Memorials . . . of Utah* (Salt Lake City, 1852), chap. 6, p. 139.

22. J. F. Kinney was appointed twice, and when removed the second time he was unanimously elected territorial delegate to Congress. His is the best documented and least known story of any of the judges.

23. Jules Remy and Julius Brenchley, *A Journey to Great Salt Lake City* (London: W. Jeffs, 1861), has delightful personal vignettes about both Kinney and Drummond. Hosea Stout was intimately connected with Judge Drummond's tangle with the law in Fillmore. Stout, *Diary.* New footnotes to the Drummond story are in Juanita Brooks, "Abraham the Jew and the Mormon War," *Proceedings of the Utah Academy of Science, Arts and Letters* 44 (Salt Lake City, 1967): 535. This is "Utah Judge Drummond" who left his wife and five children in Illinois, while parading the "beautiful, talented, skinny (whore) Ada," as his wife in the Mormon country.

24. D. P. Lowe, of Massachusetts and later Kansas. An experienced politician and jurist, he recognized the futility of trying to win any success in the face of the extraordinary gulf that divided the state.

25. Appointed in 1890, from Michigan, he had already been to Utah and had seen the speculative opportunities in Ogden.

124   WILLIAM LEE KNECHT

26. The appointment files are bulging with complaints about Judge Miner and his decisions in cases in which his close relatives had a vested interest. (See RG 60, M680, rolls 6 and 11, NA.)
27. Flenniken was a political huckster—he probably never appeared in a courtroom as advocate more than a dozen times in his life. He was a speech maker and a loyal party worker. Appointed chargé d'affaires to Denmark in 1847, then removed with a change of administrations, he besieged his party leaders (when they were in power) with pleading letters. Born in 1802, he went to Utah (Nevada) in 1860, resigned after a few years, and retired and died in San Francisco in 1879.
28. Flenniken to J. S. Black, December 12, 1860, RG 60, M680, roll 1, NA.
29. McKean and Strickland were so accused. Their defense was that the claims had been registered in their names without their knowledge by friends to escape statutory limitations on the number of claims which one man could register.
30. Strickland was "of Michigan" by way of Montana and Utah. Appointed to Judge Drake's unexpired term, he served for several years. Resigning, he settled in Washington Territory, then Idaho.
31. Also of Michigan, he made a great point of his honor and integrity in the face of threats from Brigham Young. See his address to the Oakland County Pioneer Society, in *Report of the Pioneer Society . . . of Michigan . . . with . . . Reports of County, Town, and District Pioneer Societies,* Michigan Historical Association, vol. 3 (Lansing, 1881): 592.
32. The transaction involving the sale is described by Drake to his attorney George Bates in a letter dated April 26, 1873, cited by the *Salt Lake City Herald,* May 31, 1873. The Salt Lake City papers about this time gave a great deal of space to the event.
33. Unsigned letter dated May 30, 1854. Applications and Recommendations for Public Office, 1797–1901, 331, Flenniken, RG 59, NA.
34. Ibid., McKean.
35. See note 15.
36. Salt Lake County Court House Probate Files.
37. D. Webster to P. Brocchus, April 28, 1852, quoted by Brocchus in his pamphlet, *Letter of Judge Brocchus, of Alabama to the Public, upon the Difficulties . . . of Utah* (Washington, D.C.: L. Towers, 1852), p. 5.
38. Kinney to J. S. Black, n.d., item no. 3262, RG 60, M680, roll 1, NA.
39. Kinney to J. S. Black, n.d., ca. 1857, RG 60, M680, roll 1, NA.
40. See note 22.
41. J. S. Black to Cradlebaugh, May 17, 1859, Cradlebaugh, Copies of Letters of the Attorneys General, RG 60, M680, NA.
42. Catharine V. Waite, *The Mormon Prophet and His Harem: Or, an Authentic History of Brigham Young . . . and Children* (New York: Riverside Press, 1866).
43. *Young* v. *Young,* February 25, 1875. Ann Eliza Young, *Wife Number 19: Or the Story of . . . Sufferings of Women in Polygamy* (Hartford: Dustin, Gilman, & Co., 1876), and Irving Wallace, *The Twenty-seventh Wife* (New York: Simon & Schuster, 1961), both deal with the affair, though with more rather than less bias.
44. January 5, 1879. The death certificate said "Typhoid Fever," but he was never the same vigorous person he had been before his removal. See Goodwin, *Bench and Bar of Utah,* p. 47.

45. Isaac C. Parker   3/16/75   Michael Schaeffer   4/19/76
    David P. Lowe   3/18/75   David Corbin   4/1/79
    John Coghlan   3/28/76   John A. Hunter   7/1/79
    Alexander White   8/29/76   Stephen P. Twiss   12/1/79
46. He wanted to go to Fort Smith, Arkansas. He earned the moniker "Hanging Judge Parker." See S. W. Harman, *Hell on the Border* (Fort Smith, Ark.: Hell on the Border Publishing Co., 1953), and Wayne Gard, *Frontier Justice* (Norman: University of Oklahoma Press, 1949).
47. See note 24. Also J. T. Botkin, "Justice Was Swift and Sure in Early Kansas," *Collections of the Kansas State Historical Society* 16 (Topeka, 1925): 488.
48. Appointed September 11, 1875, of Iowa. George F. Prescott wrote on January 27, 1875 (*sic*), in a telegram: "White is worse possible Judge for Utah. Deaf, conceited, obstinate. Knows no mining law. Thinks he Knows it all. Tramples on all precedents. Lawyers and Litigants panic stricken. Business and mining interests Demand Rejection." Prescott to Senators Edmunds and Frelinghuysen, Senate, 44 BA4, Papers Relating to the Nomination of Alexander White, Committee on the Judiciary, Papers Relating to Presidential Nominations, 44th Congress, RG 46, NA.
49. He was the only appointee from California. His appointment was dated March 28, 1876, but he refused the appointment and instead was made United States attorney for the District of California on April 4, 1876. See vol. 2, p. 382, Commissions of Federal Judges, 1837–88, RG 59, NA.
50. See note 7.
51. *New York Tribune,* December 28, 1877; April 3, 1879; and May 7, 1879.
52. From Lancaster County (Ohio), Washington, D.C., and St. Louis (Mo.), he was appointed to the bench in 1879. He stayed until 1884 when C. S. Zane was appointed.
53. Power of municipal government to regulate the sale of spirituous liquor: *Rosenbaum* v. *Great Salt Lake City* (The Beer Case). Titus refused habeas corpus on the ground of the absolute right of chartered cities to prohibit the sale of fermented liquor (*Daily Union Vedette,* July 17, 1865). *Englebrecht* v. *Clinton* (September term, 1870, Third District Court). McKean rejected demurrer to complaint for damages from destruction of unlicensed liquor saloon. See Whitney, *History of Utah,* 2:560–72.
54. Kinney was against them during his first term. See Kinney to C. Cushing, March 1, 1855, RG 60, M680, roll 1, NA. Eckels disapproved of them and denied their jurisdiction (D. Miller, petition for habeas corpus, unreported decision, April 1860 [?], ibid.). Kinney returned and ruled in favor of their jurisdiction (petition of James Graham for habeas corpus, unreported decision, noted in *Deseret News,* March 20, 1861). Titus succeeded Kinney and followed Kinney's rule (*Cunningham* v. *Thatcher and Robinson,* unreported decision, noted in *Daily Union Vedette,* October 29, 1867). McKean opposed and ruled against them. (James Stevens, petition for habeas corpus [October 29, 1873], granted. *Deseret News.* Frederick Bright, petition for habeas corpus [February 18, 1874], granted. *Deseret News.*)
55. Poland Act (Utah Territorial Courts Act), chap. 469, 18 Stat. 253 (1874).
56. Thomas G. Alexander, "Federal Authority versus Polygamic Theocracy," *Dialogue* 1 (1966): 85.

APPENDIX / Utah Territorial Justices

Name	Birthplace	Residence	Date of appointment	Replaced	Succeeded by	See note
Joseph Buffington	Pa.	Pa.	9/28/50	(1)	—	(2)
Perry E. Brocchus	Va.	Ala.	9/28/50	(1)	Shaver	(3)
Zerubbabel Snow	Vt.	Ohio	9/28/50	(1)	Stiles	—
Lemuel G. Brandenbury	Ohio	Pa.	3/12/51	(1)	Read	(3)
Orson Hyde	Conn.	Utah	(4)	Brocchus	—	(5)
Samuel Stokely	Pa.	Ohio	6/27/52	—	—	(2)
Lazarus Hammond Read	N.Y.	N.Y.	8/31/52	Brandenbury	Kinney	(6)
Leonidas Shaver	Va.	Mo.	9/31/52	Brocchus	Edmunds	(7)
George Edmunds, Jr.	—	Ill.	3/04/53	Shaver	Drummond	—
John Fitch Kinney	N.Y.	Iowa	8/24/53	Read	Eckels	(2)
John W. H. Underwood	Ga.	Ga.	10/03/53	—	—	—
George Perses Stiles	N.Y.	Utah	9/30/54	Snow	Sinclair	(2)
William Wormer Drummond	Va.	Ill.	9/12/54	Edmunds	Potter	(6)
Emery Davis Potter	R.I.	Ohio	7/06/57	Drummond	Cradlebaugh	(6)
Delana R. Eckels	Ky.	Ind.	7/13/57	Kinney	Kinney	(6)
Charles E. Sinclair	Va.	Va.	8/25/57	Stiles	Crosby	—
John N. Cradlebaugh	Ohio	Ohio	6/04/58	Potter	Flenniken	(3)
Robert Patterson Flenniken	Pa.	Pa.	4/09/60	Cradlebaugh	Drake	(3)
Edward Randolph Hardin	Ga.	Ga.	5/11/60	—	—	(2)
Alexander Wilson	—	—	(8)	—	—	(5)
John Fitch Kinney	N.Y.	Nebr.	6/26/60	Eckels	Titus	(3)
Henry Roberjot Crosby	Pa.	Oreg.	1/30/61	Sinclair	Waite	(3)
Charles Burlingame Waite	N.Y.	Ill.	1/27/62	Crosby	McCurdy	(6)
Thomas Jefferson Drake	N.Y.	Mich.	2/03/62	Flenniken	Strickland	(9)
John Titus	—	Pa.	1/05/64	Kinney	Wilson	—
Solomon P. S. McCurdy	Ky.	Mo.	4/14/64	Waite	Hoge	—

Name	Birthplace	Residence	Date of appointment	Replaced	Succeeded by	See note
SOLOMON P. S. McCURDY	Ky.	Utah	1/23/68	—	—	(10)
Enos Dougherty Hoge	Va.	Ill.	1/23/68	McCurdy	Hawley	(11, 3)
Edwin O. Perrin	Ohio	N.Y.	6/25/68	—	—	(5)
CHARLES C. WILSON	Mass.	Ill.	7/25/68	Titus	McKean	(3)
Obed Franklin Strickland	N.Y.	Mich.	4/01/69	Drake	Emerson	(6)
Cyrus Madison Hawley	N.Y.	Ill.	4/15/69	Hoge	Boreman	—
JAMES BEDELL McKEAN	Vt.	N.Y.	5/24/70	Wilson	Lowe	(3)
William M. Mitchell	—	Mich.	(12)	—	—	(5)
Philip H. Emerson	Vt.	Mich.	3/07/73	Strickland	Powers	(6)
Jacob Smith Boreman	Va.	Mo.	3/13/73	Hawley	Twiss	(6)

NOTE: Small capitals denote chief justices; numbers in parentheses are references to the notes below.

1. Filled a newly created seat.
2. Refused the appointment.
3. Removed from office.
4. 1852. See Brocchus, *Letter of Judge Brocchus*; and Knecht and Crawley, eds., *History of Brigham Young*, p. 122.
5. Did not serve; no record of appointment in General Records of the Department of State, Record Group 59, National Archives Building, but substantial other evidence of appointment.
6. Resigned from office.
7. Died in office.
8. May 1860. Knecht and Crawley, eds., *History of Brigham Young*, p. 308.
9. Sold his office; resigned.
10. Did not serve; rejected by United States Senate.
11. Served, but not confirmed.
12. "The President has nominated William Mitchell Associate Justice to fill the vacancy caused by the resignation of Judge Strickland." *Salt Lake City Tribune*, January 10, 1873. See *Salt Lake City Herald*, February 15, 1873, and Roberts, *A Comprehensive History of the Church of Jesus Christ of Latter-Day Saints*, 5:421.

APPENDIX—*Continued*

Name	Birthplace	Residence	Date of appointment	Replaced	Succeeded by	See note
ISAAC C. PARKER	Ohio	Mo.	3/16/75	—	—	(13)
DAVID PERLEY LOWE	N.Y.	Kans.	3/18/75	McKean	White	(6)
ALEXANDER WHITE	Tenn.	Iowa	(14)	Lowe	Schaeffer	(6)
JOHN M. COGHLAN	Ky.	Calif.	3/28/76	—	—	(2)
MICHAEL SCHAEFFER	Pa.	Ill.	4/19/76	White	Hunter	(3)
DAVID T. CORBIN	Vt.	S.C.	4/01/79	—	—	(10)
JOHN A. HUNTER	Ohio	Mo.	7/01/79	Schaeffer	Zane	—
Stephen Price Twiss	Mass.	Mo.	12/01/79	Boreman	Boreman	—
Philip H. Emerson	Vt.	Utah	(15)	Emerson	Powers	(6)
CHARLES SHUSTER ZANE	N.Y.	Ill.	7/02/84	Hunter	Sandford	—
Jacob Smith Boreman	Va.	Utah	12/20/84	Twiss	Anderson	—
Orlando Woodworth Powers	N.Y.	Mich.	1/05/86	Emerson	Henderson	(11)
Henry Perry Henderson	N.Y.	Mich.	7/20/86	Powers	Miner	—
John Walters Judd	Tenn.	Tenn.	7/09/88	(1)	Blackburn	(6)
ELLIOTT SANDFORD	Mass.	N.Y.	7/09/88	Zane	Zane	(3)
Thomas Jefferson Anderson	Ill.	Iowa	1/04/89	Boreman	Bartch	(6)
John Widener Blackburn	—	Utah	12/16/89	Judd	Smith	(3)
CHARLES SHUSTER ZANE	N.Y.	Utah	12/15/89	Sandford	Merritt	—
James Alvin Miner	Mich.	Mich.	6/20/90	Henderson	King	—
George Washington Bartch	Pa.	Utah	1/04/93	Anderson	(16)	—
Harvey Walker Smith	—	Utah	8/16/93	Blackburn	Rolapp	—
SAMUEL AUGUSTUS MERRITT	Va.	Utah	1/08/94	Zane	(16)	—
William Henry King	Utah	Utah	7/06/94	Miner	(16)	—
Henry Herman Rolapp	Denmark	Utah	12/04/95	Smith	(16)	—

NOTE: Small capitals denote chief justices; numbers in parantheses are references to notes below.

1. Filled a newly created seat.
2. Refused the appointment.
3. Removed from office.
6. Resigned from office.
10. Did not serve; rejected by United States Senate.
11. Served, but not confirmed.
13. Name withdrawn; did not serve.
14. Commission by President U. S. Grant dated September 11, 1875.
15. May 16, 1881.
16. Statehood.

Discussion of Sources

MARION M. JOHNSON

THE APPOINTMENT RECORDS in the National Archives relating to territorial supreme court judges, as well as to United States attorneys and marshals in the territories, are a fertile source of information concerning both the men who were responsible for the administration of justice in the territories and the conditions under which they performed their duties. The files of applications and recommendations for these offices before 1853 are in the general series of Applications and Recommendations for Public Office, in General Records of the Department of State, Record Group 59. Beginning in 1853 the attorney general took over from the secretary of state the task of handling correspondence relating to judicial and legal offices; thereafter the files for territorial supreme court judges and United States attorneys and marshals are in the Appointment Papers, 1853–1903, and in the Applications and Endorsements, 1901–33, in General Records of the Department of Justice, Record Group 60.

The letters of application and recommendation for judges, attorneys, and marshals in these files of the Departments of State and Justice were addressed to the president, the secretary of state, or the attorney general, senators, representatives, and others, and are often accompanied by endorsements by the addressees. The files also include oaths of office and protests against incumbent officers or prospective appointees. Documents submitted in support of recommendations or protests often include petitions and memorials from citizen groups, bar associations, and legislative bodies. The papers also frequently contain documents relating to the termination of service, including protests against reappointment, charges preferred against incumbent officers, resignations, and removals from office.

The Applications and Recommendations for Public Office are arranged approximately by presidential administration and thereunder alphabetically by name of applicant. The Appointment Papers and the Applications and

Endorsements are arranged by state, territory, or judicial district; thereunder by presidential administration in the Appointment Papers and by title of position in the Applications and Endorsements; and by name of applicant thereunder. The files of applications and recommendations for the administration of George Washington are in the Manuscript Division of the Library of Congress, having been deposited there by the Department of State in 1909. They are described in *Calendar of Applications and Recommendations for Office During the Presidency of George Washington*, by Gaillard Hunt (Washington, D.C., 1901).

Related appointment records of the Department of State include letters of resignation and declination, Senate confirmations and rejections of presidential nominations, acceptances and orders for commissions, record copies of commissions, letters sent, and indexes, registers, and lists relating to applications and appointments. Information concerning appointments is also found in the records of the Department of Justice in letters received and filed in the Attorney General's Papers, 1790–1870, and the Source-Chronological Files, 1871–84; registers of letters received; letters sent by the attorney general; lists of judges, United States attorneys and marshals for various periods, 1846–83; lists of assistant attorneys and special assistant attorneys general, 1870–98; and registers of nominations submitted to the Senate by the president, 1887–1905. Fragmentary records concerning appointments and nominations are in Records of the White House Office, Record Group 130. The records of Congress include Senate papers relating to presidential nominations listed in a special list published by the National Archives[1] as well as other relevant records described in Mr. South's paper in this conference.

In addition to records concerning appointments of territorial judges and United States attorneys and marshals, the records of the Department of Justice also contain general correspondence with these officials and related records in the Attorney General's Papers; the Source-Chronological Files; the Year Files, 1884–1904; the Numerical Files, 1904–37; the Administration Files for Judicial Districts, 1912–38; and the Classified Subject Files, 1914–37. The first two of these series of records are arranged by source and chronologically thereunder. The other three are organized in case files. Related chronological series of letters sent consist of volumes of handwritten and letterpress copies, including General and Miscellaneous Letters, 1818–1913; Instructions to United States Attorneys and Marshals, 1867–1904; Letters to Executive Officers and Members of Congress, 1871–1904; and Letters to Judges and Clerks, 1874–1904. Before the establishment of the Department of Justice in 1870, the secretary of state also corresponded with attorneys and marshals. This correspondence is in General Records of the Department of State, Record Group 59. Correspondence of the solicitor of the Treasury with attorneys, marshals, and clerks of courts is in Records of the Solicitor of the Treasury, 1801–1934, Record Group 206.

Fiscal records relating to the administration of justice in the territories are in various record groups. Records of the General Accounting Office, Record Group 217, includes settled accounts of marshals, clerks of courts, and judges for salaries and judicial expenses in the Miscellaneous Treasury Accounts, 1790–1894; Emolument Returns, 1842–1906, consisting of semiannual statements of accounts of marshals, attorneys, and clerks of courts; and Territorial Accounts, 1894–1907, including accounts of marshals and other territorial officials. In General Records of the Department of the Treasury, Record Group 56, are correspondence with United States judges, attorneys, marshals, and clerks of courts, 1833–1910, and letters received from executives of territories, 1833–56, comprising letters and other documents relating to lawsuits, actions arising out of evasion of customs, salaries, court sessions, and the depositing or withholding of court fees and fines.

The records of the Department of State include some early correspondence relating to payment of expenses of courts and marshals. The records of the Department of Justice include inherited correspondence of the Department of the Interior, 1849–70, and correspondence of the department itself after 1870 relating to the administration of the judiciary fund and the supervision of the accounts of marshals, clerks, and other judicial officers. The accounting records of the Division of Accounts of the Department of Justice comprise many series and concern the various appropriations under the attorney general's control, including those for the courts, and the receipts from fees collected by marshals, attorneys, United States commissioners, and clerks of courts. Much of the material relates to the disbursing functions of the marshals. The few series antedating 1870 were transferred to the Department of Justice by the Department of the Interior. They deal with requisitions from and advances to marshals and with the emoluments of attorneys, marshals, and clerks of court. These records were continued by the Department of Justice.

Material concerning legal affairs in the territories is also available in the State Department Territorial Papers up to 1873 and thereafter in the Interior Department Territorial Papers in Records of the Office of the Secretary of the Interior, Record Group 48, and in Records of the Office of Territories, Record Group 126. Included are reports, correspondence, and enclosures relating to such subjects as law enforcement, crime and criminals, offers of rewards, pardons and commutations of sentences, and the protection of the rights of Mexican citizens. The land entry papers in Records of the General Land Office, Record Group 49, provide some information about legal proceedings in the territories in such matters as litigation over private land claims, contested land entries, and rights of inheritance. Many of the homestead case files contain records concerning naturalization proceedings. Records relating to the extradition of accused persons are among the records of the Department of State. Records concerning the confinement of prisoners are in General Records of the Department of Justice, Record Group 60, and in Records of the Bureau of Prisons, Record Group 129, 1914–43. Records relating to pardons and commutations of sentence are among the records of the Department of State up to 1893; from 1893 to 1938 they are in Records of the Office of the Pardon Attorney, Record Group 204.

Records of the Supreme Court of the United States, Record Group 267, 1790–1933, includes case files, dockets, and minutes relating to cases appealed from territorial supreme courts. The case files include a transcript of the records of the case in the lower court, papers filed during the progress of the case before the Supreme Court, and correspondence concerning the case. The docket for each case consists of a chronological list of the steps in the progress of the case from the initial filing to the conclusion of the case. The minutes record the daily proceedings of the Court, including those in cases before the Court. The attorney rolls, a related card index, and the minutes of the Court contain information concerning the admission of attorneys to the bar of the Court.

When territories became states the territorial court records were transferred to state courts. The records of the territorial supreme courts were usually turned over to state supreme courts, and records of the district and probate courts to the local superior, district, or county courts of the state. Records relating to unfinished federal cases in the territorial courts, however, were transferred to United States district courts in the new states. Information concerning territorial supreme court records that have been microfilmed is in *A Guide to the Microfilm Collection of Early State Records* by the Library of Congress Photoduplication Service (Washington, D.C., 1950).

In Records of the Work Projects Administration, Record Group 69, there is a collection of materials relating to the Survey of Federal Archives. Some of the inventories of records of federal courts prepared by the Survey of Federal Archives include entries for records of territorial courts. These inventories describe the contents and physical condition of available records and indicate their location at the time the inventories were compiled, about 1940. Information concerning the location of records of courts of ten territories existing at the time of the Civil War is given in the National Archives publication entitled *Guide to Federal Archives Relating to the Civil War,* compiled by Kenneth W. Munden and Henry P. Beers (Washington, D.C., 1962), pages 117–25. The records of the Court of Private Land Claims, which was created by an act of Congress approved March 3, 1891, to hear private land claims derived from Spanish or Mexican grants in areas acquired from Mexico, are in custody of the New Mexico State Office of the Bureau of Land Management at Santa Fe, New Mexico.[2]

NOTES

1. U.S., National Archives and Records Service, *Papers of the United States Senate Relating to Presidential Nominations, 1789–1901,* Special List no. 20, comp. George P. Perros, James G. Brown, and Jacqueline A. Wood (Washington, D.C., 1964).
2. The final report of the United States attorney for the court is published in U.S., Department of Justice, *Annual Report of the Attorney General of the United States for the Year 1904* (Washington, D.C., 1904), pp. 95–99.

Comment on Justice in the Territories

KENT D. RICHARDS

HISTORIAN AND LAWYER have presented contrasting views of the territorial bench in the Far West with, perhaps surprisingly, the historian defending the judges and the barrister leading the attack. Mr. Guice asserts that "as a body, the jurists were builders and makers of the law who contributed substantially to the development of the territories." Mr. Knecht concludes that in Utah, at least, "where delicate discretion was required to avoid total involvement on one side or the other, the appointees were very poor choices." Further, whereas Mr. Guice offers some generalizations on the territorial courts, Mr. Knecht presents a more detailed account of the judiciary in one territory. Both, however, point to the need for increased examination of the role of the federal judiciary within the territorial system. Several competent studies of individual territories have appeared in the past fifteen years, but they accord the federal courts scarcely more than a passing glance.[1] It is startling that Earl Pomeroy's excellent introduction to the subject, contained in a chapter of his *The Territories and the United States,* published in 1947, remains not only the first but almost the last word on the subject. This morning's papers each take a step toward rectifying this neglect.

Mr. Guice has assumed a position which may properly be termed revisionist. All serious scholars will applaud his thrusts at the myopic antiquarianism that has marked the "hanging judge" school of territorial history. But all will not agree with his assertion that the territorial judge was the carrier of common law, a stabilizing force in the community, and an innovator who modified the law to conform to the needs of the environment; with all this accomplished under adverse political and financial conditions.

It is difficult for me to quarrel with the last conclusion—territorial judges labored under conditions which ranged from tolerable to abominable. The difficulty in receiving salary due, the political acrimony, and the physi-

135

cal difficulties imposed by the environment have been detailed by both speakers. At times judges, who acted with the best of intentions, found it physically impossible to carry on their duties. An example is Robert P. Flenniken, whose appointment as justice for western Utah in 1860 was opposed by the local bar. Led by the brawny future senator, William H. Stewart, the legal profession escorted the judge to the telegraph office, dictated his resignation, persuaded him to sign it, and placed him on the next stage to the East.[2] But to admit that the territorial judges faced a multiplicity of difficulties does not necessarily lead to the conclusion that they successfully overcame their liabilities.

Mr. Guice has taken issue with those who characterize territorial judges as carpetbaggers. It would appear that this epithet correctly describes the majority of territorial officials. For example, Mr. Knecht's list of the fifty-two men appointed to the Utah supreme court between 1850 and 1890 shows only five who resided in the territory at the time of appointment.[3] Perhaps the important distinction between carpetbagger and old settler was not the period of time spent in the territory before appointment, but the political orientation of the appointee. Was he keyed to the problems of the Far West or was he tied to the East and a national political party? An examination of territorial judges will show the latter inclination as the prevalent one. Mr. Knecht observes that for Utah, in "the first thirty years or so, it is safe to say that the men appointed were political hacks who had worn out their welcome at home. . . ." Mr. Guice further argues that the historian who accepts the carpetbagger theme forces himself into a narrow interpretive position. It would seem that a case could be made for drawing the opposite conclusion—to recognize carpetbaggery as a fact of territorial life indicates the close relationships between the territorial politician and the national parties and the need to examine those relationships. Robert Johannsen's *Frontier Politics and the Sectional Conflict* indicates the potential fruitfulness of this approach. I would certainly agree with Mr. Guice that care should be taken not to use "carpetbagger" as a blanket term of opprobrium applied to western judges.

Mr. Guice argues quite correctly that "a considerable degree of national-local interplay existed" in the territorial system. But did this interplay flow both ways, or was it a one-way stream limited to influence and control exerted by federal politicians over territorial actions? Although direct intervention in legislation or judicial decisions was relatively infrequent, the judges worked under the threat of a federal veto or removal. The interplay increased during the Civil War, but again this took the form of greater federal control over the courts rather than the new opportunities which Mr. Guice seems to suggest.[4] The organic acts which created Colorado, Dakota, and Nevada territories in 1861 specifically stated that judges were subject to removal at any time by the president, a power previously implied but not clearly stated. In addition, appeals from territorial supreme courts to the United States Supreme Court were denied in certain cases. Democrats in Congress, led by Sen. Stephen A. Douglas, argued that, taken in context with the removal provision, more power was placed in the hands of the president. Douglas condemned the organic acts of 1861 as denials of popular sovereignty and implied that they constituted a power grab by the executive branch.[5]

Mr. Guice raises other provocative points which in the space of his necessarily brief paper do not receive the amplification they deserve. For example, the western judge as innovator. It appears, when the more prominent examples of legal innovation are considered, that others beat the judges to the draw. The western code of mining law was formulated and developed in the mining districts of California and Colorado. Provisions for selecting, marking, filing, and working claims were well defined before they became part of territorial statutes or judicial decisions. The same miners replaced the law of riparian rights with the doctrine of prior appropriation. Another example is provided by the cattlemen's associations that formulated range laws for Wyoming and other territories—procedures later approved by territorial courts and legislatures. It is Mr. Knecht's judgement that in Utah "no innovators" and "no explorers in the world of law" appeared on the territorial bench. It would seem that legal ramifications of the church-state relationship in that territory would have provided fertile ground for a competent judge. Perhaps further examination is needed to show the territorial judge to be an innovator or carrier of institutions.

And finally, Mr. Guice notes the eagerness with which the western populace awaited the territorial courts. There is no doubt of this, for although some of the extralegal political organizations of the pre-territorial period had successfully protected property and dispensed justice, the belief persisted that official United States sanction was needed to secure land claims and judicial decisions. But this eagerness quickly turned to disillusion as citizens reacted to the judges' machinations. A typical reaction was that of the *Territorial Enterprise* of Virginia City, Nevada, which welcomed the judges, but soon thereafter claimed that Judge George Turner's very presence was suggestive of "flattery, fawning, treachery, and dishonesty. . . . 'For Sale' is written on his countenance as plainly as on a house, and he has grown wealthy by virtue of that sign. If the balance of our lovely judges can be induced to retain their seats we shall be a stout advocate for Judge Turner remaining in his—for in such a body of Judicial excellence, the Chief Justiceship, as a matter of right, should be filled by a low, slimy, intriguing imbecile like himself."[6] This kind of rhetoric appeared in most territories soon after the judges arrived.

My comments on Mr. Knecht's paper will be substantially briefer. Two points in particular piqued my curiosity. First, the role of the probate court, and especially its opposition to and competition with the federal courts. It would seem that Mr. Knecht's conclusions might hold for other territories, and, in any event, the probate courts are worthy of further examination. Secondly, as any student of territorial history is aware, each western territory faced pressing problems that came in many variations—Indian wars struck Washington Territory a few months after its formation; complex problems of claim litigation beset Nevada; Wyoming struggled against the political power of the Union Pacific; and in Utah the domination of the Mormons added an extra dimension. Mr. Knecht places the territorial judiciary in the context of this Mormon-Gentile conflict, and I only regret that he did not have the time to pursue further some of the threads of this conflict.

And as a final point, comparing the two papers once again, Mr. Guice is concerned with the judiciary as an institution in which the collective judges represented tradition and legalism in a flexible and open society—the rocks of stability in a sea of change. But an examination of judges as individuals, as Mr. Knecht has done, reveals that the ideal was seldom obtained—the judges too became products of the environment, engaging with contemporaries in a scramble for wealth and position. If the judges were mercilessly attacked by politicians and a political press, it was because the judges were political creatures. Although the territorial judges may have had the power to significantly shape the destiny of the territories, as Mr. Guice believes, they seldom used that power for the general welfare. Twenty-two years ago Earl Pomeroy wrote, "the judicial system was one of the weakest parts of the territorial system. Its weakness did not lie in any formal discrimination against the territories. . . . Territorial courts did not suit because the territories were of the West. Likewise, being typically western, the territories resisted—and survived—the experience. . . . It was tolerable and lasted only because it fitted loosely though badly, and because the prospect of early statehood lay always before westerner and easterner alike."[7] Or as one westerner of the nineteenth century observed, "The judges knew just enough of judging to cause trouble." I support both Mr. Pomeroy and this anonymous westerner in their assessment of the territorial judiciary.

NOTES

1. For example: Howard R. Lamar, *Dakota Territory 1861–1889* (New Haven: Yale University Press, 1956) and Lewis L. Gould, *Wyoming: A Political History, 1868–1896* (New Haven: Yale University Press, 1968).

2. Eliot Lord, *Comstock Mining and Miners* (Washington, D.C.: Government Printing Office, 1883), pp. 104–8.

3. Seven of the last eight judges appointed were residents of Utah at the time of appointment. This same pattern can be seen in other territories, perhaps reflecting increased stability as the area moved out of the frontier period.

4. Claims of western politicians who asserted they saved their territory for the Union should be viewed with skepticism.

5. U.S., Congress, Senate, *Congressional Globe,* 36th Cong., 2d sess., February 28, 1861, pp. 1205–7.

6. *Virginia City* (Nev.) *Territorial Enterprise,* July 26, 1864.

7. Earl Pomeroy, *The Territories and the United States, 1861–1890: Studies in Colonial Administration* (Philadelphia: University of Pennsylvania Press, 1947), p. 61.

DISCUSSION NOTE

In general discussion at the conclusion of the session the "cracker-barrel theory" of law was mentioned. Some persons support the theory, it was said, holding that judges often do well in rustic situations, with little or no legal training and without access to law books or codes, when they are forced to rely upon their own common sense and are free to innovate in the administration of justice. Insofar as Guice seemed to support this theory, the speaker disagreed with him, holding that early territorial judges were more likely to make mistakes than to produce worthwhile innovations in law. Knecht was asked if poorly trained judges did not often take a cue from leading members of the territorial bar in arriving at their decisions, and if he had not oversimplified the problems involved in collection of court fees. He responded by general agreement with the former suggestion, and the observation that there were indeed many reasons, in addition to fee problems, causing probate courts especially to suffer. Political rivalries were especially troublesome, but all the problems could not be analyzed in that day's brief paper.

With reference to the provision that a wife cannot be forced to testify in court against her husband, the question was raised of what happened in the case of polygamous marriages. Knecht commented that procedures in such cases were not codified in territorial Utah, but the general principle was followed that only the first wife was granted immunity from forced testimony.

Referring to the work by Clark Spence, *British Investments and the American Mining Frontier, 1860–1901,* a questioner pointed out that Spence held that there were innovations in mining law in the mining frontier while Knecht indicated there were not. Knecht agreed that the scope of his research was more limited than that of Spence, and in broad terms he could be mistaken, but he continued to believe that western American

140

territorial courts did not introduce significant changes in mining law through court decisions and accumulation of precedents.

Arthur Bestor raised questions so broad as to defy resolution by further discussion: Was court experience in far western territories fundamentally different in any way from experience in earlier territories to the east? How about the Canadian West—were early courts conducted there in a fashion superior to that of the American West? What were the crucial factors in determining the length of service of territorial judges? How about carpetbag judges sent from London into the thirteen colonies?

The conference consensus was clearly that much more research needs to be pursued in the areas touched upon in this session.

THE TERRITORIES:
LAND AND POLITICS

EDITOR'S NOTE

The following two essays, in the order given here, were presented at luncheons on the two days of the conference. Thomas G. Alexander was introduced by Paul W. Gates of Cornell University, who commented on the great significance of the study of landholding in the West to an understanding of its history. He pointed out that this is a subject which was common to the development of both territories and states, although the latter may have been in a better position to defend their interests in the halls of Congress than were the former. Vernon Carstensen of the University of Washington, in introducing Kenneth N. Owens at the second luncheon, discussed Owens's paper as an important pioneering effort to bring order into the analysis of political functions where chaos sometimes seems to be the chief characteristic. No opportunity was available at either luncheon for formal commentary on the essays.

The Federal Land Survey System and the Mountain West, 1870–1896

THOMAS G. ALEXANDER

BETWEEN 1861 AND 1868, the federal government defined the boundaries of all the future eight Rocky Mountain states, and settlers began pushing into the region in such numbers that population increased 430 percent between 1870 and 1900. Like an amoeba, settlement spread and divided over an extensive and disconnected area—principally in mining districts and along rivers and streams. By 1890 four major concentrations had been established. One stretched northward from the Rio Grande and Pecos valleys in New Mexico through central Colorado to the North Platte in Wyoming. Another spread from the Virgin River in Nevada northward through Utah to the Snake River of Idaho. A third dogged the northward course of the Snake River along the Oregon border, and followed its tributaries northward and eastward. The fourth could be covered by a circle of a 200-mile diameter drawn around Helena, Montana. Smaller colonies were found particularly in river valleys of these territories and in Nevada and Arizona.[1]

In July 1870, with the creation of a separate surveying district for Arizona Territory, Congress completed organization of the land survey districts in the Mountain West. Under the system as it stood in 1870, citizens could own land only after it had been surveyed. These surveys were completed under the direction of the surveyor general of the territory or state either under congressional appropriation or by special deposits which the citizen made to cover the cost of the survey. In the case of mineral claims only the cost of surveying, platting, and filing the actual claim had to be deposited; but in the case of the rectangular surveys a settler had to pay

The author expresses appreciation to the Woodrow Wilson Foundation, the University of California Committee on Research, and the Brigham Young University Research Division for financial help in the preparation of this study. He appreciates also the comments of James B. Allen of the Brigham Young University History Department.

for the survey of the entire township in which his land was situated. In either case, congressional appropriations were necessary to tie the survey to the rectangular survey system, or, in the case of mineral surveys, to special mineral survey markers if the rectangular survey were too far distant.[2]

The people of the territory, the surveyor general, territorial governors and legislatures, the territorial delegate, and the commissioner of the General Land Office all placed pressure on Congress for funds to complete surveys. Despite the squatters' rights which obtained at the time of settlement, very often, as one correspondent put it, citizens did not feel "sufficiently encouraged to make good improvements" without the security of a clear title.[3] The reason for this is obvious. Land grant railroads in all the territories posed adverse claims, and rapid settlement meant an influx of people anxious to get the best land they could for themselves. Such challenges could mean costly litigation and possibly loss of the claim.

Because they were on the scene in Congress, the territorial delegates bore the brunt of the efforts. In the early 1870s delegates such as Richard C. McCormick of Arizona, Jacob K. Shafer of Idaho, and George Q. Cannon of Utah had some success in securing appropriations through their personal influence and through help from commissioners of the General Land Office such as W. W. Drummond and powerful congressional leaders like James A. Garfield, chairman of the House Appropriations Committee. Representative Henry H. Starkweather, floor manager of the sundry civil appropriations bill in 1875, attested to their efforts when he said that "the Delegates, who are clever gentlemen, came to the committee and each one wished an increase of the appropriation for his particular Territory." Even though he believed that "substantial justice" would be served with a reduced appropriation, Arizona received $20,000 and Idaho and Utah $30,000 each for surveys for fiscal 1876.[4]

The success of the Democratic party in the House elections of 1874 and the desire for reductions in expenditures meant lower appropriations beginning in 1876. Leaders such as Samuel J. Randall of Pennsylvania and William S. Holman of Indiana set the tone of Congress. Holman secured the adoption of a House rule which allowed amendments if they effected a reduction in expenditures but which prohibited any amendment that increased appropriations. In the debate on the legislative appropriation bill in 1876, Randall called upon Garfield to support the democratic majority and to assist in reform and retrenchment. Garfield refused to cooperate in this sort of "reform." To him, the "supreme end" of congressional action was:

to sustain the Government wisely. If economy can be had too,
that is well; but if larger expenses are needed to carry on the

Government wisely Congress ought to have full liberty to do
that. And to shackle a committee so that it can only reduce,
without having any power to enlarge in case of necessity, is to
say that we are not fit to be trusted, and that we need to be
shackled in advance.[5]

Holman demonstrated his attitude toward surveys and the attitude of
many easterners and midwesterners, particularly Democrats, in a debate
with Thomas W. Bennett of Idaho. The Indianan moved to reduce the
annual salaries of the surveyors general from $3,000 to $2,000. He considered the land surveys both useless and wasteful. The federal government,
he pointed out, had surveyed more than 25 million acres of land in the
sixteen public land states and sold only 3 million acres. "The surveys," he
said, "in every State and Territory having public land are far beyond what
is required by emigration and settlement." Martin Maginnis of Montana
then objected, and after he had a heated dispute with Randall, the House
decided to pass over the section of the bill dealing with surveys and consider
it with the sundry civil appropriations bill. The Senate, however, still controlled by Republicans and, with a larger representation from the public
land states, restored the appropriation.[6]

In an apparent attempt to prevent logrolling, Holman and the members
of the appropriations committee began the practice of voting a lump sum
for surveys. The committee recommended only $200,000 for fiscal 1877,
though Congress had appropriated $800,000 the year before. Delegate
Maginnis complained that Congress had just voted $145,000 for geological
surveys which he believed were "chiefly for the purpose of taking photographs and sticking pins through bugs," renaming "the historic old romantic
landmarks of the country," and bestowing on mountains "the names of the
parties belonging to their expedition." He considered it a gross injustice
to give only "$200,000 for the benefit of the actual settlers of sixteen States
and Territories." Though he obviously did not understand its purpose,
Maginnis said he favored the geological survey work because it "advertises
the country," but when the House regarded the interests of "actual settlers"
as inferior to "fanciful work of making photographs and handsomely-colored
maps," in his opinion, it made a mistake. The House rejected his plea and
those of Thomas M. Patterson of Colorado and others, and after the Senate
and the conference committees had finished the bill, Congress had voted
only $300,000 for surveys, instead of the $820,000 the commissioner of
the General Land Office had recommended.[7]

From 1876 through 1891, Congress continued to keep the appropriations low. Between 1877 and 1886, the estimates of the surveyors general
of Idaho, Utah, and Arizona ranged between $15,000 and $60,000, with

the estimates of La Fayette Cartee and William P. Chandler of Idaho ranging the highest and those of John Wasson of Arizona the lowest. By 1884, however, Royal A. Johnson of Arizona, one of Wasson's successors, said that settlers had been so inconvenienced by scattered surveys that he needed $60,000. Even Surveyor General John Hise of Arizona, who appears to have been somewhat sympathetic with the economy move, conceded that settlers demanded surveys which he could not supply.[8]

In the meantime, representatives and delegates from the Far West argued and cajoled, but Holman and the Democrats, together with Republicans in harmony with them such as Greenbury L. Fort and Joseph G. Cannon of Illinois, held the line. Holman argued that surveys merely advanced speculation, the interests of deputy surveyors, and frauds in general. Only because of the Senate, in which the West had greater representation and which was more often controlled by sympathetic Republicans, did Congress vote lump sums ranging from $300,000 to $425,000 between 1877 and 1885.[9]

From these appropriations Arizona, which had been the territory most slighted before, averaged more than $18,000 per year; Idaho received an average of just over $12,000; and Utah got an average of just under $13,000 during the period from 1876 to 1885. In 1886, however, Holman and his supporters, with the approval of the commissioner, William Andrew Jackson Sparks, reduced the total appropriation to $50,000, and none of the three territories received anything for surveys for fiscal 1887 or 1888.[10]

Holman had the correct factual information on the status of land purchases in each of the three territories studied. More land had been surveyed and offered for sale than settlers would purchase. Yet, requests came to the surveyors general for more surveys than they could possibly make, and despite mounting appropriations before 1876, they never kept up with the petitions. Even in Utah, which had less difficulty than Arizona or Idaho, Surveyor General Nathan Kimball found the appropriations inadequate.[11]

The core of the problem, that the land distribution and survey laws suited for the humid East or even the arid plains could never work in the dry rugged Mountain West, some refuse to admit even today. As early as 1876, Kimball had admitted that what Holman said of Utah and other Mountain territories and states was eminently true, but contrary to the views of the representative from Indiana he concluded in a report that:

the reason is obvious, and these lands will remain unsold and
unproductive and valueless to the Government and people, until
Congress removes the restrictions which prevent their sale and
occupancy. Under existing laws no one can obtain title to public
lands excepting under the preemption and homestead laws, limiting
the settler to 160 acres, and requiring actual settlement, &c . . . .

The law limiting the settler to 160 acres necessarily compels selections altogether along and near the springs and streams, where irrigation can be had at little cost, thus leaving the upper or mesa land, equally as valuable, unoccupied and unsold, because of the greater labor and cost of irrigation. If Congress would remove the restriction by amending the preemption and homestead laws, and permit sale for cash . . . by use of their money [settlers] would make these lands productive, and return millions of dollars to the national and State treasuries and benefit all classes of citizens.

Existing restrictions, as Surveyor General Wasson pointed out in the same publication, made it impossible for a man to carry on legal cattle ranching except by the subterfuge of obtaining "possession of a large range by examining the country and finding a spring or digging a well, and . . . [making this] watering place the headquarters of his business."[12]

In addition, land legislation made the use of timberland in any but an illegal way practically impossible. Settlers could legally cut timber only on their own land, but because timber stands in the Mountain West were generally found in the mountains and mountainous land could not legally be surveyed, westerners simply cut the timber in defiance of the law. Even though enforcement was sporadic, many citizens opposed payment for the trees owing to the high cost of cutting and transporting timber. Both Surveyors General Wasson of Arizona and Cartee of Idaho asked that the government allow the survey and sale of timberland because they believed that if private citizens had a financial interest in timber they would economize it.[13]

Simply by following instructions, surveyors could subdivide a great deal of land which settlers could not acquire. Surveyors general were ordered to try to meet the needs of settlement, but when they extended surveys into new areas, they had to connect the new lines with the previous surveys. Instructions by which the General Land Office aimed to prevent frauds required surveyors to complete an entire township once they had started surveying it, even though no settlers lived on the remaining land. The only exception was made on land such as mountainous land which was unsurveyable by law because it was assumed it could not be settled.[14]

Congress appeared to answer one of the objections in 1876 when it slashed the appropriations. It enacted a provision which allowed surveyors to pass over sterile land by triangulation. By the same act, however, Congress set up categories of land for which the appropriation for land surveys might be used, and triangulation was excluded. In other words, deputy surveyors might triangulate over unsurveyable lands if they did so at their own expense![15]

Before the administration of Commissioner James A. Williamson began in 1876, the General Land Office had been quite lax in enforcement of many regulations. The reduced appropriations and the desire for a more efficient system, however, forced reform. Williamson began to demand assurances that settlers actually occupied the land. In an attempt to correct the problem of inaccurate surveys, Williamson began to send outside investigators or disinterested third parties to check the surveys. The General Land Office suspended the accounts of surveyors under investigation until a determination of the accuracy could be made. Commissioner Noah C. McFarland continued this practice and also required different deputies to survey section and township lines to check on one another.[16]

Williamson tried to deal with the problems caused by depredations on the timberlands. He found, however, that westerners needed timber for homes and buildings, and the methods he used neither ended depredations nor brought any money into the Treasury. He suggested that the government withdraw all timberland from settlement and survey and then sell it.[17]

Early in 1878 the territorial delegates agreed to press Congress for action on the timber question. The resultant Timber Cutting Act allowed residents of Colorado, Nevada, and the territories to cut timber for domestic purposes from unsurveyed government mineral lands. Both Carl Schurz and Williamson opposed the legislation, failed to catch John Wesley Powell's vision of a sustained-yield timber policy, and construed "domestic purpose" so narrowly that even small lumber companies without specific authorization from individuals could not legally cut and sell timber for the local market.[18]

In an attempt to deal with some of the problems caused by unsatisfactory conditions, Williamson and Schurz, with the assistance of Congress, undertook the consideration of alternative survey systems in 1877 and 1878. Williamson believed the consolidation of all land surveys under a surveyor general in Washington would be more satisfactory.[19]

In March of 1878, the House Committee on Public Lands held hearings on Williamson's suggestions and on the general question of the need for a change in the survey system.[20] Powell, Professor Julius E. Hilgard of the Coast and Geodetic Survey, Lt. George M. Wheeler, and Ferdinand V. Hayden testified on the problem. Powell argued that because "much of the irrigable lands have been surveyed, and as important portions of the surveyed lands had already been settled, a change in the system of parceling . . . [was then] a matter of but little importance." To alleviate the problem of oversurveying he suggested that triangulation be used. He also asked for surveys of grazing lands, but pointed out that this did not need to be done before entry. As the system stood, the

owners of stock are squatters on the public lands, and they roam
about from point to point with their herds; and because they are

unable to obtain titles to the lands they are not interested in local improvements, in the making of homes, and the building of school-houses, churches, roads, &c.

He asked also that mineral surveys be connected to the rectangular system by triangulation and accepted Commissioner Williamson's recommendation that the present system be abolished in favor of a system of salaried professionals with central direction.

Wheeler and Hilgard found many faults in the existing system but saw, as Wheeler said, "simplicity" as "one of its greatest advantages and safeguards. . . ." He agreed triangulation would be possible, but said it would be expensive and doubted the federal government could find the surveying talent to use the system.

Both westerners and the surveyors general appear to have opposed the centralization in Washington. They feared, perhaps quite realistically, a further loss of contact with actual western needs. As the situation stood, what was needed was not a sweeping reorganization of the land survey system, but a realistic modification and more money. Surveyors already had the authority to pass over wastelands by triangulation and to tie mining claims into the regular rectangular surveys. They could do nothing, however, until Congress voted funds for the purpose. Sufficient appropriations would also have allowed adequate inspection of surveys. A change in the eastern and midwestern attitude toward grazing and timberlands would have wrought a salutory change also.[21]

Unfortunately, Congress had lashed out at "extravagance" and "fraud" without bothering to consider the actual problems which existed. In spite of the new triangulation system, surveyors still had to survey entire townships; and owing to the disconnected settlements this regulation, together with the requirement of pushing surveys into areas where actual settlers had established themselves, continued to produce the survey of unsalable land during a time when more people clamored for surveys to acquire permanent titles than could be accommodated. Regulations concerning cattleland and timberland had not changed and, where poor surveys had been made previously, resurveys could not be made under existing appropriation policy.

During McFarland's term, allegations were made of frauds in the use of special deposit surveys in Arizona and Idaho. Prior to 1879, certificates of deposit could be used to purchase land only in the township which a claimant designated for survey. In 1879, however, Congress amended the law to allow the certificates to be used in payment for any land. Claims came to McFarland that the system produced fraud and that surveyors and others interested in obtaining land entered into conspiracies to purchase surveys and use the certificates for land which they wanted. In an attempt to deal with the problem, Secretary of the Interior Samuel J. Kirkwood and Commissioner McFarland both recommended repeal of the special deposit system. McFarland also issued orders providing for special scrutiny of all contracts under special deposits and requiring all certificates to be sent to Washington for validation before any land could be purchased with them. Congress repealed the provision allowing their use anywhere in 1882. In the meantime, McFarland's investigation showed the Idaho and Arizona charges to be unfounded, in as far as they applied to special deposits.[22]

Despite the reform measures of Williamson and McFarland and the expressed desires of westerners to improve the system, suspicion grew about the motives of people of the West and fraudulent surveys. In 1885 Grover Cleveland's new commissioner, William Andrew Jackson Sparks, undertook a program of administrative reform unprecedented in the annals of the General Land Office. He moved against abuses which he believed existed in the surveying system, particularly those under special deposits. He discontinued the practice of allowing higher rates for rough terrain. He tried to stamp out the lax enforcement of contract regulations, especially the acceptance of surveys without field examinations. His first report was filled with such words as "unauthorized," "unwarranted," and "illegal."[23]

At the root of Sparks's conception of the evils of the existing practices lay an almost paranoid fear of monopoly. He suspended final action on all land entries in the arid region and recommended repeal of the Preemption, Timber Culture, and Desert Land Acts, and the commutation feature of the Homestead Act. He charged that the land office had been "largely conducted to the advantage of speculation and monopoly, private and corporate, rather than in the public interest"; and that "large bodies of land" had been "monopolized" by "cattle ranges." He was convinced that a syndicate of banks and surveyors had financed and performed surveys. Because he feared these interests would control the land and exclude homesteaders, he opposed any surveys in advance of actual settlement.[24]

Sparks failed to understand the nature of the western cattle industry and to see the impossibility of using much of the land which cattlemen had "monopolized" for any other purpose. He apparently thought that by refusing to allow surveys of any land that cattlemen might use for grazing he could in some way defeat the conspiracy which he believed existed against the small homesteader. He refused in Arizona, for instance, to allow the survey of claims of about three hundred twenty acres because he thought that this was a "somewhat extensive range for cattle." When Surveyor General Hise learned of this, he advised the commissioner that the best way to protect any small settler was to survey the land. He counseled Sparks's informant to "repair to some crystal stream and be 'baptized anew in the true faith' [then] he would be a wiser and perhaps a better man, and cease to be the advocate of a policy that *he does full well know* is in the interest of the monopolists and against the mass of the people" On another occasion Sparks told Hise that: "Herders of cattle will not be considered as *settlers* or permanent residents, nor will their cabins, 'dugouts or shelters' be regarded as improvements."[25]

He tightened the reins on deputy surveyors by changing the contract form and prohibiting any further surveys from special deposits. Both of the regulations were designed to end what he considered to be frauds in the surveying process. In spite of remonstrances on the suspension of deposit surveys because settlers could secure surveys in no other way, Sparks, with Secretary L. Q. C. Lamar's support, refused to allow them.[26]

To insure the accuracy of all surveys, Sparks ordered all accounts suspended until agents from Washington could examine surveys in the field. By the end of 1886 Sparks had begun investigations only in Arizona. He had been unable to complete any probes in Utah or Idaho, and congressional economy moves, which included an appropriation of only $25,000 for examinations in fiscal 1887, made it appear unlikely that he could do so very soon. The examiner, George W. Lechner, found some surveys in Arizona within the limits of accuracy and "well done," and others that were far out of alignment and "exceedingly defective," which Sparks properly refused to accept until they were corrected.[27]

By 1887 Sparks's policies had created numerous enemies for him in the West and problems in the General Land Office. In November President Cleveland refused to support him, and his assistant S. M. Stockslager replaced him, only to continue his policies. One of the Utah deputies, Edward W. Koeber, was particularly anxious to secure his money because local banks from which he had borrowed working capital were charging him a high rate of interest. Not until June 1888 did Examiner R. B. Rice accept one of Koeber's surveys as "fairly well made." Rice then proceeded to examine several other surveys in Utah and rejected them as inaccurate. After the Sparks-Stockslager era, Commissioner Lewis A. Groff, who had received numerous complaints about Rice's work, ordered the surveys reexamined by Archibald Carr. Carr found that Rice had made careless mistakes in his examinations, and the department accepted the suspended surveys in March 1890.[28]

From the results of examinations in Utah, Idaho, and Arizona, it is evident that not only were the wholesale surveying frauds which Sparks had anticipated not perpetrated, but Bureau policies had hurt innocent people with the guilty. Some surveys were found to be "unusually well executed," while others were found to be defective and had to be redone. By suspending action on all surveys, however, with insufficient funds for examination, Sparks forced the very settlers whom he professed to love to wait for years before they could obtain titles to their lands. This was particularly damaging in the Mountain West, because under the land withdrawal feature of the act of October 2, 1888, establishing the Irrigation Survey, many settlers who had been unable to secure titles to their land had to wait until 1891 and later to do so.[29]

In early 1887, under authority of a House resolution providing for the abolition of all surveyors general on July 1, 1888, as an economy measure, the House subcommittee on the legislative appropriation bill began to reinvestigate the system. Instead of Powell, Wheeler, Hilgard, and Hayden, the star witness was James Edmunds, Sparks's survey division chief. Edmunds testified that no contracts were being let in the Mountain West and that no more would be let until it could be shown that "settlers" demanded them. Edmunds left the impression that he knew little of what the surveyors general actually did, and questions and comments of William Holman and Joseph Cannon showed that they shared his ignorance of both procedures involved and examinations required.[30]

When Surveyor General Joseph C. Straughan of Idaho learned what was happening, he memorialized Congress in opposition. He then wrote Sparks explaining why the abolition of the offices would be a disaster. As Edmund Rice of Minnesota said on the floor of Congress, the surveyors general were "just as necessary to the practical conducting of the public land system as the engineer department is to the management of the railroad."[31]

Even after the end of the first Cleveland administration, and in spite of pleas by the surveyors general, delegates, senators, representatives, and governors such as Arizona's Lewis Wolfley, a surveyor by profession, the territories still had considerable trouble. The commissioner was reluctant to authorize surveys in Arizona, on land which settlers were trying to irrigate, because it was not yet agricultural! Surveyor General Royal A. Johnson said that settlers would not want to invest money to improve the land if they "are told right in the outset that the land cannot be surveyed, [and they cannot] be protected in their titles before the land becomes 'agricultural' and productive." Utah and Idaho appear to have had less difficulty. In all three territories, however, surveyors general had difficulty securing enough money for clerks and draftsmen to complete surveys and for the connection of mineral monuments to the general survey system.[32]

The appropriations in 1892 improved, but the panic of 1893 and the ensuing depression forced reductions even below the meager level of the years of 1890 and 1891. Sen. Fred T. Dubois of Idaho castigated the congressional leadership for suggesting an appropriation of only $80,000 for surveys. His new state had been unable to obtain the grants of land which the federal government had given it at the time of entry into the Union owing to the stingy appropriation policy. Dubois pointed out that he had "cheerfully voted $20,000,000 for a river and harbor bill," from which his state received no help and $300,000 "for a naval display in New York." Sen. Joseph M. Carey of Wyoming went so far as to suggest the possibility of the dissolution of the two national parties in the public land states unless more attention were paid to their needs.[33]

By 1894 Secretary Hoke Smith and Commissioner Silas W. Lamoreaux recognized that long delays in the land office procedures resulted from the lack of congressional appropriations. In 1895, a joint congressional committee reported that it took at least two years for settlers to gain titles to their claims after the General Land Office had inaugurated its tardy surveys. Lamoreaux lamented that "not infrequently" appropriations lapsed into the treasury and a deficiency appropriation became necessary owing to the lack of money to complete the drafting and filing of survey plats.[34]

Settlers could take some solace from the attempts of Commissioners Groff, Lamoreaux, and Thomas H. Carter to ease the situation. They began to allow local deputies and employees of the surveyors general to examine surveys. They found, just as Sparks and his predecessors Williamson and McFarland, that some surveys were poorly made and others well done. By 1892 Surveyor General Johnson of Arizona commented that it was "possible for deputies to get the pay for surveys executed according to their contracts, without waiting until they are bankrupt." Still, as the congressonal report of 1895 showed, the situation was far from acceptable.[35]

At the basis of the difficulty in the application of the land system to the Mountain West was an eastern and midwestern conception of the nature of the arid region which bore about as much relationship to reality as the Flat Earth Society's view of the recent exploration of the moon. The Flat Earth Society's secretary said that the whole moon exploration exercise was a conspiracy to defraud the public by NASA, contractors, and globe makers because the moon is a disk situated less than 2,700 miles from the earth.[36] According to W. A. J. Sparks and congressional leaders like William S. Holman and "Uncle Joe" Cannon, the Mountain West was a replica of the East and Midwest, and if settlement patterns did not appear to follow those of the Midwest, it was because conspiratorial groups of surveyors, bankers, and cattlemen were trying to empty the public treasury and monopolize the land. Involved in their view was also a conception of the nature of progress which included the belief that the epitome of development was the independent yeoman, and that cattle ranching was an inferior occupation.

The tragedy of the whole story is that the policies which were followed actually retarded development. Because surveyors could not tie mineral surveys into the general land survey network, some surveys overlapped and mining claims became entangled in costly litigation. In order to make use of otherwise unusable resources, cattlemen and lumbermen had to become common thieves. Because surveys could not be completed, platted, and filed, smaller settlers had difficulty securing titles to their lands, and in many cases feared to make substantial improvements.

It has been argued elsewhere that the people of the Far West were out of touch with reality during this period and that they were the ones demanding adherence to policies which could not work.[37] In fact, however, they tried with the means at their disposal to change the land survey and disposal system to meet their needs, but resistance from midwesterners and easterners who held an erroneous conception of conditions in the Mountain West made life for the westerner much harder than it need have been.

NOTES

1. Leonard J. Arrington, *The Changing Economic Structure of the Mountain West* (Logan: Utah State University Press, 1963), pp. 30–32; Randall D. Sale and Edwin D. Karn, *American Expansion: A Book of Maps* (Homewood, Ill.: Dorsey Press, 1962), pp. 18–25.

2. Columbus Delano to Commissioner of the General Land Office, February 8, 1871, Record of Letters Sent by the Lands and Railroads Division, Records of the Office of the Secretary of the Interior, Record Group 48, National Archives Building, Washington, D.C. (hereafter referred to as NA). Delano to President, February 4, 1871, ibid. M. M. Curtis to John Wasson, February 7, 1871, Record of Letters Sent concerning Surveys in Arizona, General Land Office, Records of the Bureau of Land Management, Record Group 49, NA. (Hereafter, correspondence from this source will be cited as: Arizona [Utah, Idaho, or New Mexico] Letter Book, GLO, RG 49, NA.) For a more detailed discussion of the process of the creation of surveying districts, see: Thomas G. Alexander, "The Federal Frontier: Interior Department Financial Policy in Idaho, Utah, and Arizona, 1863–1896" (Ph.D. diss., University of California at Berkeley, 1965), pp. 56–63. The most recent study of land law development is Paul W. Gates and Robert W. Swenson, *History of Public Land Law Development* (Washington, D.C.: Government Printing Office, 1968).

3. On the pressure for surveys, the evidence is voluminous, but consult: James H. Martineau to Courtland G. Clements, March 16, 1870, and Clements to J. W. Wilson, March 28, 1870, GLO, RG 49, NA. U.S., Department of the Interior, *Annual Report of the Secretary of the Interior,* 1872, 2 vols. (Washington, D.C.: Government Printing Office, 1872), 1:160. (Hereafter, these annual reports will be cited as *Interior Department Report,* with the year, volume, and page.) Ibid., 1874, 1:156; newspaper clipping, May 23, 1868, Hubert Howe Bancroft, "Bancroft Scraps: Idaho Miscellany," p. 102, in Bancroft Library, University of California, Berkeley;

Arizona Citizen (weekly, Tucson), October 15, 1870; U.S., Congress, *Congressional Globe,* 38th Cong., 2d sess., 1865, p. 1261. In this paper, Arizona, Utah, and Idaho will be used as cases for illustrative purposes.

4. *Arizona Miner* (weekly, Prescott), September 14, 1867; clipping, n.p., n.d. [1871], in Benjamin Ignatius Hayes, "Hayes Scrapbooks: Arizona," 6 vols. (unpublished, in Bancroft Library), vol. 3; *Idaho Tri-weekly Statesman* (Boise), March 16, 1867, and March 9, 1871; Drummond to McCormick, May 16, 1872, Arizona Letter Book, GLO, RG 49, NA; S. S. Burdett to George Q. Cannon, January 18, 1875, Utah Letter Book, GLO, RG 49, NA. The annual appropriations are cited in Alexander, "Federal Frontier," table 3, p. 406.

5. U.S., Congress, *Congressional Record,* 45th Cong., 2d sess., 1878, pp. 2982–83; *Dictionary of American Biography,* s.v. "Holman, William Steele."

6. *Congressional Record,* 44th Cong., 1st sess., 1876, pp. 2790, 3594, 4107.

7. Ibid., pp. 4102–4. Wallace Stegner lumps Maginnis, Patterson, and others from the Mountain West together as "tubthumpers of homestead settlement." *Beyond the Hundredth Meridian: John Wesley Powell and the Second Opening of the West* (Boston: Houghton Mifflin Co., 1954), p. 340. For a critique of this view see: Thomas G. Alexander, "The Powell Irrigation Survey and the People of the Mountain West," *Journal of the West* 7 (January 1968): 48–54.

8. S. S. Burdett to John Hailey, June 18, 1874, Idaho Letter Book, GLO, RG 49, NA. *Interior Department Report,* 1873, 1:174; Wasson to Drummond, July 8, 1873, Letters Received, GLO, RG 49, NA. Drummond to Nathan Kimball, February 18, 1874, Utah Letter Book, GLO, RG 49, NA. Fred Salomon to J. A. Williamson, July 8, 1878, and July 1, 1880, to Noah C. McFarland, June 24, 1881, and July 19, 1882; Cartee to Williamson, July 5, 1877, and July 5, 1878; Chandler to Williamson, May 2, 1879, and April 17, 1880, to McFarland, May 2, 1882, June 4, 1883, June 3, 1884, and to Sparks, June 1, 1885; Wasson to Williamson, June 21, 1878, and June 25, 1880, to McFarland, June 28, 1881; Johnson to McFarland, June 25, 1884; Johnson to Sparks, June 19, 1885, Letters Received, GLO, RG 49, NA. *Interior Department Report,* 1886, 2:475.

9. *Congressional Record,* 44th Cong., 2d sess., 1877, pp. 1787–92, 1950, 2094.

10. See Alexander, "Federal Frontier," table 3.

11. This fact is eloquently attested by the annual reports of the surveyors general in *Interior Department Reports,* 1877–86.

12. *Interior Department Report,* 1876, 1:278. This was two years before John Wesley Powell's *Report on the Lands of the Arid Region of the United States, with a More Detailed Account of the Lands of Utah* (Washington, D.C.: Government Printing Office, 1878) appeared. Cattle ranching and mining were both extremely important industries in the Mountain West. See Arrington, *Changing Economic Structure,* pp. 51–53; *Arizona Citizen,* November 28, 1874.

13. Wasson to J. W. Wilson, January 5, 1871, and to Drummond, July 8, 1873, Letters Received, GLO, RG 49, NA; George Q. Cannon to Brigham Young, June 16, 1876, Cannon Congressional Correspondence, Historical Department of the Church of Jesus Christ of Latter-Day Saints, Salt

Lake City; *Interior Department Report,* 1872, 1:160; *Arizona Citizen,* January 17 and August 29, 1874.

14. Wilson to Cartee, July 29, 1870, Idaho Letter Book, GLO, RG 49, NA.

15. U.S., 19 *Statutes at Large,* 120.

16. Williamson to Wasson, May 12 and June 4, 1879, and August 13, 1878; McFarland to Wasson, October 26, 1881, Luther Harrison to Joseph W. Robbins, August 29, 1882, McFarland to Robbins, February 2, 1883, Arizona Letter Book, GLO, RG 49, NA. Williamson to Salomon, March 9, 1881, Utah Letter Book, GLO, RG 49, NA. Williamson to Cartee, May 8 and September 13, 1877; Uri J. Baxter to Cartee, June 29, 1877, Idaho Letter Book, GLO, RG 49, NA. Wasson to Williamson, May 24, 1879, and July 29, 1878; Cartee to Williamson, May 18 and July 30, 1877; Wasson to Commissioner, October 17, 1881, Letters Received, GLO, RG 49, NA.

17. U.S., Congress, Senate Executive Document 9, 45th Cong., 2d sess., Serial 1780; *Interior Department Report,* 1877, 1:18–25; Harold Hathaway Dunham, *Government Handout: A Study in the Administration of the Public Lands, 1875–1891* (Ann Arbor: Edwards Bros., 1941), pp. 52–53; Cannon to Young, January 28, 1877, Cannon Congressional Correspondence, Historical Department of the Church of Jesus Christ of Latter-Day Saints, Salt Lake City; *Interior Department Report,* 1877, 1:300; Powell, *Lands of the Arid Regions,* pp. 23–24.

18. U.S., 20 *Statutes at Large,* 88; *Idaho Statesman* (Boise), February 16, 1878; U.S., Congress, Senate Report 122, 45th Cong., 2d sess., Serial 1789; Dunham, *Government Handout,* pp. 54–55; *Interior Department Report,* 1878, 1:345; ibid., 1880, 1:577, 550; ibid., 1881, 1:384; *Idaho Statesman* (Boise), April 3, 1879. See also Alexander, "Federal Frontier," pp. 379–81. Teller loosened the restrictions somewhat, but not a great deal. Powell believed that timber could be saved from fires if the federal government would treat it as a crop to be harvested rather than as a treasure to be guarded.

19. *Interior Department Report,* 1877, 1:9–10; U.S., Congress, House Miscellaneous Document 55, 45th Cong., 2d sess., Serial 1818, p. 15.

20. The investigation is House Miscellaneous Document 55, 45th Cong., 2d sess., Serial 1818. For further consideration of proposed reforms see Alexander, "Federal Frontier," pp. 186–87; Dunham, *Government Handout,* pp. 69–73; and Henry Nash Smith, *Virgin Land: The American West as Symbol and Myth* (New York: Random House, Vintage Books, 1957), pp. 231–33.

21. Dunham, *Government Handout,* pp. 69–70, 74–75; *Congressional Record,* 45th Cong., 2d sess., 1878, p. 2675; *San Francisco Chronicle,* October 16, 1880, in Hubert Howe Bancroft, "Bancroft Scraps: Utah Miscellany," 2 vols. (Bancroft Library), 2:490.

22. U.S., *Revised Statutes,* secs. 2401–7. Dunham, *Government Handout,* pp. 68, 79–80; *Interior Department Report,* 1881, 1:xv–xvi, 6–8; *Idaho Statesman* (Boise), May 23, 1882. For a detailed account of the Arizona and Idaho situation see Alexander, "Federal Frontier," pp. 193–96. A certificate of deposit is a receipt for the deposit of money with a federal depository.

23. *Interior Department Report,* 1885, 1:163–64, 291, 325, 330; Dunham, *Government Handout,* pp. 242–43; Roy M. Robbins, *Our Landed Heritage:*

The Public Domain, 1876–1936 (Lincoln: University of Nebraska Press, Bison Book, 1962), p. 291.

24. *Interior Department Report,* 1885, 1:155, 167–68; and see note 26.
25. Sparks to Royal A. Johnson, October 8 and November 24, 1885; Sparks to John Hise, January 7 and 14 and March 31, 1886, Arizona Letter Book, GLO, RG 49, NA. Hise to Sparks, April 12, 1886, Letters Received, GLO, RG 49, NA. See also petition of settlers, April 26, 1886, in ibid., and Sparks to Johnson, October 10, 1885, Arizona Letter Book, GLO, RG 49, NA.
26. *Interior Department Report,* 1885, 1:166–67, 313, 325, 327; Sparks to Chandler, June 30 and July 18, 1885, Idaho Letter Book, GLO, RG 49, NA; Sparks to Salomon, July 17, 1885, and to Richmond S. Dement, April 1 and July 22, 1886, Utah Letter Book, GLO, RG 49, NA; Sparks to Johnson, May 19, 1885, Arizona Letter Book, GLO, RG 49, NA; Sparks to Surveyor General of New Mexico, June 6, 1885, New Mexico Letter Book, GLO, RG 49, NA.
27. Sparks to Dement, December 4, 1885, Utah Letter Book, GLO, RG 49, NA; Sparks to Johnson, December 8, 1885, and to Hise, December 14, 1885, February 16 and June 29, 1886, Utah Letter Book, GLO, RG 49, NA; Alexander, "Federal Frontier," pp. 204, 303–4.
28. Koeber to Sparks, January 6, 1887, Letters Received, GLO, RG 49, NA; Sparks to Koeber, January 28, 1887; Stockslager to Koeber, March 7, 1888, to Richardson, March 7, 1888, to Edmund Wilkes and Charles S. Betts, March 30, 1888, to William G. Bowman, June 7 and July 9, 1888, and to Surveyor General, January 18 and 30, 1889; Groff to Koeber, November 14, 1889, Groff to Ellsworth Daggett, March 8, 19, and 20, 1890, Utah Letter Book, GLO, RG 49, NA.
29. See Alexander, "Federal Frontier," pp. 305, 341–45.
30. U.S., Congress, House Report 3916, 49th Cong., 2d sess., Serial 2501, pp. 31–35.
31. Straughan to Sparks, February 10, 1887, Letters Received, GLO, and Sparks to Straughan, February 19, 1887, Idaho Letter Book, GLO, RG 49, NA. From Sparks's letter it is obvious that either Edmunds did not speak for the administration or Sparks had changed his mind after reading Straughan's letter. *Congressional Record,* 50th Cong., 1st sess., 1888, pp. 1281–83.
32. Louis Wolfley to John Noble, July 17, 1889, Letters Received, GLO, and William M. Stone to Wolfley, August 2, 1889, Miscellaneous Letters Sent, GLO, Division E, RG 49, NA; *Interior Department Report,* 1892, 1:409. There appears to have been a slight relaxation of this treatment under Commissioner Thomas H. Carter. Carter to Surveyor General, May 16, 1892, Arizona Letter Book, GLO, RG 49, NA. For a more detailed treatment of this problem, see Alexander, "Federal Frontier," pp. 314–17.
33. *Congressional Record,* 52d Cong., 1st sess., 1892, pp. 4148–49; ibid., 2d sess., 1893, pp. 2487–89. See also Alexander, "Federal Frontier," pp. 305–10.
34. Hoke Smith to President of the Senate, July 31, 1894, and S. W. Lamoreaux to Smith, July 18, 1894, Senate Executive Document 168, 53d Cong., 2d sess., Serial 3163; "Joint Commission of Congress to Inquire into the Status of Laws Organizing the Executive Departments," House Report

1954, 53d Cong., 3d sess., Serial 3158; *Interior Department Report,* 1894, 1:105; ibid., 1895, 1:50–52.

35. *Interior Department Report,* 1892, 1:411; Alexander, "Federal Frontier," pp. 311–12.

36. *Salt Lake Tribune,* June 25, 1969, p. A5.

37. See especially Smith, *Virgin Land,* and Stegner, *Beyond the Hundredth Meridian.*

Pattern and Structure in Western
Territorial Politics

KENNETH N. OWENS

A GENERAL DISCUSSION of western territorial politics may begin most appro-
priately with tribute to Clarence Carter, that nearly perfect gentleman and
most dedicated scholar whose memory this conference helps to honor. Obviously, the study of territorial history has been deeply influenced by Dr.
Carter and the work he first undertook as editor of *The Territorial Papers
of the United States*. He brought territorial history fully to professional
attention, and began making available to future generations of students the
essential documentary materials for territorial studies.[1]

Before Carter's time scholarly writing about territorial government had
tended to reflect uncritically the current intellectual fashions among historians. At an early point, before the Progressive era, there was concern
with origins and growth of territorial forms as evidence of institutional evolution, stage by stage, a concern that derived of course from nineteenth-
century Germanic historiography and doctrines of Social Darwinism.[2] This
emphasis gave way in time to a more nationalistic, noninstitutional interpretation of the territorial process, an interpretation founded upon a Progressive faith in frontier democracy and the natural goodness of men when
placed in a wilderness setting.[3] But these interpretive themes did more to
illustrate broader movements of American historical thought than to eluci-
date materials of territorial history. It remained for Carter first to show us
the richness of these materials. Without exaggeration, one may say that
Clarence Carter opened the field of territorial history to modern scholarly
investigation.

I

Less obvious perhaps is the manner in which Carter's own interpretive
view of territorial government has lent direction to scholarly studies in this

field. With his eyes fixed upon the federal documents he was editing with such meticulous care in the National Archives, Clarence Carter saw territorial government essentially as a federal system of colonial administration. The territorial system he called a system of colonialism in the continental United States which—for all of its disunified, decentralized, irrational organization—provided an effective means of governing newly settled areas and bringing them eventually into the federal Union. The American territorial system, he concluded in his 1948 article, has proved "the most successful experiment in the administration of colonies that the modern world has witnessed. . . ."[4]

This rather beneficent view of territorial administration, reflecting a federal perspective, has guided the approach many of us have taken to territorial history since the 1940s. We have been concerned to understand and explain the manner in which territorial institutions actually took shape as a means of frontier government under federal authority. Our accounts, not only of the territorial system itself but also of territorial law and constitutional growth, of executive administration and the emergence of territorial political institutions, have generally been written with an attitude which strongly seconds Carter's claims. Perhaps Earl Pomeroy, the man who first followed Carter into the then disorganized, dusty, and fragrant files of territorial records, has best summed up this attitude. In a brilliant early article which is still too little known, "The Territory as a Frontier Institution," Professor Pomeroy in 1944 pointed out that the territory was the official American unit of expansion. Its distinctive quality, he declared, was that "it carried not only national authority in facilitating settlement, but also American forms and ideas of self-government." The territory, he added in a fortunate phrase, "has been an omnibus vehicle of American institutions and loyalties. . . ."[5]

The essential truth of these claims no one will dispute. As a system for expansion, a system that had as an ultimate goal the full integration of newly settled regions into the national political structure, the American territorial system was a unique and successful innovation in colonial government. On another occasion it was my argument that the accomplishment of statehood alone could not be taken as conclusive evidence for success of the territorial system. For by the same line of reasoning, one could claim that a Saturday night drinking spree should be counted successful if the hungover sinner reaches church on Sunday morning. But from a federal perspective, as Carter and Pomeroy have clearly understood, entrance into the sanctuary of statehood was certainly a sufficient test of territorial government's effectiveness as a system for expansion.

On that earlier occasion my criticism sprang from a failure to distinguish clearly the federal perspective from a different point of view: a territorial perspective that is rightly concerned with the character of institutions, the nature and quality of government, the pattern and structure of political life which territorial agencies helped establish along the borders of frontier settlement. From this territorial perspective the system of government has a different aspect. It is not primarily a system of colonial administration for expansion of American forms and ideas of government. Rather, it appears as a system of emerging political relationships in the individual territories. Territorial government, considered from a territorial perspective, was fundamentally concerned with allocation of political power and the rewards of power in control over public policy.

The difference between these two views is basic in territorial historiography. Among western historians W. Turrentine Jackson was first to recognize the essential issues of political power that underlay petty quarrels of governors, judges, and legislative assemblies over territorial affairs of every sort.[6] Since the pioneering studies of Professor Jackson, such other scholars as Howard Lamar, Merle Wells, Herbert Schell, T. A. Larson, Lewis Gould, and Robert Larson—all writing from a territorial perspective—have helped make us aware of questions of local power and political control that were implicit in the history of territorial government in the American West.[7] In their published works and in the research of a number of other students, one can see that territorial history contains the origins of modern politics in western states. And though contemporary western politics may remain to the uninitiated something of a puzzle, an understanding of territorial political arrangements has great relevance to the study of more recent periods in western political history. Hence, it remains a task of highest importance for western historians to explain the pattern and structure of western political life during territorial years.[8]

For scholars interested in the general scene from a territorial perspective, however, there has of course been a difficulty in finding a forest hidden among all those trees. The first impression one forms in examining western territorial histories is that lines of political growth in the separate territories were divergent, disparate, and bewilderingly different. In each territory peculiarities of political experience seem to mark every case as distinct and dissimilar from every other. Yet it is my intent to describe not one uniform pattern but rather a few standard variations that can be observed throughout western territorial political history. The concern first is for the pattern of political organization and second for the structure of the political order that took shape under territorial authority.[9]

II

In each western territory the early years of organization were characterized by disruptive, confused, intensely combative, and highly personal politics that can best be described by the term *chaotic factionalism.* But in time this disorderly style of politics was replaced by a more stable and enduring organizational pattern, either a *one-party system,* a *two-party system,* or a *no-party system.* One or another of these variant patterns came to characterize the politics of each western territory—except in Nevada, a territory that achieved statehood while still in an underpopulated stage of chaotic factionalism.[10] Each of these party systems had its special characteristics, and in every instance the dominant type of party system deeply stamped the later growth of political institutions in the territory and state.

For anyone who has even a nodding familiarity with territorial history, the term chaotic factionalism needs no explanation as a descriptive label for the earliest type of frontier politics. Whether one examines the Sibley administration in Minnesota, the Stevens administration in Washington, the Campbell administration in Wyoming, or a comparable period during the first years of organization in any other western territory, the conclusion is plain that a condition of chaotic factionalism could not be averted. The reasons may be less plain. It will not suffice to account for this general type of politics in terms of specific local peculiarities or disruptive personalities in one territory or another. Nor is the general case explained by reference to administrative and legal idiosyncrasies in a particular territory, or even as a consequence of the disorderly and permissive framework for political activity provided by territorial government.

The common reasons for chaotic factionalism may be found instead in common features of the frontier condition in every western territory. The population was small, and the number of persons actively interested and involved in politics—persons who may be designated by the term *political community*—was even smaller.[11] Settlements were few, widely dispersed in most cases, and isolated from one another by rivalry and competition as well as by distance and physical barriers. Moreover, in these individual communities, as Allan Bogue has explained with great insight, a settled social and political order had not yet taken form.[12] The people were most often new to one another as well as to the country. They were concerned mainly with the hard task of making a living in a land where there was little experience to guide them—and where there were virtually no community resources, no social welfare agencies or kindly millionaire philanthropists to see them through hard times. There had not yet developed, in short, the social and economic infrastructure necessary to sustain orderly political life.

In these frontier circumstances, it may be further observed, politics impinged upon real and vital concerns of only a relatively few individuals. For the great number of early settlers, political issues and political organizations had only peripheral importance, providing them perhaps with some supposed tie to their earlier life back in the states.[13] The few with vital political concerns were persons who sought through politics some degree of personal advantage. Federal officials, from land office registrars to the governor and territorial judges, must be counted among them. Also included ordinarily were locally posted army officers and local supervisors or agents for such major nonterritorial enterprises as transcontinental railroads. Preeminent among political activists, however, were newly minted local boosters, frontier newspaper editors, lawyers, and other professional men whose careers would prosper as the country attracted more immigrants. Most important of all were frontier businessmen who had come to a new location on speculation, who were anxious through governmental means to speed the rapid growth of their business, their town, their region.

It is these sorts of frontier entrepreneurs, the business and professional men, whose participation was most important in setting the tone of early territorial politics. They comprised the largest, most influential element in the political community of each new territory. Moreover, they brought into territorial politics a very pragmatic understanding of basic facts of political life in a new country: control over public policy could be achieved through political power; and with this control went authority over natural resources and economic privileges that could entail magnificent fortunes for the fortunate, or the shrewd. The chaotic factionalism of early territorial politics was partly a reflection of struggles among such would-be local leaders—struggles reminiscent of the state of nature described by Thomas Hobbes as the war of every man against every man, in which force and fraud are the cardinal virtues.[14]

The movement to a more stable party system took place when these men began to unite their separate interests and coalesce into recognizable, relatively enduring combinations and power groupings. This point was reached in each locality as western communities began to acquire permanent character. Even fairly small towns soon assumed a kind of ethnic and class division, and people concerned about respectability had to live on the right side of the tracks. By the same token it became important to have the right sort of men in political office—men whose claim to leadership the community could accept as legitimate. To cite but one sociopolitical index, at least in mining and cattle country, this point of development seems to have coincided generally with the first citizen crusades against bordellos. Propriety, we may assume, took precedence over pleasure, and the virtue of tolerance was subverted in a struggle—perhaps more symbolic than substantive—over which groups would determine the new community's social ethos.[15] From the original condition of chaotic factionalism, local political wars over just such causes and others, great and small, provided materials for a party system. For these wars brought together pioneer members of the political community into alliances that could be identified as political interest groups, headed by men with a secure right to political leadership in the opinion of their associates.

Territorial party systems were built by an agglomeration of various political interest groups to form coalitions that translated into political terms the social and economic demography of the territory. These systems did not arise haphazardly. Indeed, there may be found substantial uniformity in conditions which encouraged growth of each pattern.

The establishment of a one-party system required most obviously that a substantial majority of voters throughout the territory could be persuaded to support consistently one national party.[16] This condition could be met most easily where population was relatively homogeneous and not sharply divided by sectional jealousies. A measure of local control over territorial patronage was a second requirement; but such control could only be assured when the dominant territorial party was also the normal majority party in the nation. Under favorable circumstances the territorial delegate then normally became the local party's patronage monger in the national capital. Finally, a one-party system could flourish only if territorial politicians welcomed into their local leadership councils men who represented the major social and economic interest groups in the territory. Under these conditions the one-party system could effectively represent the territory's political community, and the opposition party was restricted to little more than a ceremonial role.

These conditions were found in both Minnesota and Oregon after 1853, and in Kansas by the time of the admission movement in 1861. In each case the result was formation of a one-party system under local management that gained a virtual monopoly of political power. The administration Democrats led by Henry M. Rice became the agency of one-party rule in Minnesota, while in Oregon during the same period Joe Lane and his allies, the "Salem Clique," established a similar control over territorial affairs.[17] New political strains, related to the nation's sectional crisis, were threatening to disrupt these party patterns by the eve of statehood in both Minnesota and Oregon; but Rice and Lane nevertheless succeeded in their long-term ambitions to become the first United States senators from their new states. Meanwhile the struggle over "Bleeding Kansas" had resulted in triumph for Free State forces by 1859, when Free State leadership formally organized the Republican party in Kansas Territory. The inauguration of a Republican national administration in 1861 and a reconciliation of sorts between Samuel C. Pomeroy and James H. Lane, the two most prominent Free State leaders, prepared the way for Kansas's admission as a state under one-party control. Naturally, Pomeroy and

Lane were pleased to enter the Senate together as beneficiaries of the Kansas one-party system.[18]

In Washington and Dakota Territories a pattern of one-party government can also be traced from the late 1860s through the troubled 1880s to the time of statehood. The territorial electorate, responding to national influences, made the Republican party dominant in both territories, and Republican leadership came to be exercised in large part by men who moved to these territories first as federal appointees. Washington Republicans after 1872 came under the careful direction of a "Federal Ring" at Olympia, headed by Governors Elisha P. Ferry and Watson C. Squire. The opening of eastern Washington to settlement produced new sectional strains upon this system of party control; then the rise of strong anti-monopoly sentiment directed against the Northern Pacific Railroad and agitation of class issues by workers in Northern Pacific coal mines added to the complexities of the situation. But Ferry and Squire, now firmly attached to the Northern Pacific interest, found an issue in the working-men's anti-Chinese agitation which enabled them to rally conservative support, split Democratic leadership, and restore one-party Republican rule by the time of Washington's admission to the Union. Ferry was rewarded by election as first governor of the new state, Squire was made first United States senator, and a conservative Republican associate from eastern Washington, John B. Allen, became Squire's colleague in the Senate.[19]

Leadership among Dakota Republicans was more frequently disturbed by factional and personal disputes, sectional divisions within the territory, and ambitions of new federal appointees to take over party control. Throughout the territorial period it seemed true, as James J. Hill once remarked, that Dakota's politicians were interested in nothing except loaves and fishes.[20] During the late 1860s a Republican "Yankton Ring," including among the ringleaders Governors Newton Edmunds and A. J. Faulk, along with Faulk's son-in-law, Delegate W. A. Burleigh, attempted to assume control of party affairs in the territory. But a series of carpet-bagger appointees during the Grant administration interfered with their plans, bringing an era of bitter factionalism and unabashed corruption. Republican disunity resulted in election of a Democratic delegate in 1870 and 1872, while opening the Black Hills and northern section of the territory during the late 1870s introduced new, heterogeneous elements into Dakota politics.

To protect southern Dakota interests, in the 1880s a revived and substantially reformed "Yankton Oligarchy" took the initiative in sponsoring a division movement to secure statehood for South Dakota under an extralegal constitution. The opposition during the Arthur and Cleveland administrations was led by a bipartisan "Bismarck Ring," including Governors Ordway and Pierce but headed by Alexander McKenzie, identified with the Northern Pacific Railroad and the business community of St. Paul-Minneapolis. But in 1886 a politically potent Farmers' Alliance movement first challenged the McKenzie machine for control of the Republican party in the northern part of the territory, made common cause with South Dakota statehood leaders, and helped provide local enthusiasm which convinced Congress to approve admission of both North and South Dakota in 1889.

South Dakota statehood men succeeded in consolidating their power by assuming the highest offices in the new state upon admission. But in North Dakota, though Alliance men were able to write a state constitution with many liberal reformist provisions and elect a pro-Alliance candidate as first state governor, McKenzie forces controlled selection of North Dakota's first congressional delegation. Former Governor Pierce and a wealthy bonanza farmer, Lyman R. Casey, went to the United States Senate, while Lyman C. Hansborough, a newspaper editor known as a McKenzie man, entered the House of Representatives.[21]

The brief political history of Oklahoma, last of the western territories to be organized, offers an interesting example of a nominal one-party system. Except briefly during President Cleveland's second administration, Republican appointees had command of all territorial offices. In every territorial election except one, Oklahoma voters sent as their emissary to Congress the Republican candidate for territorial delegate. In light of overwhelming Democratic majorities subsequently in the first state elections, the apparent Republican party dominance during the territorial period deserves explanation. The superior organization of the local Republican party and the willingness of Republican national administrations after 1889 to appoint Oklahoma residents to territorial positions help to account for this one-party pattern. The two Republicans who served a number of successive terms in Congress, Dennis Flynn and Bird S. McGuire, successfully identified themselves with the popular issues of Indian land allotment, free homesteads, and joint statehood for Oklahoma and Indian Territory. Moreover, during a period of extremely rapid population growth and strong agitation for statehood, one may suppose the Oklahoma electorate recognized the expediency of returning to Washington the candidates who might best influence the national administration. Only in 1906, during the state constitutional convention, did Oklahoma Democrats become well organized, under leadership of William H. Murray and Charles N. Haskell, the political figures most responsible for bringing Oklahoma into the Union under Democratic control.[22]

As a means of territorial self-government, one-party systems were the summum bonum of professional politicians. When all went well for party managers, these systems were marked by continuity of leadership, certainty of tenure, and relative immunity from embarrassing disclosures. Under a one-party system fundamental decisions on public policy were made by party leaders, not by the electorate. There was a tendency for the party to become a cooptive institution that excluded amateurs while recruiting into the organization as professionals the promising new men in territorial politics. And for politicians, whatever their personal interests and extrapolitical associations, a one-party system had the great virtue of allowing them to represent themselves as spokesmen for all people of their territory.

Two-party systems entailed fewer advantages for politicians, a fact which helps to account for the appearance of a true two-party pattern only in Nebraska and Colorado. Even in these territories existence of a two-party system can be regarded as provisional and temporary. In Nebraska the two-party era lasted only from 1860 until 1872, from the last years of the territorial period through the earliest years of statehood. This period can be considered transitional between the first years of Democratic dominance and the later years of Republican ascendancy. After 1872 Republican power went without serious challenge until William Jennings Bryan led the forces of Nebraska Democracy against the illiberal, railroad-dominated Republican machine in 1890.[23]

In Colorado, on the other hand, territorial Republicans had already made clear their overwhelming strength at the polls by 1864, when a regular party organization was formed. Establishment of a one-party system in that territory was delayed only by divisive rivalry between Jerome Chaffee's so-called "Denver Crowd" and the "Golden Crowd" led by Henry Moore Teller. Once this Republican schism was repaired during the statehood movement, Colorado also developed a Republican one-party system that carried both Chaffee and Teller into the Senate when Colorado joined the Union in 1876. This system remained effective until Republicans were again divided by the Free-Silver movement in the 1890s.[24]

By contrast with the one-party pattern, political leaders were used up at a much higher rate in two-party territories, if only because voters periodically exercised their option to throw the rascals out. The power of the electorate to decide between rival organizations and rival candidates was the most distinctive feature of two-party politics. Competition between parties for popular support, however, was usually accompanied by an instability of leadership within separate party organizations. Since selection of party managers depended ultimately upon electoral validation, such organizations tended to remain looser, less structured than those in a one-party system, and to resemble a collection of ambitious personal cliques more than a disciplined, efficient engine of government. To this extent, it may be observed, two-party government in territories more easily became a battleground for contending economic interests, since apparently there was always at hand a large supply of pliable and ambitious men who were ready to accept backing from any source, and in any amount. And to this extent, moreover, the two-party system was a less effective agency for representing to the federal government and other nonterritorial agencies the concerns and demands of the territory's political community.

With Nevada discounted as a territory which never emerged from a stage of chaotic factionalism, attention can be directed to four territories in which a no-party pattern of territorial politics took shape: Utah, Montana, Wyoming, and New Mexico. In each case the institutions of party government came to be managed by a coalition of local interests that cut across party lines. Utah provides an obvious first case, since the Latter-Day Saints' church hierarchy remained the decisive political influence throughout the territorial period.[25] In New Mexico the well-known "Santa Fe Ring" led by Stephen Elkins and Thomas B. Catron became the effective decision-making body after 1872. Though this group was predominantly Republican in party allegiance, it also brought into the inner circle a number of New Mexico's leading Democrats, including representatives of the Hispano-American community. After a brief episode of two-party contests during the 1890s, a revived Santa Fe Ring reclaimed power and guided New Mexico to statehood finally in 1912, making only slight concessions to reform-minded Roosevelt progressives.[26]

By the 1870s both Montana and Wyoming were developing combinations at least as effective as the Santa Fe Ring. The political history of Montana Territory can be written largely in terms of operations of one man, Samuel T. Hauser of Helena, who achieved a position as the territory's most eminent capitalist and leading Democrat. Although he held office only briefly and reluctantly on one occasion, when President Cleveland appointed him territorial governor, it is no exaggeration to say that Hauser and his associates—including the perennial Democratic delegate, Martin Maginnis, the long-time Republican governor, Benjamin F. Potts, and later the successful Butte mining engineer, Marcus Daly—managed Montana's governmental affairs with a thoroughness their enemies could only admire.[27] In Wyoming, as Professor Gould has recently demonstrated, a rather similar role was taken by Francis E. Warren and his colleague Joseph M. Carey. So long as these two men maintained their friendship, they and their supporters in the Wyoming business community were able virtually to dictate Republican policy and keep the sympathetic Wyoming Democratic leadership in fee.[28]

A more detailed explanation is needed for the politics of two territories,

Idaho and Arizona, in which a distorted pattern of two-party politics, best termed a mixed-party system, evolved into a no-party system. In both cases territorial elections from an early date were normally dominated by Democrats; yet through most of their territorial history federal patronage was controlled by Republican national administrations, and that patronage helped nurture small, sometimes desperately beleaguered Republican organizations. Consequently, Democratic leaders in Arizona and Idaho found reason to complain most vehemently of their colonial status under Republican officials, most of whom were nonresident appointees. But in both territories during this era of mixed-party government there grew a strong tradition of accommodation and shared power that often made party lines less important than personal interest.

During the 1880s, however, shrewd Republican newcomers introduced new political issues which disrupted—at least temporarily—the traditional arrangements. In Idaho United States Marshal Fred T. Dubois originated an anti-Mormon movement that became a means to split Democratic ranks, disfranchise a substantial Mormon bloc of Democratic voters, force anti-Mormonism upon the Idaho Republican party, and secure Dubois's own election as delegate. Another tactic succeeded in Arizona, where Nathan O. Murphy began in 1885 to promote an anti-Apache Indian removal movement that became a vehicle for Republican popular success.

The Idaho anti-Mormon movement and the Arizona anti-Apache movement served a similar function in territorial politics. They gave local Republicans, now securely in charge of territorial party organizations, a broadened base of popular support. But these movements did not result in a system of one-party rule in either Idaho or Arizona. Idaho's conservative non-Mormon Democratic leaders drew together with Republicans, forming an anti-Mormon and prosilver alliance which controlled the statehood movement and brought Idaho into the Union. Significantly, Dubois was elected chairman of the state constitutional convention in 1889, though in the allocation of state offices upon Idaho's admission in 1890 he had to defer his higher ambitions temporarily to two old-line frontier capitalists and Republican conservatives, George M. Shoup and William J. McConnell.[29]

Arizona failed in the parallel attempt to gain statehood at the same time, and after the Populist excitement of the 1890s another newcomer, Mark A. Smith, restored the Democratic party to a position of power in Arizona. Under the machine rule of Smith and his clique of "Corporation Democrats," however, the tradition of accommodation remained strong in Arizona, as it did in Idaho. Arizona capitalists of every political persuasion remained assured of a congenial climate of government. Only in 1910, during a renewed drive for statehood, did progressive liberalism threaten Smith's leadership of the Arizona no-party system. Democratic insurgents and a few Republican allies, led by progressive Democrat George Hunt, took control of the constitutional convention that year and fashioned a charter of state government that incorporated progressive reform provisions. When Arizona entered the Union two years later, the struggle between progressive liberalism and corporate illiberalism, fought mainly within the Democratic party, still divided politicians in the new state. Hunt secured the governorship, Smith went to the Senate, while all factions were able to agree upon selection of Henry Fountain Ashurst to be Smith's Senate colleague and young Carl Hayden to serve in the House of Representatives. The remarkable political longevity of all four men after 1912 is a tribute perhaps to the enduring tradition of accommodation that continued to mark politics in that state.[30]

One distinct condition helps to account for emergence of a no-party pattern in these last six territories. In each a community of joint interest grew among leading men, fashioned out of their common concern for material development and social welfare of their regions, and for immediate prosperity of their own enterprises. These concerns, they came to believe, could not be adequately safeguarded by the machinery of government available under territorial authority. From the perspective of Santa Fe, Salt Lake City, Cheyenne, or the other territorial capitals, there was too much at stake in determining control of public policy to entrust these decisions to ordinary vicissitudes of party politics as practiced in western territories. Business communities in these territories, or Mormon church leaders in the case of Utah, were intent upon advancing a limited few vital interests. These groups made political coalitions virtually coterminous with the effective political community of their separate territories. The device of a no-party system was their solution to problems of governmental weakness and political instability that were endemic to territorial status.

Under a no-party system the direct influence of either the electorate or the federally appointed professional politicians in both national parties was minimized. The identifying feature of no-party government as practiced in these territories was not in lack of party organizations or political contests, but in management of public policy by agencies other than political parties and strict party politicians. Officeholders had to be malleable in such a system and able to rationalize their conceptions of the public good with the welfare of the interests they served—whether those interests were tied to local business and industry, alien corporate enterprise, or religious and social institutions that supervened party lines. In this type of system political leadership was normally determined by prescriptive means, rather than cooptive or elective. In Montana, for example, when Martin Maginnis became independently ambitious and attempted to secure the governorship for himself in 1885, Sam Hauser simply crossed him off and made himself a candidate for the appointment.[31] And while material rewards of successful political service might also be great in other systems, invariably politics became for loyal politicians a road to greater wealth in a no-party system. From a federal perspective, the federal territorial system subsidized frontier expansion and western settlement by grants of political power to leading men of the territories. And from this perspective, the no-party pattern of politics represented an ultimate achievement by these enterprising westerners.

III

From a summary of party patterns in western territories a few simple conclusions may be drawn. Apparently territorial conditions did not encourage growth of two-party political systems. The alternatives of a one-party or a no-party pattern proved far more viable under the territorial form of government once a region had outgrown the early stage of chaotic factionalism. But this conclusion should surprise only those whose view of American politics has been derived from the dream world of civics textbooks, a world in which all men are honest, all politicians are statesmen, and all governments invariably express popular will through the two-party system. After 1848, it can be pointed out, and certainly after 1865, actual two-party systems were scarcely less prevalent in older states than in western territories. Only at the national level, where all the myriad forces of local politics came together, did the concept of two-party government have approximate validity. It remained true, as James Madison had written in the Federalist, no. 10, that an enlarged Republic, comprehending a wider diversity of interests, provided the one possible check upon the baleful influence of faction and party in local governments.

Regarding the difference between one-party and no-party patterns: territories with a relatively homogeneous population, a lack of sharp intraterritorial sectional divisions, a relatively diversified structure of economic development, and a fairly rapid and continuous rate of settlement tended toward a one-party system. By contrast, where ethnic and sectional differences were greater and where growth of settlement and development of the territorial economy were retarded by isolation and a lack of immediately productive resources, a no-party pattern was likely to appear. In those territories, moreover, that were least economically diversified, in which local economy rapidly became dependent upon one or two major industries, a no-party system most quickly became characteristic of territorial politics. Viewed in this way, though pioneer western buncombe manufacturers could scarcely be expected to announce it on the Fourth of July, one might conclude that territorial party managers helped fix politically a form of internal colonialism upon frontier societies whose representatives they claimed to be.

Once territorial politics began to overcome the wide-open factional turmoil of the earliest years, the structure of western government assumed a marked elitist character. For these western territories there is every reason to affirm the conclusion that various scholars have advanced regarding Anglo-American politics at other times and places: political affairs were essentially the concern of a rather small, restricted leadership stratum that was identified with upper-class interests. Except during occasional periods of wide social and economic discontent, factional and party divisions did not reflect class lines; nor did movements of discontent ever bring about a general demand for fundamental, radical alterations in the structure of upper-class politics. Under every party system, territorial politics involved ambitions of upper-class leaders who secured broad support from all sectors of the territorial electorate.[32]

If one reads the roll of new senators from the West who took their places as each state entered the federal Union, it is necessary to agree that these men were wonderfully well qualified to join that "Millionaires Club" in the national capital.[33] As successful frontier entrepreneurs in a political as well as an economic sense, these men constituted with few exceptions a class of territorial magnates who naturally assumed direction of public policy for their regions. Even as territorial populations increased and western society matured beyond conditions of the early frontier settlement era, these western leaders continued to maintain their influence over the limited political community they had become accustomed to supervise under territorial authority.

These conclusions of course do damage to the progressive, Turnerian image of the American West as a realm of natural democracy. But they may offer a further validation for the claim that territorial government was a successful agency of Anglo-American expansion. As a system of political relationships, territorial government provided the means by which a resident, upper-class leadership could fashion structures of government congruent with those in the older states. And this conclusion, finally, may be found entirely consistent with Frederick Jackson Turner's early statement that the history of frontier politics provides a rich body of materials for the study of American political forms and their evolution.[34]

NOTES

1. Carter explained his work principally in three articles intended as progress reports: "The United States and Documentary Historical Publication," *Mississippi Valley Historical Review* 25 (1938): 3–24; "The Territorial Papers of the United States," *American Archivist* 8 (1945): 122–35; "The Territorial Papers of the United States: A Review and Commentary," *Mississippi Valley Historical Review* 42 (1955): 510–24.

2. Works in this school include John M. Merriam, "The Legislative History of the Ordinance of 1787," *Proceedings of the American Antiquarian Society,* n.s., vol. 5 (1888), pp. 303–42; Jay Amos Barrett, *Evolution of the Ordinance of 1787 . . . of the Northwest Territory* (New York: G. P. Putnam's Sons, 1891); Max Farrand, *The Legislation of Congress for the Government of the Organized Territories of the United States, 1789–1895* (Newark: W. A. Baker, 1896); and Alpheus H. Snow, *The Administration of Dependencies: A Study of the Evolution of the Federal Empire with Special Reference to the American Colonial Problems* (New York: G. P. Putnam's Sons, 1902). For a summary of earlier writings see Ray A. Billington, "The Historians of the North West Ordinance," *Journal of the Illinois State Historical Society* 40 (1947): 397–413.

3. Representative treatments include Frederick Jackson Turner, "Western State-Making in the Revolutionary Era," *American Historical Review* 1 (1895): 70–87, 251–69; Theodore C. Pease, "The Ordinance of 1787," *Mississippi Valley Historical Review* 25 (1938): 167–80; Roy F. Nichols, "The Territories: Seedbeds of Democracy," *Nebraska History* 35 (1954): 159–72; and John D. Barnhart, *Valley of Democracy: The Frontier versus the Plantation in the Ohio Valley, 1775–1818* (Bloomington: Indiana University Press, 1953). Compare also Turner's remarks in *The Frontier in American History* (New York: H. Holt & Co., 1920), pp. 168–70.

4. "Colonialism in [the] Continental United States," *South Atlantic Quarterly* 47 (1948): 28. In addition to the 1955 article cited above, see also Carter's earlier essay, *Apprenticeship for American Statehood*, Department of State Bulletin, vol. 12, no. 312 (1945), pp. 1109–14.

5. "The Territory as a Frontier Institution," *Historian* 7 (1944): 41. Cf. Frederick Merk, *Manifest Destiny and Mission in American History: A Reinterpretation* (New York: Knopf, 1963), pp. 4–6; and Francis S. Philbrick, *The Rise of the West, 1776–1830* (New York: Harper & Row, 1965), pp. 130–33.

6. Among Professor Jackson's writings on territorial politics see particularly "Indian Affairs and Politics in Idaho Territory, 1863–1870," *Pacific Historical Review* 14 (1945): 311–25; "Montana Politics during the Meagher Regime, 1865–1867," *Pacific Historical Review* 12 (1943): 139–56; "Dakota Politics during the Burbank Administration, 1869–1873," *North Dakota Historical Quarterly* 12 (July 1945): 111–34; "The Administration of Thomas Moonlight, 1887–1889," *Annals of Wyoming* 18 (1946): 139–62; "The Wyoming Stock Growers' Association: Political Power in Wyoming Territory, 1873–1890," *Mississippi Valley Historical Review* 33 (1947): 571–94; and "The Wyoming Stock Growers' Association: Its

Years of Temporary Decline, 1886–1890," *Agricultural History* 22 (1948): 260–72.

7. For Professor Lamar's principal works, see notes 21 and 24 below. A selection of Dr. Wells's writings on Idaho politics is cited in note 29 below. Schell's volume on South Dakota is cited in note 21 below, though not his earlier writings. The works of Professor T. A. Larson and Professor Gould on Wyoming are listed in note 28 below, while Professor Robert Larson's treatment of New Mexico politics is cited in note 26 below.

8. Cf. Owens, "Research Opportunities in Western Territorial History," *Arizona and the West* 8 (1966): 7–18.

9. This general approach to territorial politics is closely related to the Namier school of historiography. For a number of years I have been engaged in a program of research that is intended to develop an analysis of frontier political leadership and western government consistent with the Namierian form of investigation. For a comparable survey treatment of Anglo-American colonial politics, which has been in part a model for this paper, see Jack P. Greene, "Changing Interpretations of Early American Politics," in Ray A. Billington, ed., *The Reinterpretation of Early American History: Essays in Honor of John Edwin Pomfret* (San Marino: Huntington Library, 1966), pp. 151–83. In the following footnotes I have attempted to cite only a few general published accounts dealing with the political histories of the various territories, although my general conclusions are based in large part upon research in documentary materials too extensive for citation in this context.

10. The classic literary account of Nevada territorial history of course is found in Mark Twain, *Roughing It.* A more sober account is found in Myron Angel, *History of Nevada* (New York, 1881), pp. 75–81. That the state has never entirely outgrown a condition of chaotic factionalism is one conclusion which may be derived from the recent popular history by Gilman M. Ostrander, *Nevada: The Great Rotten Borough, 1859–1964* (New York: Knopf, 1966).

11. The term *chaotic factionalism* I have found used first in a formal descriptive sense by Professor Greene in the article cited in note 9. The concept of the *political community* is derived from Sir John Namier's application of the term *political nation* to describe the active participants in eighteenth-century English political life.

12. Allan G. Bogue, "Social Theory and the Pioneer," *Agricultural History* 34 (1960): 21–34. My thinking in this connection has also been particularly informed by Barrington Moore, Jr., *Political Power and Social Theory* (Cambridge: Harvard University Press, 1958); Seymour M. Lipset, *Political Man: The Social Bases of Politics* (New York: Doubleday, 1960); and Professor Lipset's article, "Some Social Requisites of Democracy: Economic Development and Political Legitimacy," *American Political Science Review* 53 (1959): 69–105. Another work of seminal importance for the understanding of frontier relationships between social change, economic growth, and political organization is E. E. Hagen, *On the Theory of Social Change: How Economic Growth Begins* (Homewood, Ill.: Dorsey, 1962). An important line of comparative study has been explored by Earl Pomeroy in his essay "The West and New Nations in Other Continents," in J. A. Carroll, ed., *Reflections of Western Historians* (Tucson: University of Arizona Press, 1969), pp. 237–61.

13. Cf. Bogue, "Social Theory and the Pioneer," pp. 30–34; Chilton Williamson, *American Suffrage: From Property to Democracy, 1760–1860* (Princeton: Princeton University Press, 1960), pp. 209–22.
14. *Leviathan* (var. ed.), chap. 13. For a similar atomistic view of frontier society see Turner, *Frontier in American History,* p. 212.
15. Unfortunately, there is to my knowledge no scholarly study of this important topic.
16. At this point I am not concerned with the issues regarding patterns of voting behavior and the determinants of party allegiance. The importance of these issues and the possibilities for further analysis are emphasized in Samuel P. Hays, "The Social Analysis of American Political History, 1880–1920," *Political Science Quarterly* 83 (1965): 373–94. For further comment see Owens, "Research Opportunities," pp. 15–18.
17. William Watts Folwell, *A History of Minnesota,* 4 vols. (St. Paul, Minnesota Historical Society, 1921–30), still provides the most satisfactory account of Minnesota territorial politics. Among general works of particular importance for Oregon territorial history see especially Walter C. Woodward, *The Rise and Early History of Political Parties in Oregon, 1843–1868* (Portland: J. K. Gill Co., 1913); Charles H. Carey, *A General History of Oregon Prior to 1861,* 2 vols. (Portland: Metropolitan Press, 1935–36), 1:317–60, 2:466–520; and the recent biographical study by James E. Hendrickson, *Joe Lane of Oregon: Machine Politics and the Sectional Crisis* (New Haven: Yale University Press, 1967). Also of importance is Robert W. Johannsen, "Oregon Territory's Movement for Self-Government, 1848–1853," *Pacific Historical Review* 18 (1949): 485–99.
18. Kansas territorial politics receive detailed coverage in William E. Connelley, *History of Kansas: State and People,* 5 vols. (New York: American Historical Society, 1928); Alice Nichols, *Bleeding Kansas* (New York: Oxford University Press, 1954); and G. Raymond Gaeddert, *The Birth of Kansas* (Lawrence: University of Kansas, 1940). For social analysis see also James C. Malin, *John Brown and the Legend of Fifty-six* (Philadelphia: American Philosophical Society, 1942); and Paul W. Gates, *Fifty Million Acres: Conflicts Over Kansas Land Policy, 1854–1890* (Ithaca: Cornell University Press, 1954).
19. There is no adequate general account of Washington Territory's political history, though the outlines are presented best in Clinton A. Snowden, *History of Washington: The Rise and Progress of an American State,* 4 vols. (New York: Century History Co., 1909); and Hubert Howe Bancroft, *Works of Hubert Howe Bancroft,* 36 vols. (San Francisco: History Co., 1890), vol. 31.
20. Quoted in Joseph Gilpin Pyle, *The Life of James J. Hill,* 2 vols. (Garden City: Doubleday, Page & Co., 1917), 1:426–27.
21. Cf. Howard R. Lamar, *Dakota Territory, 1861–1889: A Study of Frontier Politics* (New Haven: Yale University Press, 1956), 244–84 et passim; Herbert S. Schell, *History of South Dakota* (Lincoln: University of Nebraska Press, 1961), pp. 203–22; Elwyn B. Robinson, *History of North Dakota* (Lincoln: University of Nebraska Press, 1966), pp. 197–216. Before the work of these modern scholars the basic history of Dakota politics was found in George W. Kingsbury, *History of Dakota Territory,* 5 vols. (Chicago: S. J. Clarke Publishiing Co., 1915), a work still useful for descriptive details.

22. Although no published studies provide a detailed account of Oklahoma territorial politics, the most important summaries are found in Joseph B. Thoburn and Muriel Wright, *Oklahoma: A History of the State and Its People,* 4 vols. (New York: Lewis Historical Publishing Co., 1929); and Roy F. Gittinger, *The Formation of the State of Oklahoma (1803–1906)* (Berkeley: University of California Press, 1917). Also compare the evaluations in Grant Foreman, *A History of Oklahoma* (Norman: University of Oklahoma Press, 1942), pp. 261–72, 310–26; and Edwin C. McReynolds, *Oklahoma: A History of the Sooner State* (Norman: University of Oklahoma Press, 1954), pp. 292–323.

23. Detailed basic accounts of Nebraska territorial politics are available in J. Sterling Morton and Albert Watkins, *Illustrated History of Nebraska,* 3 vols. (Lincoln: J. North & Co., 1905–13); and Addison E. Sheldon, *Nebraska: The Land and the People,* 3 vols. (Chicago: Lewis Publishing Co., 1931). A modern summary appears in James C. Olson, *History of Nebraska* (Lincoln: University of Nebraska Press, 1955), pp. 82–92, 122–33. Also useful is Professor Olson's biography of the pioneer Democratic leader, *J. Sterling Morton* (Lincoln: University of Nebraska Press, 1942).

24. Cf. Howard R. Lamar, *The Far Southwest, 1846–1912: A Territorial History* (New Haven: Yale University Press, 1966), pp. 205–301, Elmer Ellis, *Henry Moore Teller: Defender of the West* (Caldwell, Idaho: Caxton Printers, 1941), pp. 62–97. Among general accounts reference may also be made to Wilbur F. Stone, *The History of Colorado,* 5 vols. (Chicago: S. J. Clarke Publishing Co., 1918–19); and LeRoy R. Hafen, *Colorado and Its People: A Narrative and Topical History of the Centennial State,* 4 vols. (New York: Lewis Historical Publishing Co., 1948).

25. The most recent account of Utah territorial history appears in Lamar, *The Far Southwest,* pp. 305–411. Also of particular importance are Leland Creer, *Utah and the Nation* (Seattle: University of Washington Press, 1929); Leonard J. Arrington, *Great Basin Kingdom: An Economic History of the Latter-Day Saints, 1830–1900* (Cambridge: Harvard University Press, 1958); Norman Furniss, *The Mormon Conflict, 1850–1859* (New Haven: Yale University Press, 1960); and Thomas F. O'Dea, *The Mormons* (Chicago: University of Chicago Press, 1957).

26. The basic modern account is provided in Lamar, *The Far Southwest,* pp. 23–201, 486–501. The standard older treatment, still convenient for details, appears in Ralph E. Twitchell, *The Leading Facts of New Mexico History,* 5 vols. (Cedar Rapids: Torch Press, 1911–17). Also of interest are Calvin Horn, *New Mexico's Troubled Years: The Story of the Early Territorial Governors* (Albuquerque: Horn & Wallace, 1963); and two volumes by William A. Keleher, *Turmoil in New Mexico, 1846–1868* (Santa Fe: Rydal Press, 1952), and *Violence in Lincoln County, 1869–1881* (Albuquerque: University of New Mexico Press, 1957); and the recent study by Robert W. Larson, *New Mexico's Quest for Statehood, 1846–1912* (Albuquerque: University of New Mexico Press, 1968). Professor Lamar's article, "Political Patterns in New Mexico and Utah Territories, 1850–1900," *Utah Historical Quarterly* 28 (1960): 363–87, should also be consulted.

27. Montana territorial politics are best outlined in Helen Fitzgerald Sanders, *A History of Montana,* 3 vols. (Chicago: Lewis Publishing Co., 1913). A

sketchy account appears in the modern multi-volume state history, Merrill G. Burlingame and K. Ross Toole, *A History of Montana*, 3 vols. (New York: Lewis Historical Publishing Co., 1957). More informative for the early years is the treatment in James M. Hamilton, *From Wilderness to Statehood: A History of Montana, 1805–1900* (Portland: Binsford & Mort, 1957).

28. Lewis Gould, *Wyoming: A Political History, 1868–1896* (New Haven: Yale University Press, 1968). Other valuable accounts are found in T. A. Larson, *History of Wyoming* (Lincoln: University of Nebraska Press, 1965), and an older work, Frances B. Beard, *Wyoming from Territorial Days to the Present,* 3 vols. (Chicago: American Historical Society, 1933). An extremely important reference work is Marie H. Erwin, *Wyoming Historical Blue Book: A Legal and Political History of Wyoming, 1868–1943* (Denver: Bradford Robinson Print Co., 1946).

29. Idaho's political history is best summarized by Merle Wells in Merrill D. Beal and Merle Wells, *History of Idaho,* 3 vols. (New York: Lewis Historical Publishing Co., 1959); but see also the following more detailed accounts by Wells for the events emphasized in my treatment: "Origins of Anti-Mormonism in Idaho, 1872–1880," *Pacific Northwest Quarterly* 47 (1956): 107–16; "The Idaho Anti-Mormon Test Oath, 1884–1892," *Pacific Historical Review* 24 (1955): 235–52; and "The Idaho Admission Movement, 1888–1890," *Oregon Historical Quarterly* 56 (1955): 27–60.

30. This treatment follows principally the account in Lamar, *The Far Southwest,* pp. 415–85, 494–504. Thomas J. Farish, *History of Arizona,* 8 vols. (San Francisco: Filmer Brothers Electrotype Co., 1915–18), provides a wealth of detail, while a satisfactory brief treatment appears in Rufus K. Wyllys, *Arizona: The History of a Frontier State* (Phoenix: Hobson & Herr, 1950).

31. J. K. Toole to Hauser, March 30, April 24, 27, May 1, and July 5, 1885; and G. G. Vest to Hauser, June 19, 1885, in the Samuel T. Hauser Papers, Historical Society of Montana, Helena.

32. Cf. Greene, "Changing Interpretations," pp. 170–72; Alfred F. Young, *The Democratic Republicans of New York: The Origins, 1763–1797* (Chapel Hill: Published for the Institute of Early American History and Culture, Williamsburg, Va., by the University of North Carolina Press, 1967), pp. 83–105 et passim.

33. See David J. Rothman, *Politics and Power: The United States Senate, 1869–1901* (Cambridge: Harvard University Press, 1966), pp. 159–90, and particularly Professor Rothman's accounts of such western senators as Fred Dubois, Richard Pettigrew, Henry Moore Teller, and Francis Warren.

34. Cf. Turner, "Problems in American History," in *The Early Writings of Frederick Jackson Turner,* ed. Fulmer Mood (Madison: University of Wisconsin Press, 1936), and the different attitude in Turner, "Contributions of the West to American Democracy," in *Frontier in American History,* pp. 243–68.

THE TERRITORIES

IN THE

TWENTIETH CENTURY

EDITOR'S NOTE

*The following two essays, with ensuing commentary
and discussion, were delivered at the closing session of
the conference. Oliver W. Holmes, in introducing the
speakers, commented on the two great parts into which
the overall history of the American territorial system
may be divided, "the first being the story of that system
as it worked within the contiguous boundaries of a
country characterized by an advancing frontier, and the
second the story of the application of the system to
overseas territories that, except for Alaska, were characterized by conditions that represented almost the reverse
of frontier societies." He posed the question, "Were
there significant changes in the old system in the emerging twentieth century?" He pointed out that the first
paper provided a last look at some earlier aspects of the
system by examining one of the last territorial governorships of nearly the last of the contiguous territories, New Mexico, while the second paper was devoted
entirely to the application of the system to overseas
jurisdictions.*

*The address by the Honorable Harrison Loesch,
Assistant Secretary of the Interior for Public Land Management, was delivered at the formal dinner of the
Conference on the History of the Territories of the
United States. This took place on Monday evening, November 3, 1969, at the Hotel Washington, in the presence of the participants in the conference, their guests,
and a group of distinguished guests from the United
States House of Representatives, the Department of the*

Interior, and the General Services Administration. Dr. James B. Rhoads, Archivist of the United States, introduced the distinguished guests, including the Honorable Robert L. Kunzig, Administrator of General Services, who spoke briefly in a personal vein in introducing Mr. Loesch.

After concluding his address Mr. Loesch entertained from the audience many questions which were not recorded, and conducted an active period of discussion. Mr. Loesch's address was released to the press on the morning of Tuesday, November 4, 1969.

George Curry of New Mexico: Territorial Governor in a Changing Era

ROBERT W. LARSON

CAPTAIN GEORGE CURRY, while governor of Samar province during the Philippines campaign, received an urgent cablegram from President Theodore Roosevelt on April 1, 1907. ". . . Have today appointed you Governor of New Mexico. You must accept. Have designated the Territorial Secretary as Acting Governor until your arrival. Complete your business as early as possible."[1] Few territorial governors have had the dubious distinction of being commanded to assume their posts. During the Gilded Age, eastern politicians had often eagerly sought the chief executive office under the territorial system. Older states competed with states bordering the frontier, as Earl S. Pomeroy has pointed out in his pioneering study on territorial administration from 1861 to 1890, to see which could garner the most territorial appointments. Politicians boasted of their ability to deliver territorial governorships or judgeships, as examples of their personal political power.[2]

A number of significant changes had occurred, however, as the old century gave way to the new. When Curry first arrived in New Mexico, in 1879, moving to Lincoln County a year after the famous range war, territories were still regarded by Washington as remarkable outlets for the yet uncurbed spoils system. The Department of the Interior, which had assumed responsibility for the territories in 1873, much to the delight of the secretary of state, was carefully cultivating its policy of indifference toward the territories, notwithstanding laudable efforts, in 1879, of Secretary Carl Schurz to do otherwise.[3] There were nine contiguous territories, including unorganized Indian Territory, making up the continental territorial empire that comprised the last frontier. Resource development and settlement were pursued very largely under laissez faire conditions.

But even during Curry's first decade in New Mexico, when the young, Louisiana-born man in his twenties was ranching and holding offices in Lincoln County, changes were taking place. During the 1880s Washington began to accede to a growing local demand that the president appoint residents as governors and judges of territories.[4] Governors Edmund G. Ross and LeBaron Bradford Prince, appointees of Cleveland and Harrison, were both residents of New Mexico at the time of appointment. A modest effort was begun to restrict the often freewheeling activities of western empire builders when the national administration, during Cleveland's first term, restored 80,000,000 acres of land, illegally entered, to the public domain, and directed that private fences be removed from public land, a blow to large cattle interests.[5]

In the nineties, while Curry was gaining governmental experience by service in the legislature, acting as president of the territorial senate in 1896,[6] America's great conservation program began developing. In the General Land Revision Act of 1891 the frequently abused timber culture acts and preemption laws were repealed and the Desert Land Act was revised, and, almost as an afterthought, the General Revision Act was amended to allow the president to set aside forest reserves by proclamation. Under this new authority, President Harrison created New Mexico's first national forest on March 3, 1891, on the headwaters of the Pecos River, launching a program which would eventually result in having 12 percent of New Mexico's domain in national forests.[7] Soon the government would be charging grazing fees and determining boundaries for the expanding forest reserves. In the Carey Act of 1894 the federal government came to the rescue of the West, following the irrigation boom-and-bust of 1887 to 1893, by granting millions of acres of land to western states and territories to finance irrigation.[8] And, in the Forest Management Act of 1897, the secretary of the interior's power over western resource development was greatly increased by new authority "to regulate the occupancy and use" of national forests. In a territory such as New Mexico, one of four remaining contiguous territories by 1897, the secretary of the interior not only had overall political supervision, but now also had a great deal more to say about how the inhabitants would develop their forest and grazing resources.

During the period from 1898 to 1907, while Curry was serving as a Rough Rider and later as an officer and military governor in the Philippines, the conservation program became more of a crusade. President Theodore Roosevelt enthusiastically embraced it as "my policy." Water power conservation was given a solid boost by passage of the Right-of-Way Act of 1901. The Reclamation Act of 1902, needed because so few projects were launched under the Carey Act by the late nineties, brought about direct federal financing of irrigation. The transfer of forest reserves from the Department of the Interior to the Department of Agriculture in 1905 further increased the power of that ardent conservationist and soul mate of Roosevelt in "the strenuous life," Gifford Pinchot, the chief forester. The rash of conservation legislation was forcefully implemented by President Roosevelt who, among other actions, withdrew millions of acres of forest land as part of the national reserve.[9]

The president urgently needed Captain Curry in 1907 because of a conservation scandal in New Mexico which had received national attention. Involved were a piece of congressional legislation meant to help the territory and a well-meaning but inexperienced governor, Herbert J. Hagerman. The Fergusson Act of 1898, sponsored by a popular former territorial delegate, Harvey B. Fergusson, was to grant immediately to the territory sections 16 and 36 of every township for support of public education, with sections 2 and 32 to be granted later, when New Mexico was admitted as a state. This new measure was essential, for the court of private land claims, established in 1891 to adjudicate conflicting claims of ownership over large Spanish and Mexican land grants, had through its decisions opened up a vast amount of acreage to settlement. The territory had been fearful that, if a measure such as the Fergusson Act were not passed, all good land would be gobbled up, leaving the territory only worthless desert acreage. Disposal of this land was to be for the benefit of the small homesteader. An individual purchasing such land from the territory was entitled to 160 acres only. In-lieu selections by the territory were permitted, except for mineral land and land set aside by the federal government for other purposes.[10]

Governor Hagerman, a progressive, reform-minded young man recommended to Roosevelt by his first secretary of the interior, conservationist Ethan A. Hitchcock,[11] was to expose himself to his enemies in New Mexico by administering the Fergusson Act in an illegal way, but in a way that citizens of the territory wanted it administered. One hundred and sixty acres was hardly sufficient to make a living in semiarid New Mexico, where 98 percent of the land was inadequate for crop production.[12] Extractive industries in New Mexico had fallen into the practice of having their employees acquire adjoining 160-acre plots, which when consolidated would comprise a sizeable tract. Employees of the Pennsylvania Development Company (a group of capitalists from the Keystone State), the Santa Fe Central Railway, and the New Mexico Fuel and Iron Company had purchased thousands of acres of valuable timberland in Valencia County this way. Hagerman ratified questionable Valencia County purchases by turning over deeds of ownership to the attorney representing these three corporations, taking approximately eleven thousand dollars in payment. The Progressive movement, another movement to which President Roosevelt gave full support, was growing rapidly throughout the country, and

Hagerman had felt, prior to coming to the territory, that he had a mandate from the president to clean up New Mexico politics. He made bitter enemies in the process, alienating Holm O. Bursum, the most powerful Republican in the territory at this time, whom he removed as superintendent of the territorial prison because of an alleged mishandling of funds. Roosevelt, who wanted to stabilize the New Mexico situation, apparently saw a way of eliminating a serious political liability by removing Hagerman on the pretext that he had broken the law by delivering controversial deeds to the Pennsylvania Development Company and the other two corporations.[13]

Curry had been contacted regarding the New Mexico governorship as early as February 1907, weeks before the president compelled Hagerman to resign. Roosevelt had great faith in Curry, holding him in higher esteem than almost all other Rough Riders, a group for which he had boundless affection.[14] Captain Curry was a resident, as had been all of New Mexico's territorial governors since 1885, but he had been away from the politically torn territory continually for eight years. ". . . Curry is as straight as a string," the President wrote Ormsby McHarg, one of two special investigators sent by the Justice Department to investigate violations of the Fergusson Act and other alleged land fraud cases.[15] Curry's absence from the territory had not, however, changed his attitude toward the way New Mexico should be governed. The new governor was a product of the era of laissez faire in New Mexico and had been away while most of the significant changes in public policy regarding resource development had been made, changes which tended to erode private prerogative in livestock, mining, and lumber industries. Lumbermen, for instance, used to cut on public domain and on unconfirmed land grants without fear of reprisal until, in the 1880s, the federal government began to demand stumpage fees and threaten suits to recover value taken. From 1898 to 1905, when Curry had been absent from the territory every year but one, 4,726,201 acres of New Mexico timberland had been added to the 311,040 acres set aside in forest reserves prior to his departure.[16]

Evidence of wrongdoing and questionable conduct uncovered by McHarg and his fellow investigator from the Department of Justice, Peyton Gordon, involved some of Curry's old friends and associates. During Curry's first months in office he deeply resented the interference of these outside federal agents, and, playing on his friendship with Roosevelt, he threatened to resign once. His attitude in this regard was not much different from that of Gov. Samuel B. Axtell some thirty years earlier when he protested federal intervention in New Mexico's Lincoln County War and insisted that the government had "no control over him—and that he [would] not be investigated."[17] Curry, unlike Axtell, had presidential support in this situation. Roosevelt ordered the two Justice Department agents to complete their investigation by December 1907, and turn their evidence over to the new United States district attorney, Capt. David J. Leahy, another old Rough Rider comrade and New Mexico resident. Nineteen indictments which had been drawn up by McHarg against persons accused of fraudulent coal land entries in the northwest part of the territory, including Cleveland A. Dodge of the Phelps-Dodge Company, were eventually dropped.[18]

Professor Pomeroy has pointed out that during the late nineteenth century the most important attribute for a territorial governor was his ability to get along with his constituents. A petition asking for the removal of Wyoming's territorial chief executive in the early 1870s insisted that the governor did not "mingle with our people, and get acquainted with our wants and our interests, or identify in any way with our citizens."[19] Curry had shown that he could do all of these things during his first eight months as governor. His harmonious relations with the legislature were in sharp contrast to the struggle that Governor Hagerman had had with the powerful supporters of Bursum, who dominated the legislature and blocked him at every turn. Where Curry erred was in his failure to recognize that territorial government was in a period of transition. More pressure was now coming from the federal government than had, perhaps, ever been the case. The period of studied indifference that had characterized the attitude of most of the secretaries of the interior toward their territorial responsibility had passed. The program of conservation had paved the way for a truly significant intervention on the part of the Department of the Interior, and the Department of Agriculture and other executive departments to a lesser extent. The reform spirit engendered by progressivism only sharpened public interest in any misuse or abuse of territorial resources, as illustrated by the widely published Hagerman affair.

But Curry's concern at first was to advance the interests of the territorial citizenry, and he quickly came into sharp conflict with Pinchot over grazing rights and cutting in national forests. As owner of a ranch in southern New Mexico adjacent to Lincoln National Forest, which was established on July 26, 1902, he was in complete agreement with his neighbors, many of whom were of Spanish extraction, that users' rights to graze stock on public domain were incontestable. He, too, agreed that federal grazing fees, instituted after 1906, were too high. When a local lumber firm, the Alamogordo Lumber Company, was accused of fraudulently acquiring twenty thousand acres of timberland, Curry protested and offered to resign—the first of several such gestures during his term of office, a rather impressive show of independence for a territorial chief executive. His stubborn stand was due largely to the influence of his attorney general and closest adviser, Albert Bacon Fall, a man with scant sympathy for conservation. Roosevelt placated his old comrade-in-arms by issuing orders to federal officials in the territory not to interfere in local matters, even dropping the case against the Alamogordo company in October 1907, and eventually arranging a conference between his chief forester and Curry, Bursum, and Solomon Luna, the largest sheep raiser in New Mexico. Luna had attended the Public Lands Convention, an anticonservation meeting held in Denver in June 1907, and was a sincere critic of federal policy regarding forest uses.

At this conference between Pinchot and his detractors, held in January 1908, a spirit of understanding and cooperation was launched. To placate the angry governor, several thousand acres of a proposed addition to national forests south of Albuquerque were opened for entry. Curry responded by working with, rather than fighting, Pinchot, and soon this cooperation blossomed into a warm friendship. The governor took the leadership of the conservation movement in New Mexico, establishing a temporary Territorial Conservation Commission in May 1908, which became permanent as a result of legislative action about a year later. The wealthy Luna, leader of the Hispano community in the territory, was made a member.[20] Curry visited President Roosevelt at Oyster Bay to present him with an especially engraved invitation to attend the National Irrigation Congress, hosted by the territory of New Mexico and scheduled to convene in Albuquerque on September 29, 1908.[21] In March 1909, Pinchot addressed the territorial legislature at the invitation of Governor Curry. W. A. F. Jones, a good friend of Pinchot, was chosen by Curry to be New Mexico's delegate to the first National Conservation Congress held in Spokane, Washington, in August 1909. Adjusting the boundaries of huge forest reserves in the West was always a problem, and Curry successfully mediated between Forest Service officials and sheepmen in the Cuba, New Mexico, area, who demanded the elimination of 150,000 acres from neighboring forest reserves.[22] The governor boasted in his report to the Department of the Interior on September 15, 1909, of the "perfect harmony" he enjoyed in working with Pinchot and stressed the importance of caring for the "Territory's forests, streams, and soil which are heritages of the people and should be handed on to future generations undissipated."[23] After Pinchot's dismissal, following his celebrated dispute with Richard A. Ballinger, Curry wrote Pinchot a warm letter recalling their early disputes and admitting that he had been "absolutely wrong" in the position he had first taken.[24]

The governor not only mediated effectively between territorial citizens and federal bureaus and departments in charge of conservation, but also took great care in administering domain directly under territorial administration. By the Fergusson Act, the territory received a total of 5,589,186.46 acres of land for support of common or public schools, the university and colleges, institutions such as the penitentiary, and water reservoirs and other territorial projects. With passage of the Fergusson Act in 1898 the territory had also received land it was entitled to under the Morrill Act of 1862.[25] By September 15, 1910, shortly after Curry left office, about twenty thousand acres of land had been set aside under the Carey Act.[26] Much more exciting was the construction, in the southern part of the territory, of huge Elephant Butte Dam, which Curry claimed would create the "largest reservoir in the world" when completed. Although a federal project built under the Newlands Act of 1902, it would benefit private irrigation projects of importance to growth of the territory as well as place under cultivation thousands of acres of productive land.[27]

Another challenge to the territorial governor of New Mexico, eagerly accepted by Curry, was the expanding authority of his office. It would have been interesting to see how much growth would have occurred in other territorial administrations by 1907 as a result of the conservation program and the decline of laissez faire, but Oklahoma was admitted that year, leaving Arizona as the only other continental, contiguous territory to survive into the twentieth century. Of course, there was the recently acquired overseas empire which, when added to Alaska, extended the size of the United States immensely. As a result of the *Insular* cases of 1901 the self-government of these lands, with their alien, largely Spanish-speaking populations, was significantly limited, creating a new American territorial system for the modern age. Fortunately for New Mexico a distinction was drawn between these new acquisitions and the older territories. New Mexico and her sister territories were regarded as "incorporated" or "organized" territories, entitled to retain old territorial prerogatives, while the new territories were considered "unincorporated" and Congress, in governing them, was not bound by all the constitutional restrictions applicable in the case of the incorporated ones.[28] Psychologically, however, the Spanish background of many of these new subjects did not help New Mexico, which, because of its large Hispano population, had never been fully integrated into the United States socially or politically. Statehood had been denied New Mexico on this score for almost a half century prior to the new American imperialism, which began to surge at the time of the Spanish-American conflict. Howard R. Lamar has suggested that Senator Albert J. Beveridge, the staunchest foe of New Mexico statehood and an outspoken advocate of new expansionist policy, refused to differentiate between New Mexico Hispanos, long-time citizens of the United States, and Spanish-speaking people of Puerto Rico or the Philippines. Undoubtedly his insistence on demeaning the Hispanos of the Southwest further impeded the struggling statehood movement in New Mexico.[29]

The dampening of statehood prospects, a trend which Curry worked diligently to reverse, only made expansion of responsibilities of New Mexico's territorial government more essential. Inadequate as territorial government was, in the opinion of most New Mexicans, it might be around for some time to come, and the new, expanded role of governments in this changing age required innovative policies and more creative administration. The governorship of New Mexico had assumed a far more important role since 1885, when President Cleveland, in offering the offices of governor or surveyor general to a prospect, claimed that the latter was the more important.[30]

Curry, although a man with no particular intellectual breadth, seemed to sense the new and growing significance of the territorial governorship. As a rancher himself, he paid great attention to activities of the Cattle Sanitary Board, appointing Cole Railston, a colorful cowboy and ranch manager who had inspired Eugene Manlove Rhodes in several of his novels, to a vacancy on the commission.[31] The board had been established in 1889, with the passing of open range and the increased competition that resulted, and by its supervision it was to provide health protection and prevention of theft. A Sheep Sanitary Board was created by the territorial legislature in 1897 for much the same purpose.[32] Curry retained the very able Robert P. Ervien, a Hagerman appointee, as territorial land commissioner. Exercising his option under the Fergusson Act to make in-lieu selections for those donated lands already homesteaded, Ervien blocked out for the territory vast areas of land, rich in resources, in eastern and southeastern New Mexico. Curry placed the office of territorial coal inspector on a salary basis; coal inspectors had been earning about forty thousand dollars a year in fees, the money being used to reward party workers throughout the territory with jobs as assistants or field deputies.[33] Early in Curry's tenure as governor a good roads commission was created, to be financed by a small tax levy.[34] The governor took great interest in the work of this commission, making long trips throughout the territory with the territorial engineer, Vernon L. Sullivan, to study the feasibility of more and better roads. The famous highway over La Bajada Hill, which cut many miles off the trip between Santa Fe and Albuquerque, was built under Curry.[35] New Mexico's seventeenth territorial governor, although he was not able to eliminate the scandal and alleged corruption that seemed to mark most of New Mexico's long tenure as a territory, did make quite a remarkable adjustment to new, twentieth-century demands on his office, concerning himself with a multitude of concerns from low county assessments to territorial immigration and reclamation projects.[36]

Unfortunately for this striving and remarkably flexible administrator, his tenure as governor was not to end on a happy note. When President Taft took office Curry's confidence began to wane quite dramatically. Blustering William H. "Bull" Andrews, territorial delegate, noticed this change several months later, remarking that Curry "is so nervous he does not know what he is doing."[37] Curry's change of character was not due to apprehension regarding Taft; he had worked under the new president when Taft was civil governor of the Philippines and felt he enjoyed the president's confidence.[38] But his relationship with Ballinger, new secretary of the interior and his immediate superior, was another matter. He had gone over Ballinger's head in 1908, when the new secretary had been commissioner of the General Land Office, and was convinced that Ballinger had never forgotten it. Ballinger in this incident had rather arbitrarily directed that homesteaders in the Clovis area surrender their claims, many of which had been improved by construction of homes and barns, and file on public domain elsewhere. Curry protested and, finding Ballinger adamant, went to his old Rough Rider colonel, Theodore Roosevelt, who directed Secretary of the Interior James R. Garfield, Ballinger's predecessor, to order the land commissioner to rescind the order.[39] Knowing how deeply Ballinger resented the affront, Curry began writing probing letters to his superior four days after Taft's inauguration to clarify his position.[40]

It might be suspected that differences over conservation alienated the governor from Ballinger, but no evidence has been found to indicate that Curry disagreed with Ballinger over the withdrawal of water power sites, the issue (aside from the Alaskan coal lands controversy) that so sharply divided Pinchot from Ballinger and Taft. Actually, Curry was a simple man whose conversion to conservation, although genuine, was based upon admiration for Roosevelt and flattering attention paid to him by Pinchot. The rather naive but sincere governor, who made such a commendable adjustment to the new demands on his office, was to become a victim of the increased interest of the federal government in territorial affairs. His two immediate predecessors, Hagerman and Miguel A. Otero, had been compelled to resign because of the new emphasis. Pressure on Curry was not to come from his constituency that, for the most part, approved of his course, but from the secretary of the interior who disliked him.

This dislike was apparent when Curry requested his first leave of absence in March 1909 so he could travel to Washington to talk to Ballinger and Taft about territorial matters, including New Mexico's statehood prospects, and later make a trip to the Philippines during the months of May and June.[41] Permission for such leave had become quite automatic during the past several decades. When the telegraph came into greater use in the late nineteenth century, territorial governors had merely wired ahead for permission to come to Washington; "perfunctory explanations" were usually accepted and very often, if there was any question, "burden of proof rested with the [Interior] department" rather than the governor.[42] Curry never had difficulty receiving permission for such leave when Roosevelt was president,[43] but Ballinger refused Curry's request, whereupon the angry governor, in characteristic fashion, threw the territory into consternation by submitting his resignation.[44]

Governor Curry's precipitous action showed that he had carefully cultivated the friendship and confidence of Republican leaders of the territory. Bursum and Maj. William H. H. Llewellyn, Roosevelt's favorite New Mexico Rough Rider and power in the territorial party, and several leading businessmen wrote or telegraphed Ballinger and the president not to accept the resignation.[45] Powerful western senators such as Thomas H. Carter of Montana, Frances E. Warren of Wyoming, and Simon Guggenheim of Colorado were contacted by a railroad executive in the territory and asked to intervene in behalf of Curry.[46] In the end Taft, recognizing Curry's close relationship with his predecessor and not wishing a political crisis so early in his administration, talked the governor out of resigning.[47]

During the next several months Curry was able to pursue his duties as governor in relative peace, although always aware of Ballinger's hostility. As for the frequently Byzantine nature of New Mexico politics—political conduct in the territory was never up to Progressive standards—there was comparative calm. The usual "mass of accusation and rumor" against officers under the territorial system was, of course, present in New Mexico.[48] Curry was accused in June 1909 of appointing as district attorney of McKinley County a man under indictment in Arizona.[49] It wasn't until the fall of that year, following Ballinger's visit to New Mexico in September, that the secretary decided to take certain of these accusations, most of which were filed on September 11 with the Interior Department by A. M. Jackley of Alamogordo, as serious enough to warrant an investigation. The governor was accused of all sorts of misdeeds, such as ignoring financial shortages in several district courts, covering up a scandalous assault on a blind girl by one of the directors of the territorial blind institution, appointing to high office ex-convicts, using his pardoning power for political purposes, and even releasing prisoners serving life terms for murder as well as pardoning a convict to marry a woman employed in the governor's mansion.[50] Ballinger's willingness to study these charges was serious enough, but when it was reported in newspapers that the secretary had left Santa Fe on the same train with Jackley, after his official visit to the territory,[51] Curry really got upset.

The governor responded in a most typical way. He resigned for the final time, giving the unsatisfactory condition of his financial affairs as the reason.[52] But Ballinger remained vindictive and refused to accept Curry's resignation until the charges filed by Jackley were discussed with Taft, who was on a political tour in the South. He even refused to grant the governor a thirty-day leave of absence so he could go to a lower altitude and recover his health, unless a formal application was made, which would be given "due consideration."[53] The deliberate Taft, however, already having his problems with other Roosevelt lieutenants, decided that the charges were too "indefinite and sweeping in nature," and that he would therefore ignore them.[54] The president wrote Curry a friendly letter on November 4 accepting his resignation and praising the governor for "honesty and loyalty."[55]

Curry, whose resignation was to be effective on February 28, 1910, remained bitter during the last months of what should have been a successful territorial administration throughout. He was disappointed in Taft and, in his mind, believed Ballinger to be a machine politician not unlike old-line Interior Department secretaries, such as Columbus Delano and Zachariah Chandler who had served under the permissive Grant.[56] Ballinger and Frank H. Hitchcock, Taft's postmaster general, were regarded by Curry as "hatchet men" who were going to eliminate all of Roosevelt's friends from positions of prominence in the territory, as part of a national campaign to build up a "straight Taft organization." He talked of information to the effect that Roosevelt had been openly critical of Taft in letters he had written to his brother-in-law.[57] It was no surprise that Curry's sympathies would be with Pinchot, when the latter was dismissed by Taft in January 1910, and that the governor in 1912 would be one of the earliest participants in the greatest party schism in the twentieth century. Elected as one of New Mexico's two United States representatives after statehood, Curry became the first congressman to follow his old colonel into the newly formed Progressive party.[58]

Governor Curry had accomplished much in this twilight period for the old, incorporated territories of the Union. Challenges not met by territorial governors of the late nineteenth century had to be faced by him. Conservation, the decline of laissez faire coupled with the demand for government regulation, and the reform spirit engendered by progressivism, not to mention the demeaning effect on the territory of the newly acquired colonial empire, with its large Spanish-speaking population, all made the job of governing New Mexico more difficult. Most of these problems were not localized, of course. State governors in the West and throughout the country had to face them, as did other officials from the municipalities right up to the presidency. Curry stumbled when it came to dealing with corruption and scandals, proverbial problems for the territory of New Mexico. His popularity with most of his constituents may have resulted because he was a pliable, affable individual whom some territorial leaders felt they could use. Not all of his conservation methods were approved by easterners; too often he would appoint representatives of livestock or extractive industries to conservation commissions. But because of his great admiration for Roosevelt, largely reciprocated, and his ability to work with and learn from governmental officials such as Pinchot, he was able to grow and adjust and meet squarely the issues of the modern age. Ironically, Curry became a victim of one of the products of this new age, the expanded interest of the federal government in its territorial responsibility. Two other twentieth-century New Mexico governors had been forced to resign, compared to only one during the nineteenth century. When a hostile person was appointed to head the crucial Department of the Interior, Curry, notwithstanding his growth and new understanding, was gradually forced to vacate a post in which he had served with a distinction far greater than might have been expected from one of his ability and background.

NOTES

1. George Curry, *George Curry, 1861–1947: An Autobiography*, ed. H. B. Hening (Albuquerque: University of New Mexico Press, 1958), pp. 186–87. Capitalization is that of the author's.
2. Earl S. Pomeroy, *The Territories and the United States, 1861–1890: Studies in Colonial Administration* (Philadelphia: University of Pennsylvania Press, 1947), p. 68.
3. Ibid., pp. 15, 27.
4. Earl S. Pomeroy, *The Pacific Slope: A History of California, Oregon, Washington, Idaho, Utah, and Nevada* (New York: Knopf, 1965), p. 70.
5. Roy M. Robbins, *Our Landed Heritage: The Public Domain, 1776–1936* (New York: P. Smith, 1950), pp. 293–94.
6. Curry, *Autobiography*, p. 83.
7. Frank D. Reeve, *History of New Mexico*, 2 vols. (New York: Lewis Historical Publishing Co., 1961), 2:258; Howard R. Lamar, *The Far Southwest, 1846–1912: A Territorial History* (New Haven: Yale University Press, 1966), p. 487.
8. Samuel P. Hays, *Conservation and the Gospel of Efficiency: The Progressive Conservation Movement, 1890–1920* (Cambridge: Harvard University Press, 1959), p. 9. The act specifically extended to the territories of New Mexico and Arizona, in addition to the western states. *Digest of Public Land Laws* (Washington, D.C.: Government Printing Office, 1968), p. 206.
9. Hays, *Conservation and the Gospel of Efficiency*, pp. 12–15, 18–21, 36–48, 74–75.
10. *Digest of Public Land Laws*, pp. 224–25. For details regarding the introduction of the Fergusson Act and the debate over it see Robert W. Larson, *New Mexico's Quest for Statehood, 1846–1912* (Albuquerque: University of New Mexico Press, 1968), pp. 193–94.
11. Curry, *Autobiography*, pp. 192–93.
12. Warren A. Beck, *New Mexico: A History of Four Centuries* (Norman: University of Oklahoma Press, 1962), p. 258.
13. Larson, *New Mexico's Quest for Statehood*, pp. 254–57. Hagerman vigorously defended his action in delivering the deeds and answered other accu-

sations made by the president in a series of letters, which Hagerman organized and published in a privately printed book in 1908, entitled *A Statement in Regard to Certain Matters concerning the Governorship and Political Affairs in New Mexico in 1906–1907*, copies of which are in the private papers given to the National Archives, National Archives Gift Collection, Record Group 200, Social and Economic Branch, National Archives Building, Washington, D.C. (Hereafter records in the National Archives Building are indicated by the symbol NA. The symbol RG is used for record group.) Herbert J. Hagerman Papers, State Records Center and Archives, Santa Fe; and Special Collections Division, University of New Mexico Library, Albuquerque.

14. The close relationship between Curry and Roosevelt is examined in Robert W. Larson, "Ballinger vs. Rough Rider George Curry: The Other Feud," *New Mexico Historical Review* 63 (October 1968): 271–90.

15. July 31, 1907, Theodore Roosevelt Papers, Manuscript Division, Library of Congress, Washington, D.C.

16. Reeve, *History of New Mexico,* 2:258.

17. Pomeroy, *The Territories and the United States,* p. 19.

18. *Los Angeles Times,* December 16, 1907, as quoted in Hagerman, *Statement in Regard to Certain Matters,* pp. 79–80.

19. Pomeroy, *The Territories and the United States,* p. 102.

20. Elmo R. Richardson, "George Curry and the Politics of Forest Conservation in New Mexico," *New Mexico Historical Review* 33 (October 1958): 278–82.

21. Curry to James R. Garfield, secretary of the interior, September 5, 1908; Frank Pierce, acting secretary of the interior, to Curry, September 10, 1908, Selected Documents Pertaining to Presidential Appointments, Governor of New Mexico, George Curry, 1907–13, Records of the Office of the Secretary of the Interior, Record Group 48, National Archives Microfilm Publication M750, NA.

22. Richardson, "George Curry and the Politics," pp. 281–82.

23. Department of the Interior, *Reports of the Department of the Interior for the Fiscal Year Ended June 30, 1909,* 2 vols. (Washington, D.C.: Government Printing Office, 1910), 2:640.

24. January 12, 1910, as quoted in Richardson, "George Curry and the Politics," p. 283.

25. Victor Westphall, *The Public Domain in New Mexico, 1854–1891* (Albuquerque: University of New Mexico Press, 1965), pp. 98–99, 149. A breakdown of the number of acres granted to the territory in the Fergusson Act is on page 149, under various categories such as the "common schools."

26. U.S., Department of the Interior, *Reports of the Department of the Interior for the Fiscal Year Ended June 30, 1910,* 2 vols. (Washington, D.C.: Government Printing Office, 1911), 2:419.

27. *Reports of the Department of the Interior . . . , 1909,* 2:639. A few years earlier leaders of the territorial government were very miffed because the federal government brought suit against a private corporation, heavily financed by foreign capital, which wanted to build a dam and reservoir at the same site as the Elephant Butte project, and never recompense the territory for the loss of private capital. Ralph Emerson Twitchell, *The*

Leading Facts of New Mexican History, 5 vols. (Cedar Rapids: Torch Press, 1912), 2:528–29.

28. William Franklin Willoughby, *Territories and Dependencies of the United States: Their Government and Administration* (New York: Century Co., 1905), pp. 7–23, 53–60; Foster Rhea Dulles, *America's Rise to World Power, 1898–1954* (New York: Harper, 1954), pp. 56–57. The author, in the first account, provides an interesting analysis of the old, contiguous territories and the new overseas possessions, plus Alaska, using the terms "organized" for the old and "unorganized" for the new in his comparison. For a contemporary, critical analysis of the Insular Cases, particularly of decisions reached in *DeLima* v. *Bidwell* and *Downes* v. *Bidwell,* see John W. Burgess, "The Decisions in the Insular Cases," *Political Science Quarterly* 16 (September 1901): 486–504.

29. Conservation and progressivism were other movements with which the statehood effort became entangled, according to Lamar in a stimulating discussion about the frustrations met by New Mexico and Arizona in their struggle for admission. Lamar, *The Far Southwest,* pp. 486–89. A detailed account of Beveridge's stubborn opposition to New Mexico statehood is found in Larson, *New Mexico's Quest for Statehood,* chapters 13, 14, 15, and 17 being especially pertinent. The importance of American nativism as an obstacle to statehood is argued, in a summation, on pp. 303–4.

30. Westphall, *The Public Domain in New Mexico,* p. 33.

31. Curry, *Autobiography,* pp. 211–12.

32. Reeve, *History of New Mexico,* 2:221, 227–28.

33. Curry, *Autobiography,* pp. 206–7, 202–13.

34. *Reports of the Department of the Interior . . . , 1909,* 2:640.

35. Enclosed newspaper clipping, Fred W. Carpenter, secretary to the president, to Richard A. Ballinger, secretary of the interior, April 21, 1909, and Curry to Ballinger, May 17, 1909, General Correspondence Files, 1907–53, RG 48, NA; Curry, *Autobiography,* pp. 213–14.

36. Curry to Ballinger, May 17, 1909, General Correspondence Files, 1907–53, RG 48, NA. An opportunity to see how a territorial governor regards his responsibilities is provided in this long, rather interesting letter.

37. Andrews to Ballinger, October 28, 1909, General Correspondence Files, 1907–53, RG 48, NA.

38. Curry believed that Taft, while serving as secretary of war under Roosevelt, suggested to the president that he would make a good governor of New Mexico, because of his "exceptionally good" record in the Philippines. As civil governor of the islands, Taft had appointed Curry to the post of chief of police of Manila in 1901. Curry, *Autobiography,* pp. 159–60, 187. In all probability, though, a letter of recommendation from Maj. William H. H. Llewellyn, a Rough Rider for whom Roosevelt had the greatest affection, was the deciding factor. Llewellyn to Roosevelt, February 27, 1907, General Correspondence Files, 1907–53, RG 48, NA.

39. Curry, *Autobiography,* pp. 225–26.

40. Curry to Ballinger, March 8, 1909, General Correspondence Files, 1907–53, RG 48, NA. Curry may have been disturbed over a March 5, 1909, newspaper clipping in the Interior files, which claimed that as soon as Taft got around to it there "would not be a Rough Rider holding an office in New Mexico that is subject to the President." The governor, in his March

8 letter to Ballinger, complained that a clerk of Senator Beveridge's had been reported as making indiscreet inquiries about when Curry would be removed and that Beveridge, himself, was feeding "democratic and anti-Roosevelt" newspapers with stories to discredit him. Ballinger's response to Curry was a noncommittal one. March 15, 1909, General Correspondence Files, 1907–53, RG 48, NA.

41. *Muskogee Times-Democrat,* March 22, 1909; *Omaha Daily Bee,* March 23, 1909; unidentified newspaper clipping, Carpenter to Ballinger, April 21, 1909, General Correspondence Files, 1907–53, RG 48, NA. There is some disagreement, among the reports found in these three news clippings, as to whether Curry wished to discuss statehood with the president and his secretary of the interior. Considering Curry's determination to see New Mexico admitted while he was governor, it would be most surprising, indeed, if Curry did not plan to argue New Mexico's qualifications for statehood while in Washington. The governor's proposed trip to the Philippines is discussed in an April 15, 1909, letter to Taft, forwarded by the president's private secretary, Fred W. Carpenter, in his April 21, 1909, letter to Secretary Ballinger. General Correspondence Files, 1907–53, RG 48, NA.

42. Pomeroy, *The Territories and the United States,* p. 20.

43. Curry had no difficulty receiving a leave when he requested, in a letter of September 5, 1908, permission to travel to Oyster Bay to deliver to Roosevelt a special invitation to attend the National Irrigation Congress in Albuquerque. See Frank Pierce, acting secretary of the interior, to Curry, September 10, 1908, General Correspondence Files, 1907–53, RG 48, NA.

44. Ballinger was informed in a March 22, 1909, telegram from Curry that the governor had sent his resignation to Taft. Curry also had been fuming over a report, which had appeared in such newspapers as the *Washington Evening Star* and the *St. Louis Post-Dispatch,* that President Taft had told him while he was leading a delegation to lobby for statehood in Washington, to return to New Mexico and give back $3,500 that the territorial legislature had appropriated to meet the expenses of his group. When a local journalist, A. J. Loomis, editor of the *Santa Fe Eagle,* published the story, Curry hustled him out of his gubernatorial office, delivering two well-publicized swipes to his head which were duly noted in the files of the Interior Department. Such incidents, added to Ballinger's refusal to grant him a leave, undoubtedly hastened his resignation. *Omaha Daily Bee,* March 23, 1909; unidentified newspaper clipping, March 27, 1909, General Correspondence Files, 1907–53, RG 48, NA.

45. Bursum to Ballinger, March 22, 1909; Llewellyn to Taft, March 22, 1909, General Correspondence Files, 1907–53, RG 48, NA. In this source there are letters to Taft from such prominent New Mexico businessmen, bankers, and local officials as Harry W. Kelly, J. M. Cunningham, I. Sparks, Secundino Romero, and George S. Klock.

46. Identical letters from Robert Law, president of the New Mexico Central Railroad, dated March 24, 1909, were sent to each of the three senators. All three intervened, at least making an inquiry about Curry's resignation. Warren to Ballinger, March 29, 1909; Carter to Ballinger, March 30, 1909; Guggenheim to Ballinger, April 5, 1909, General Correspondence Files, 1907–53, RG 48, NA. Warren and Carter both held Law, a former Union Pacific executive, in high esteem, regarding him as a reliable, disinterested

person. Carter was impressed with Curry. "Personally I have a good opinion of Governor Curry and I believe that he has exerted himself in discharging the duties of his office to the very best of his ability."

47. The president wrote Curry on March 23, 1909, stating that he felt Curry had acted with "undue haste" and urging him to "reconsider" his action. The *Leavenworth Times* on April 14, 1909, interpreted Taft's action as a vote of confidence in the governor, and claimed that the president had also assured Curry of "early passage of the statehood bill." Curry, in gratitude, wrote a long letter to Taft on April 14, 1909, which was forwarded to Ballinger on April 21, in which he explained why he had requested a leave of absence. He also told the president that he was calling off his trip to the Philippines, one of the reasons for his request for a leave. General Correspondence Files, 1907–53, RG 48, NA. Taft even invited Curry to come to Washington where, in an hour-long conference, he was able to reassure him. Curry, *Autobiography,* pp. 242–43.

48. Pomeroy, *The Territories and the United States,* pp. 19–20. Frequently the charges were malicious and based upon hearsay evidence. Although Pomeroy's study does not go beyond 1891, these characteristics, along with the excessive volume of complaints, were projected into twentieth-century New Mexico territorial politics.

49. The man under indictment was Alfred Ruiz, who was paid $250 in advance by Apache County authorities for a job he could not complete, because the county board felt that the purchase of new record books would be too expensive. See George H. Crosby to F. W. Nelson, district attorney of Apache County, April 27, 1909; Alfred Ruiz to Ralph H. Cameron, Arizona delegate to Congress, June 6, 1909; Cameron to Ballinger, June 15, 1909; Ballinger to Cameron, June 17, 1909, General Correspondence Files, 1907–53, RG 48, NA.

50. Clipping from the *Washington Post,* n.d.; John R. DeMier to Findley M. Garrison, April 22, 1913, General Correspondence Files, 1907–53, RG 48, NA. The letter from DeMier, written to Wilson's secretary of war, was to protest consideration of former Governor Curry for a position on the Philippine Commission.

51. Clipping from the *Washington Post,* n. d.; General Correspondence Files, 1907–53, RG 48, NA.

52. Curry to Taft, October 25, 1909. Curry enclosed his letter of resignation in a letter to Ballinger, dated the same day, in which he complained that rumors had been circulating around the territory, since the secretary's visit, that Ballinger had asked for his resignation. General Correspondence Files, 1907–53, RG 48, NA.

53. Ballinger to Curry, October 30, 1909. Ballinger forwarded Curry's resignation to Taft in a letter, dated October 30, in which he alluded to Jackley's charges as being of "such a serious character" that he would have brought them up with the governor during his visit, had he known of their "gravity" at the time. Taft, writing from Birmingham, Alabama, on November 2, told Ballinger that it would be better to "withhold matters" until he returned to Washington. General Correspondence Files, 1907–53, RG 48, NA.

54. Ballinger to Curry, November 14, 1909, General Correspondence Files, 1907–53, RG 48, NA.

55. William Howard Taft Papers, Manuscript Division, Library of Congress.

56. Pomeroy classified the men serving in the Interior Department post from 1873 to 1891 as either machine politicians or conservationists, such as the exceptional Carl Schurz or the able Lucius Q. C. Lamar. Pomeroy, *The Territories and the United States,* p. 27.
57. These views were expressed to LeRoy O. Moore, chief of field division, General Land Office, in Santa Fe, who communicated them in a long, confidential letter to Ballinger, dated November 9, 1909. Ballinger responded to Moore on November 20 in a terse letter, the kind he apparently reserved for his subordinates, in which he insisted that Curry had been treated with "utmost fairness and consideration." He did thank Moore for telling Curry that his meeting with Jackley was not prearranged. General Correspondence Files, 1907–53, RG 48, NA.
58. Curry, *Autobiography,* pp. 269–70.

United States Territories in Mid-Century

ROBERT R. ROBBINS

THE ABOVE TOPIC is as potentially rich as it is sprawly. To do justice to it requires much more digested knowledge than I possess, as well as words in great quantities. In getting my topic off the ground in the context of this conference, I am led to mention a paper on "The Development of a Colonial Policy for the United States," prepared for an audience of fifteen hundred or more persons in Philadelphia on the evening of April 19, 1907: the annual address of the American Academy of Political and Social Science.[1] The distinguished speaker on that occasion displayed the virtue of getting into his subject immediately:

Administration is the principle upon which our colonial policy should proceed for a century to come. Whenever we have departed from the idea of administration as such, we have made an error which natural conditions will gradually compel us to correct. Not sudden "self-government" for peoples who have not yet learned the alphabet of liberty; not territorial independence for islands whose ignorant, suspicious and primitive inhabitants, left to themselves, would prey upon one another until they become the inevitable spoil of other powers; not the flimsy application of abstract governmental theories possible only to the most advanced races and which applied to underdeveloped peoples, work out grotesque and fatal results—not anything but the discharge of our great national trust and greater national duty to our wards by common-sense methods will achieve the welfare of our colonies and bring us success in the civilizing work to which we are called.[2]

The late Sen. Albert J. Beveridge from Indiana, went on to say that:

It was inevitable that, in the end, American control should extend

over Cuba, San Domingo, and Porto Rico. It was inevitable that
Hawaii—the halfway house of the Pacific—should become
American—witness Humboldt's prophecy concerning the Pacific.
And Hawaii once American, it was inevitable that further expansion
over the western seas should occur—for it is the genius of our race
not to stop forever at any halfway house. The people of our blood
never pause midway in the syllogism of events, but go on to its
conclusion. And so in our present and future colonial expansion,
we shall only be working out the logic of history.[3]

Many of us may find such statements very funny today. Senator Beveridge's address serves admirably as one example among many of that period to show the vast distance we have come since the early years of the century in our thinking about colonial areas and our changed attitudes in handling our responsibilities for them. In contrast to Beveridge's self-assurance was a second speech. The academy was honoring the Right Honorable James Bryce, the British ambassador, and he addressed his remarks to "Some Difficulties in Colonial Government Encountered by Great Britain and How They Have Been Met."[4] The sobering realities of administering an empire after decades of experience produced a piece much more in keeping with our own later moods and appreciation of the complexities involved in the promotion of self-government in the modern world than that of the renowned senator.

I

The previous references relate, of course, to America's ventures stemming from the Spanish-American War, with an enlargement of territorial jurisdiction and problems of providing for governance of exotic peoples far removed from our shores. These could not simply be enveloped by the mantle of the Northwest Ordinance of 1787. But in the light of the amount of territory already brought under it and still biding time for admission to the Union, it would have been strange indeed for public opinion not to have been expansion-minded. Since 1907, the United States of America has been expanded by 881,457 square miles, increasing the area of the Union by 25 percent.

The long-standing practice of punctuating the achievement of full self-government by admitting a territory into the Union has finally taken place with regard to Alaska and Hawaii after unconscionable delays. In light of this well-established practice, the United States government responded in 1946 to the request of the secretary general of the United Nations for the opinion of each member on factors to be taken into account in determining which are the non-self-governing territories referred to in chapter 11 of the United Nations Charter, and inviting the respective members to supply information on their non-self-governing territories.

The acting secretary of state responded, expressing the view that chapter 11 applied to territories "which do not enjoy the same measure of self-government as the metropolitan area of that Member." On the basis of this, information was transmitted on Alaska, Hawaii, Puerto Rico, the Virgin Islands of the United States, and the Panama Canal Zone, as well as Guam, Samoa, and other island possessions administered by the Navy Department. An agreement was concluded the following year to place the Pacific islands formerly mandated to Japan under the United Nations trusteeship system, and it was brought into force on July 18, 1947.[5] Thereby, the United States also became obligated to submit annual reports on the Trust Territory of the Pacific Islands.

The United States's generous definition of a non-self-governing territory and its willingness to report on seven territories soon caused difficulty. On November 14, 1946, the delegate of Panama declared in the General Assembly that the United States should not have transmitted information on the Canal Zone, because sovereignty there resides in the Republic of Panama. The United States led pridefully with its chin as the first member to declare its non-self-governing territories. This placed them shortly in a mix of seventy-two non-self-governing territories under eight members of the United Nations. These included such contrasting territories in varying stages of political and social advancement as Papua, Greenland, Comoro Archipelago, Pitcairn Island, Cyprus, and Hawaii. The explanation for this quick United States response was that it wished to encourage other members to transmit information on their territories, because there might be wrongdoing to dependent peoples elsewhere which should be scrutinized.

I I

Transmittal of information to the United Nations on Alaska and Hawaii produced only slight domestic ripples of complaint during the long interval between the founding of the United Nations and the final achievement of statehood for those two territories. On the contrary, transmittal of information in fulfillment of United States obligations under chapter 11 of the Charter was used as a handle by the Department of State to provide leverage in behalf of statehood for the two territories. The assistant secretary of state for United Nations affairs, John D. Hickerson, informed the Senate Committee on Interior and Insular Affairs on April 24, 1950, that

The Department of State considers that favorable action by the
Congress on the bill to provide statehood for Alaska would be in
fulfillment of this obligation and would accordingly serve to
support American foreign policy and to strengthen the position
of the United States in international affairs. The Department
of State would welcome the opportunity of conveying to the United
Nations, on behalf of the Government and people of the United
States, the information that the Territorial status of Alaska had
terminated with the admission of Alaska into the United States as
a State with full and equal rights and participation in the Union
with other States.[6]

When the Eisenhower administration took over in 1953, the Department of State's usual letter in support of statehood for Alaska and Hawaii had to be revised by qualifying its support with the phrase: "whenever the Congress and the President determine."[7] This step backward was necessary because President Eisenhower was unwilling throughout the major portion of his eight years in office to press for the political package which would bring the two territories into the Union. The Eisenhower administration, and particularly those members responsible for handling United Nations business, were unaware of how fortunate they were that a survey report, *Alaska's Health,* was not used as reference material when the United Nations General Assembly's Committee on Non-Self-Governing Territories prepared its summaries and analyses of information on Alaska. This 300-page report was prepared for the Department of the Interior by the Alaskan Health Survey Team of the University of Pittsburgh, the chief of which was Dr. Thomas Parran, former surgeon general of the United States. "White Alaska," with "a relatively young, vigorous, generally urbanized population, [which] shows a record of life-expectancy as favorable as that in the majority of the states" was contrasted with "Native Alaska," described in part as follows:

In tragic contrast, the indigenous peoples of Native Alaska are
the victims of sickness, crippling conditions and premature death to
a degree exceeded in very few parts of the world. Among them
health problems are nearly out of hand.[8]

Eskimos, Indians, and Aleuts received little coverage in the anticolonial outpourings from White Alaska politicians prior to statehood, and there are continuing reminders that the grave problems of those indigenous peoples remain and should trouble the American conscience.

III

A new dimension was added to American federal government when Puerto Rico emerged in mid-century (1948–52) as a free and associated state or commonwealth. The process by which it came about seems to have approached the ideal as an application of the vaunted principle of self-determination in comparison with any other case study that might be drawn from the world's horizon.

One might expect to find here some reference to early chapters of United States administration of what was once the "fair-haired" colony of the Spanish Empire; to belated interest in the plight of the island in the era of Franklin Roosevelt;[9] and to the emergence of a poet as a dynamic political leader, Luis Muñoz Marin. He was not merely the first elected governor, but also the politician and statesman par excellence who led in building the Popular Democratic party's overwhelming majority. He became the architect of the commonwealth relationship.

We might continue with the phenomenal development program, "Operation Bootstrap"; Muñoz Marin's political thinking regarding Puerto Ricans which ultimately came to stress "Operation Serenity"; the emergence of the "crown prince," Roberto Sanchez-Vilella, who was elected in 1964 to succeed Muñoz Marin; and the later split in the ranks of the Popular Democratic party that made possible the election of Luis Alberto Ferre of Ponce, a wealthy industrialist, member of the Republican National Committee and long-standing advocate of statehood.

The latter of these themes will not do, however. Our fellow citizens from Puerto Rico have no objection to living in United States territory under the Stars and Stripes, yet under no circumstances will they tolerate referring to it as a *territory* with a capital *T*. Therefore, the cutoff date for discussing Puerto Rico should be July 25, 1952, the day the new commonwealth was proclaimed at San Juan.

President Truman signed Public Law 447 approving the constitution of the new commonwealth on July 3, 1952, completing a process begun by adoption of Public Law 600 of July 3, 1950, "an act to provide for the organization of a constitutional government by the people of Puerto Rico." Section 2 of Public Law 600 provided that "This Act should be submitted to qualified voters for acception or register in an island-wide referendum . . . ," which was held June 11, 1951. The law was approved, and elected members of the constitutional convention met from September 17, 1951, to February 6, 1952. The constitution drafted by the convention was approved by 81 percent of the voters, approved by the United States Congress, and signed by the president. The new constitution was then proclaimed by Governor Muñoz Marin, symbolizing, in his words, that the people of Puerto Rico "have attained their political majority."

The Puerto Ricans maintain that more than local self-government was achieved by the 1950–52 legislation, asserting a new legal entity with a unique status in American law. This fascinating legal and political issue and developments relating to it have received recent scholarly treatment by Arnold H. Leibowitz, former general counsel of the United States–Puerto Rico Status Commission.[10] Suffice it to say here that when Puerto Ricans first began to explain their conceptions of the new commonwealth as not a "territory" covered by the "territorial clause" of the United States Constitution but rather a "state" in the generic sense, a political entity sui generis whose judicial bounds are determined by a "compact" which cannot be changed without the consent of both Puerto Rico and the United States, there were people in government who could not comprehend their interpretation of the new political and constitutional relationship.

Thus it is understandable why devoted friends of Puerto Rico in Washington should have advised its leaders and spokesmen to hold their horses for a while and allow time for an understanding of the new constitutional arrangements to become better appreciated on the mainland. Puerto Ricans could appreciate the wisdom of this advice in general, but there was in their minds one matter on which action had to be taken at once; namely, that the United States government should cease reporting on the commonwealth to the United Nations pursuant to article 73(e) of the Charter. So insistent were they that the government was obliged to make forthwith a *political* decision that Puerto Rico had achieved "a full measure of self-government," the stated objective set forth in chapter 11 of the Charter, and to draw up the case to back up this decision.

In the autumn of 1952 the commonwealth government and the Departments of State and the Interior joined in preparations for advising the secretary general that the United States intended to cease transmitting information on Puerto Rico.

A considerable amount of nervousness marked the work. Legal doubts provoked the notion that the only safe way to proceed was to seek an advisory opinion from the United States attorney general on the new constitutional arrangements. The counterargument, which prevailed, was that to get the Department of Justice involved would be tantamount to delaying the matter for months or perhaps years. Nervousness was still prevalent when a staff officer carried the Puerto Rican case to the assistant secretary of state for United Nations affairs, covered by an instruction for signature addressed to the United States Mission in New York. The officer dutifully warned the assistant secretary of possible trouble ahead. There was profound relief when apprehensions were dispelled for the time being by the assistant secretary, who simply said, "Shucks," and then continued, while signing with a flourish: "Why, hell! This was all decided months ago." His action ensured that "Cessation of Information on Puerto Rico" would be an item on the agenda of the Eighth General Assembly.

This matter was considered during the 1953 meeting of the General Assembly's Fourth Committee—the Committee on Information from Non-Self-Governing Territories—a "technical committee" which did preparatory work for the General Assembly on chapter 11 matters. The United States case for Puerto Rico was presented by Dr. Fernos-Isern, "the midwife of the Puerto Rican Constitution," who served as deputy United States representative on the committee. The unenviable task of handling the matter in the Fourth Committee and the plenary meeting of the General Assembly was assigned to Delegate Frances Payne Bolton of Ohio, a member of Congress (Seventy-sixth to Ninetieth Congresses).

It would seem to denigrate the intelligence, steadfastness, and indomitable spirit of Mrs. Bolton to say that what she encountered in the Fourth Committee and the plenary session of the United Nations in handling the Puerto Rican item was comparable to the "Perils of Pauline." The analogy is not farfetched, however, but she never wavered. She believed that her assignment was important; she did her homework faithfully; and she was quick to grasp the significance of the Puerto Rican issue. She had special strength as a long-standing member of the House of Representatives, as ranking member of its Foreign Affairs Committee's Near East and Africa Subcommittee, and as a woman—a lady of quality and an advantaged person who had grasped her many opportunities to develop broad human horizons. The burdens she was obliged to shoulder during the Eighth General Assembly were not made easier by the fact that only a few people in the United States delegation were keyed up about Puerto Rico, and far fewer were capable of doing any explaining to sell the idea that a full measure of self-government had been achieved.

Shortly before the Puerto Rican item was reached in the Fourth Committee, the subject was discussed at one of the delegation's morning staff meetings. Symptomatic of the atmosphere and of those times was the fact that this sizable foregathering was preceded by a discussion of the propriety of inviting at least some of the distinguished Puerto Ricans to attend that meeting. Department of State planners and the advisory staff for Fourth Committee matters had considered Dr. Fernos-Isern as the key man. Had leave to invite him not been insisted upon, no one can say how much dust would have been stirred by the sizable delegation of distinguished Puerto Ricans who had come to New York to assist him "unofficially" from the sidelines.

In the Fourth Committee, the challenges Mrs. Bolton had to meet unfolded in rapid-fire succession. Before the Puerto Rican item was reached, she had to intervene twice in debate to prevent the committee from granting oral hearings for representatives of the minority Independence party and the so-called Nationalist party. She indicated that parties which could not win an election in Puerto Rico were asking the United Nations to come to the rescue. What they really wanted was a chance to exploit the United Nations by making political capital out of the new importance they would acquire if given a hearing by the world's greatest international forum.

At the conclusion of Dr. Fernos-Isern's presentation, the Polish delegation proposed that the Puerto Rican Federal Relations Act be circulated for information. While the United States delegation's pulses were skipping a beat, the secretary of the committee, Mr. Wilfred Benson, quickly intervened to say that Public Laws 600 and 447 were very short, and if there were no objection they could be circulated. These laws were referred to throughout the United States documentation, but certainly they were not the then-unfathomable Puerto Rican Federal Relations Act. The United States delegation found it expedient not to enlighten the committee on this point and no objection was raised.

I have set down some notes on but one chapter of the record of Puerto Rico's achievement of self-government, using some historical sidelights on that event. I have not gone beyond the first of eleven meetings of the Fourth Committee and a large part of the 459th plenary meeting of the General Assembly on November 27, 1953, devoted to consideration of Puerto Rico. To persist in such an undertaking would be revealing of the gulf which divided the thinking of many members of the United Nations at mid-century on matters which fall within the general category of "colonial question." It would show the attitudes of many members toward United States administration of dependent territories, and what may be expected when this nation next declares that a full measure of self-government has been achieved by a United States territory. It would reflect the profound lack of knowledge and appreciation of the Puerto Rican accomplishment on the part of the American public and officialdom only a little while ago. It was a painful process whereby the United States salvaged a final majority in the United Nations General Assembly by a vote of twenty-six to sixteen, with eighteen abstentions, on the proposition that transmission of information on Puerto Rico should cease. The Puerto Ricans, who could not be overjoyed by a successful vote made possible by eighteen abstentions, knew how much they owed this degree of success to Mrs. Bolton. Our British cousins, who abstained, said: "We think your Mrs. Bolton is quite a man."[11]

The painful but highly educational experiences of the United States and Puerto Rican governments in handling colonial questions in the World Forum in 1953 related in no small way to the agreement reached by President John F. Kennedy and Gov. Luis Muñoz Marin a decade later that the time had arrived to consult the people of Puerto Rico concerning further development of the commonwealth relationship and to establish an "unequivocal record" regarding their status preference. This agreement led to establishment of the United States–Puerto Rican Commission on the Status of Puerto Rico, to its monumental reporting after two years of extensive work,[12] and to the subsequent consultation with the Puerto Rican electorate on July 23, 1967, in which the voters expressed the desire to continue the commonwealth arrangement rather than seek statehood or independence.

Since the statehood advocate, Luis A. Ferre, won the governorship in 1968 in a four-way fight, Puerto Rican politics has continued to turn on the question of whether the island's economy and well-being would be maintained without the incentives of Operation Bootstrap, which has drawn more than one hundred of *Fortune* magazine's largest firms to Puerto Rico and helped to boost per capita income from $279 in 1950 to about $1,100 in 1968.

In looking to the future, one could reasonably conclude at this time that Puerto Rico is destined to remain in the American orbit with a strengthening of ties which bind it to the United States. It has been said in the past that all Puerto Ricans are more or less *independentista* at heart. They are also a rational and politically alive people who have been American citizens since 1917 and who have acquired an enormous amount of political experience and a capacity to assess and express themselves regarding spiritual and practical values in relationships with the United States. To help them over the rough spots are their political sagacity and good humor, which enhance their just pride in themselves and their accomplishments. Their jokingly expressed "imperialistic" tendencies reveal a knowledge of history, steadfastness in meeting current problems, and self-assurance regarding the future. When it has been suggested that the United States should annex Puerto Rico outright, the argument has sometimes been reversed: Puerto Rico should annex a large part of the United States, or at least Florida, based upon the expeditions of discovery by Ponce de León, who set out from Puerto Rico.

IV

In the context of this paper, it is appropriate to mention two international organizations with which United States territories were associated. The first was the Anglo-American Caribbean Commission established during World War II, with membership expanded on October 30, 1946, to include France and the Netherlands. This was a consultative and advisory body, to improve the economic and social well-being of the peoples of Caribbean territories.

Valuable insights into the times, and the considerations which prompted the establishment of this first arrangement in which colonial peoples were given the capacity to speak of their own affairs in an international context, are contained in the reports of the visit of President Franklin Roosevelt's emissary, Charles W. Taussig, to the British Colonial Office, December 9–19, 1942, and his conversations with Prime Minister Winston Churchill on December 17. Former Secretary of State Cordell Hull described this novel organization:

> The Commission followed the principle of encouraging active
> participation by dependent peoples in shaping the policy of
> their area. Commissioners were drawn from the area, the Caribbean
> Research Council composed mostly of local scientists and techni-
> cians was formed, and arrangements were made for biennial meetings
> of the West Indian Conference, with delegates directly representing
> the people.[13]

The Caribbean Commission operated significantly for more than a decade. It lost punch after 1952, when the West Indian Conference unanimously adopted a statement, submitted by the Netherlands Antilles delegation and strongly endorsed by Puerto Rico, which invited member governments to revise the basic agreement establishing the commission "in the light of the new constitutional relationship of the territories within the Caribbean area, and the light of the demonstrated desires and ability of the peoples of the area to accept responsibility in solving the problems of the region."[14] It took eight years to produce a new organization. Here is a challenging master's or honors topic for some bright student interested in constitutional, comparative, and international law all rolled together.

In appropriate "burial" and inaugural ceremonies at the San Juan Intercontinental Hotel on September 6, 1961, the commission was replaced by the Caribbean Organization brought into force by the signing of a joint declaration. The new organization, without active metropolitan government participation except by the Republic of France for its Departments of French Guiana, Guadeloupe, and Martinique, was short-lived. A key factor contributing to its demise was the failure, after long and prodigious efforts, to establish an independent federation of British territories in the area.

The South Pacific Commission, established in 1948, was modeled on the experience gained in the Caribbean area. Included originally in its geographic scope were fifteen Pacific Island territories administered by six metropolitan powers. The territories were listed, but it was not indicated which member governments administered them. Thus the problem of disputed titles to islands, of little significance now as compared to its potential for difficulties in an earlier period, was avoided. It did come to the fore somewhat obliquely after a supplemental agreement was concluded at Nouméa on November 7, 1951, to extend the scope of the commission to include Guam and the Trust Territory of the Pacific Islands.[15]

The South Pacific Commission continues to carry on work programs in health and economic and social development. Its operations have been marked by political overtones from time to time, despite provisions of the agreement which preclude consideration of political matters. Political changes have altered the geographic scope and membership. The Netherlands is no longer a member, due to the transfer of West New Guinea to Indonesia. The position of Western Samoa within the organization changed when the trusteeship ended in 1964 with the emergence of that territory as an "independent" state.

When the United States was actively engaged in planning for a better world after World War II, the secretary of state submitted and the president endorsed far-reaching proposals which stated that dependent peoples who desired independence should have opportunity to attain it. Machinery to accomplish this should be worked into the new system yet to be created. At mid-century's eve, the idealism of Cordell Hull had only a single institutional arrangement to provide an example of how the welfare and advancement of dependent peoples could be promoted internationally—the Caribbean Commission, an example he felt and said could be followed by other nations in other parts of the world. He looked with satisfaction upon the advent of the South Pacific Commission.[16]

If one would analyze the progress of the two regional commissions it would be strikingly revealed that the least tangible but most significant result from joint investment of very small amounts of money has been the application of the principle of good-neighborliness. This has redounded to the benefit of the peoples of the region, the area as a whole, and the metropolitan governments in promoting knowledge, friendship, and understanding.

V

The Interior and Insular Affairs Committees of Congress have in the past had a rank order for considering territorial matters and sometimes have acted as though the problems of advancement toward self-government in those territories down the list could await disposition of those at the top. This has led to such protocolaire nonsense that the governors of the Virgin Islands, Guam, and American Samoa, in that order, outrank the high commissioner of the trust territory, who has by far the most difficult and challenging assignment.

The Virgin Islands of the United States were bought from Denmark in 1917, and the inhabitants were made American citizens by mass naturalization ten years later. The governor's report to the secretary of the Interior and his 1967 State of the Territory Message answer many questions about the history, government, and economic life of this Caribbean paradise, with its free port and customs exemptions. The picture thus revealed of a considerable amount of well-being and momentum contrasts somewhat sharply with the situation a while ago.

By mid-century, the people of the British Virgin Islands had expressed themselves by ballot as desiring to be joined to the American Virgins. They were country folk, prone for decades past to go to town once or twice a year, and their historical metropole was Charlotte Amalie on St. Thomas. Spokesmen for the British embassy visited the Department of State for a meeting to discuss the restrictions on their freedom of movement, but the Department of the Interior representative said, "Good God! We have enough problems in our territories and don't want to bite off any more." Taking refuge behind the letter of the law, the United States Immigration Service had nothing constructive to offer, maintaining that relief, if any, rested with Congress. Compassionate but frustrated because our great government was unable to cope with this small problem, the Department of State representatives guarded in silence their fears of what might happen should the Department of Justice move into the South Pacific with a comparably strict interpretation of the law as applied to the free movement of people between the two Samoas.[17]

The governor of the Virgin Islands is presently appointed by the president with the advice and consent of the Senate. The government secretary also is appointed by the president and serves as acting governor in the absence of the governor. A unicameral legislature consists of eleven senators. What the Virgin Islands have wanted was set forth by the Constitutional Convention of the Virgin Islands which met in 1964 for twenty legislative days. It proposed a four-year term for an elective governor and lieutenant governor; revised electoral districts; a resident commissioner or delegate in Washington; and the right to vote for United States president and vice president in national elections.[18]

The first of these aspirations will be fulfilled next year, when the territory will elect its new governor. In the eight-year term of Gov. Ralph M. Paiewonsky, which ended in February 1969, there was a period of unparalleled prosperity built on a booming tourist business. It is difficult to foresee what an ultimate status of the Virgin Islands might be. Paiewonsky recently pointed to the current population explosion in the territory, estimating that it would reach sixty thousand by 1970. This is not enough for admission as a state. Even when that minimum figure may be reached, it doubtless would not be deemed sufficient in this age to justify the costs and overrepresentation by a congressman and two senators. It is said that the dimensions of the problems of government in the islands are comparable to those of a medium-sized municipality and could be well handled by a council-manager type of government. Such proposed status would be difficult to impose psychologically on a territory with a long and rich Western colonial history antedating that of Jamestown, Plymouth, and Monterey, whose people from time immemorial have looked to a government house in which a governor resided.

One might suggest that the United States policy of opposing political fragmentation in the international community could be applied to the British Virgin Islands to solve a small but acute human problem. But it takes real courage and conviction to express even sotto voce a serious notion that the Virgin Islands might be joined politically with the Commonwealth of Puerto Rico.

VI

The enlargement of the airstrip at Tafuna on the island of Tutuila in American Samoa to receive jet planes has brought that unorganized, unincorporated United States territory much closer to the Pacific crossroads of Honolulu. The introduction to Gov. H. Rex Lee's 1965 Annual Report stated that "The face of Samoa was undergoing change, and the Samoan people were working steadily and with energy to bring the changes along— keeping the best of the old and acquiring the best of the new." Developments mentioned, which continue as focal points of interest and signs of economic and social progress, included: dedication of the airport terminal building; opening of the Educational Television Center and development of the concept of educational television to upgrade teaching and to do it economically; and building the Intercontinental Hotel at Goat Island in Pago Pago Harbor, which was dedicated in December 1965 and had fulfilled hopes of becoming the center of a thriving, first-rank tourist area. Former Governor Lee is given much credit for securing greatly increased appropriations in the Kennedy and Johnson administrations.

This is in sharp contrast to the state of uncertainty which developed from President Truman's decisions to transfer responsibility for the administration of Guam, Samoa, and the trust territory from the secretary of the navy to the secretary of the interior.

With his proverbial self-assurance, but with a degree of restraint and inexcitability which does not at all characterize his memory, Secretary of the Interior Harold L. Ickes addressed a letter to the president dated September 12, 1945, which started the fire of an intradepartmental controversy that burned for most of a decade. He expressed the belief that immediate attention should be given to administration of newly occupied areas which might remain or be placed under supervision of the United States. He had already initiated study to draft plans for concentrating all territorial affairs in the Office of Territories and Island Possessions, Department of the Interior.

Mr. Ickes took a further step on October 18, asking the president for approval of a joint expert group "to visit the Pacific Islands for the purpose of preparing a detailed plan for interim administration, pending decisions and agreements concerning future disposition and administration of the islands." The president's notation on that letter was: "Appoint State War Navy Int." But in May 1947 Truman pointed out that he had "no report from the Cabinet Committee and no further information on the subject, except a recommendation which was published in the Sunday *New York Times* by a Civilian Committee, which the Navy had sent to make a survey." He said "I'd like very much to have the Cabinet Committee get together and co-ordinate a plan to present to me."[19] Thus was launched in earnest an extended period of planning leading to the transfer of responsibility for civil administration of Guam, American Samoa, and the trust territory from the Navy Department to the Interior Department.

The uncertainties and fears produced in American Samoa during this period were set forth in forty pages of memorandums urgently dispatched from Apia, Western Samoa, January 27, 1951, to the Department of State by the late Prof. Felix M. Keesing of Stanford University, the United States senior commissioner on the South Pacific Commission. In his analysis of the situation, he wrote:

. . . Samoan leaders have turned almost unanimously against an
Organic Act or citizenship except as an elective choice by individuals.
Even the transfer to the Interior at this time has been questioned
(below). There are the beginnings of an anti-Interior movement
(what in Samoan history has usually been called a *Mau*) which if
not most carefully handled could assume under some circumstances
the form of an anti-United States movement.[20]

The memorandums referred to above reflected the grim local situation with which the last navy governor, Capt. Thomas F. Darden, was struggling in attempting to alleviate the apprehensions of the Samoans and ease the process of navy withdrawal. The warmheartedness, compassionate interest, and understanding which characterized Captain and Mrs. Darden's concern for the Samoans was as genuine as was the obligation the governor felt not to take issue with the government policy which was causing so much local anguish.

One of the arguments advanced for replacing Navy with Interior administration was that greater continuity and stability would result when the civilians held the governorship for longer terms. The seven governors who have served in American Samoa, 1951–69, had an average term of office of 2.5 years. If the average for the first few years were taken, the average number of months in office would be far less.

During the eighteen years since the presidential order assigning Samoa to the Department of the Interior, the people of the territory have continued to be American nationals rather than American citizens. Legislation was first introduced during the Eighty-first Congress to provide organic legislation for American Samoa, and hearings were held in the territory in November 1949.

Five years later, Governor Lowe reported that "most of the leaders feel that such legislation should be postponed for some years to come or until the Samoan people are better trained to handle the problems which are likely to arise from it." He was inclined to agree, but at the same time said, "I should like to see more tangible steps taken toward self-government." That same month, on January 12, 1954, addressing a joint session of the legislature, Governor Lowe advised it that, in response to a resolution by it, Executive Order No. 10 had been issued calling for a constitutional committee. The governor told the Samoan legislators that, as they had pointed out in their resolution, a territorial constitution locally developed would "bring many of the same benefits of organic legislation and at the same time permit the people of Samoa to maintain the Territorial system of land tenure and their territorial social organization so long as it meets their needs."[21]

The Samoan constitutional committee was duly organized, but its constitution was not approved by the secretary of the interior until April 27, 1960. It became effective on December 27 of that year. The size of the *Fono* (legislature) was increased and its powers were expanded by a new constitution ratified by a popular vote in 1966.

Such has been the pace of constitutional development geared to *fa'a Samoa* (Samoan custom). In briefing sessions on February 2, 1967, former Governor Lee told the House Committee on Interior and Insular Affairs:

In the almost six years I have been Governor, I have not heard one Samoan express a desire for political independence from the United States or any other basic change in their relationship with the United States. They are proud of being Americans [*sic*].

They consider American Samoa as much a part of the United
States as any one of our States.[22]

The territory, it would seem, is destined to remain in a state of political
dependency on the United States, without American citizenship for its people and without a full measure of self-government as defined by the United
States. Who would be willing to guess what the oncoming generation of
educated American Samoans might choose to do with their political future?

VII

A monument on the beach park of the village of Umatac on Guam Island
commemorates discovery of the Ladrones (Islands of Thieves) in 1521 and
indicates how long ago contacts with the Western Christian world began.
The current public relations byword—"Guam, Where America's Day Begins"—emphasizes that the island is, indeed, United States territory—and,
it might be added, its people have been United States citizens since 1950.

By the Treaty of Paris, 1898, Guam was ceded to the United States
and Congress was committed thereby to determine the political and legal
status of the island. It did not do so for more than fifty years. During that
long interval Guam was left to the administrative authority of the president
in his role of commander in chief. President McKinley delegated that
authority to the navy on December 23, 1898. The president's instructions
to the first governor, Capt. Richard P. Leary, stated:

> It should be the earnest and paramount aim of the naval
> administration to win the confidence, respect, and affection of
> the inhabitants of the island of Guam, by securing to them in every
> possible way that full measure of individual rights and liberties
> which is the inheritance of all free peoples, and by proving to
> them that the mission of the United States is one of benevolent
> assimilation, substituting the mild way of justice and right for
> arbitrary rule. In the fulfillment of this high mission, supporting
> the temperate administration of affairs for the greatest good of the
> governed, there must be sedulously maintained the strong arm
> of authority. . . .[23]

The navy did not ignore its responsibilities for improving the condition of the Guamanians, but what was regarded by the president as the
paramount aim of the governor was regarded by his navy superiors as a
secondary responsibility."[24]

Navy as well as civilian historians have produced a rather full record of Guam during its years of administration by the navy.[25] The first postwar naval governor, Adm. Charles A. Pownall, assumed office on May 30, 1946, after President Truman had called for recommendations concerning future administration of Pacific Island territories. The Guam Congress was simply an advisory body, and the governor was free to accept or reject its advice and recommendations. In January 1947 it unanimously petitioned the United States Congress to provide United States citizenship for Guamanians and an organic act. This was the period in which former Secretary of the Interior Ickes's trumpet was blaring the loudest: "The Navy in Guam . . . for nearly half a century has prevented the fulfillment of national pledges made and accepted in good faith."[26]

In May 1947 the Hopkins Committee recommended United States citizenship and an organic act, but that administration should remain in the hands of the navy for an indefinite period.[27] A month later, however, the secretaries of state, war, navy and the interior recommended organic legislation, United States citizenship, and "the transfer of administration from the Navy Department to a civilian agency at the earliest practicable date . . . ."[28] President Truman soon issued Executive Order 10077 by which Guam was transferred from the navy to the Department of the Interior on August 1, 1950. On the same day President Truman signed the organic act of Guam. The principal concern of congressional leadership had been that there should be no implied commitment to statehood. United States citizenship was provided by amending the Nationality Act of 1940. A twenty-provision Bill of Rights contains guarantees similar to those found in the United States Bill of Rights.

The new organic legislation provided for a governor to be appointed by the president with the advice and consent of the Senate and to reside in Guam during his term of office. It also provided for a unicameral legislature of not more than twenty-one members, to hold office for two years; and it created a court of record, the "District Court of Guam," in which the judicial authority is vested, together with "such court or courts as may have been established or may hereafter be established by the laws of Guam."

Since the transfer of administration to civilians, Guamanians have exercised increased initiative and sharing in their government. The population in 1964 was 97,000, of which 58,598 were civilians. The tempo of political and economic life has been influenced by many factors, including the growing economy stimulated artificially by military activity; the positive and also negative influences of a succession of civilian governors, of whom there have been seven in the past twenty years; and the devastation by Typhoon Karen on November 11, 1962, with wind velocities of 200 miles an hour, which led to Guam's being declared a major disaster area. Funds provided for relief and rehabilitation proved to be an economic blessing, and there has been increased public and private interest in the territory as the principal gateway and metropole of the trust territory.

Three of the seven civilian governors have been Guamanians, but there was cause for mingled amusement and outrage at the antics of Gov. Bill Daniel (1961–63), brother of the former governor of Texas, who was appointed by President Kennedy.[29] In sharp contrast was the discriminating appointment to replace him of Manuel F. L. Guerrero, the secretary of Guam, who held the governorship for six years.

Continuing agitation for an elected governor culminated in the signature by President Johnson of the Guam Elective Governor Act on September 11, 1968. This was good, but Guamanians want more. The Johnson administration urged legislation to provide both Guam and the Virgin Islands with nonvoting delegates in Congress.[30] Getting no satisfaction, the Guam legislature has sent its own popularly elected representative to Washington. Antonio B. Won Pat was elected to this post on March 15, 1965, and maintains his office at 200 Maryland Avenue, NE.

Guamanians desire the right to vote in national elections for president and vice president. There have been strong negative responses to suggestions of independence, as when a United Nations subcommittee report recommended it, leading the Guam *Daily News* to editorialize, "We do not want independence kicked down our throats," and "what we have been aspiring for is closer union with the United States, not for separation."[31] Carlton Skinner, United States senior commissioner on the South Pacific Commission, Guam's former first United States civilian governor, in 1968 predicted "a day when the common interests of Guam, Micronesia (the present trust territory), and American Samoa will be so obviously joined, that they could constitute a 51st state of Pacifica . . . ." My own graduate seminar has concluded that the trust territory should eventually be joined to Hawaii as a new county, but that the situation can not be dealt with realistically without also considering the future of Guam. Sen. Hiram L. Fong of Hawaii has espoused this position, but without mention of Guam.[32]

VIII

Twenty years past the mid-century mark, no question in territorial administration is more immediate, perplexing, and challenging than that of the Trust Territory of the Pacific Islands. Ten of its political leaders were in the nation's capital for three weeks in October 1969 to caucus and consult with the government on the future status of the territory. They came to discuss the July 1969 Report of the Future Political Status Commission of the Congress of Micronesia. The commission's recommendation, which makes it imperative that the United States government give the matter of future status most serious and consecutive attention, is:

that the Trust Territory of the Pacific Islands be constituted as
a self-governing state and that this Micronesian state—internally
self-governing and with Micronesian control of all its branches,
including the executive—negotiate entry into free association with
the United States.

Some members of the Congress of Micronesia, prior to the close of the Johnson administration, were beginning to voice support for the idea of political independence. This made it necessary for the new Nixon administration to give the trust territory attention almost before it could catch its breath. Secretary of the Interior Walter J. Hickel went to Saipan on May 5, 1969, to install Edward G. Johnson as the new high commissioner. In a statement on that occasion Mr. Hickel declared: "We now, together, can eagerly look forward to a better future, a full partnership which begins today."

The significance to be attached to this statement was not that it contained anything new, but that what had been implicit for a long time in the stepped-up interest and programs for the trust territory was now being stated explicitly. For the first time, Micronesians were being told that the government and the American people desired closer association with them in the future.

The United States had administered the territory of the Pacific Islands under a United Nations strategic Trusteeship Agreement which became operative on July 18, 1947. These islands, spreading across three million square miles of ocean, were formerly mandated, colonized, and fortified by Japan, and taken by conquest in World War II by United States forces. The same day the Trusteeship Agreement became operative, military government in the territory was ended, and the Department of the Navy was made responsible for administration of the trust territory "pending the enactment of appropriate legislation by the Congress of the United States providing for the future government thereof." The United States Congress has not yet enacted such legislation. In 1954, when doubts were raised in Congress regarding legislative authority for presidential control of the trust territory government, a congressional act made explicit provision for such control (68 Stat. 330).

Administrative responsibility for the territory had been transferred from Navy to Interior on July 1, 1951, in accordance with their Memorandum of Understanding approved by the president on September 23, 1949. On the one hand were the views epitomized by Harold Ickes and others, who insisted that nobody under United States jurisdiction should be ruled indefinitely by the military. Their tactic was to damn the navy's alleged record of administration and neglect. This was grossly unfair, particularly in the several postwar years, when the navy had from the government for the first time a policy toward dependent peoples—chapters 11 and 12 of the United Nations Charter. On the other hand, there were those who felt quite strongly that the navy should continue to administer the islands and to carry on what was substantially an amphibious operation. In 1942 the navy's School of Military Government and Civil Affairs had been established, which produced several hundred officers especially trained in civil affairs and administration of Pacific Islands peoples. Many of them were convinced of the importance of the duty they were trained to perform and were disconcerted by the postwar agitation to divest the navy of such responsibilities.

Ambassador Francis B. Sayre, United States representative on the Trusteeship Council, in June 1949 argued strongly in favor of continued Navy Department management, pointing out that no other agency had "the necessary physical facilities, the trained personnel, or the technical know-how." At the same time, various senior naval officers were more concerned about winning an aircraft carrier from Congress than fighting a losing battle to retain responsibilities for island governments. In another direction, there have been odd proposals over the years, and even as recently as April 1969, for the State Department to assume administration of the Trust Territory.[33] This is in some degree frightening, because the president in a moment of absent-mindedness could accomplish such transfer of responsibility with a stroke of the pen.[34]

In any event, a "Memorandum of Understanding" approved by the president in September 1949 led to the Interior Department take-over on July 1, 1951. During the interim period a hard-working and highly motivated staff officer in the Interior Department's Office of Territories worked with frantic zeal to show that, with prudent economy and proper planning, administering the trust territory would be no more costly than it had been under the navy. He had the staunch support of a staff officer in the Bureau of the Budget, who was equally zealous in desiring to place the territory in civilian hands. They were key figures in perpetrating a deception which proved to be a grave disservice to the trust territory for years.

Partly as a result of this hocus-pocus and the policy of "retarded gradualism" which it dictated, the trust territory operated on an annual budget of $5–$7 million. During the Eisenhower years a dedicated high commissioner, qualified by training in government service, carried out the United States policy of "enlightened gradualism" and satisfied the United Nations remarkably well each year. In retrospect, however, the policy has been shown to have been retrogressive in economic and social matters. Funds to cover rising costs were not provided, to say nothing of additional funds for developmental programs. The general corrosion in the islands which occurred in this period caused observers to refer to them as "the rust territory." The tempo of life was such that, by comparison, the prior Japanese regime could be considered the age of the "Great Society" in Micronesia.

It should not be overlooked, nevertheless, that the process of developing local responsibility and institutions, to move toward the ultimate "full measure of self-government," moved ahead during this period. That process, dedicated to first building governmental institutions and service at the grass roots, is explained in great detail and constitutes a major portion of Prof. Norman Meller's recent and distinguished volume, *The Congress of Micronesia*.[35]

Since 1963, the annual appropriation by the United States Congress for the trust territory has moved sharply upward from about $7 million to $30 million in 1969. President Johnson requested $41.6 million for fiscal year 1970.

Since the early 1960s interest in the trust territory has greatly increased. Stepped-up policies and programs promised early significant changes, which are now occurring. A continuing spate of critical articles, books, and studies, beginning in the Kennedy administration, has given impetus to this acceleration. Much reporting results from on-the-spot observation, encouraged and greatly facilitated by the governments in Washington and Saipan, about a territory which was previously hemmed in by restrictions on travel from the outside. Most of such reporting has been very useful in dramatizing needs of the territory and provoking policy responses to them.

Highly significant in this connection has been the focusing of the United Nations spotlight more intensively upon the trust territory. The United Nations trusteeship system has pretty well run its course and can be closed down as soon as the last two trust territories—Papua-New Guinea and the Pacific Islands—are delivered from colonial rule.

Increased official interest in the trust territory by the administering power and subsequent increased appropriations enabled the high commissioner to upgrade staffing and to acquire expert advice and assistance on a broader scale from within the government and outside, upon which to build modernization programs. Announcement of a Peace Corps program was made jointly by the secretary of the interior, the United States representative to the United Nations, and the director of the Peace Corps on May 6, 1966.

The high commissioner contracted in April 1965 with Robert Nathan Associates, consulting engineers in Washington, D.C., for a team to conduct an extensive survey and recommend an economic plan. Its voluminous report was completed in December 1966.

The first chief of mission of the Economic Development Team, Mr. Ivan Bloch, was made sick at heart by what he saw as the dilemma of the trust territory. His basic premise was that his employers had been successful in previous work in underdeveloped countries because they had operated in places where there was something to develop. To him there obviously seemed little in the trust territory to develop, aside from oceanography and tourism, and there was little hope for such development unless political decisions were taken to open the territory for development and to invest large amounts of public capital within a short period of time. Through his influence largely, Robert Nathan Associates suggested that the United States economy would not be burdened if the United States Congress appropriated $1,500 per Micronesian to raise the standard of living in the trust territory to a reasonable level. Bloch resigned from his post for reasons of health, and his withdrawal doubtless averted a case of apoplexy. But his ideas and conclusions were not lost on his teammates in the field and employers in Washington.

Another study prepared under contract for the trust territory is the report on *Planning for Education and Manpower in Micronesia,* 1967, by the Stanford Research Institute of Menlo Park, California. Of unusual satisfaction and long-range importance to the trust territory, as well as to anyone else interested in political and judicial modernization, should be the recent publication of *Trust Territory Reports* containing the opinions of the High Court of the Pacific Islands, Appellate and Trial Divisions: Volume I (1951–58), Volume II (1959–65), Volume III (1965–68), Volume IV (1968–69), and Volume V (forthcoming) edited by Sharon N. Ruzumma, Thomas L. Whittington, and Donald T. Bliss, all lawyers working in the Peace Corps Legal Services.[36]

By far the greatest amount of reporting, indicating an increase in the pulse beat of the trust territory and its people, ensues from the Congress of Micronesia—its annual volumes of *Laws and Resolutions,* congressional *Journals,* interim committee reports, *Manual* of the Congress, *Report of the Joint Committee on Governmental Organization*—together with frequent press releases and the semimonthly *Highlights,* a newsletter issued by the Office of the High Commissioner.

The greatest change in the trust territory during a quarter century of American jurisdiction occurred on July 12, 1965. On that day, a movie theater was transformed into a place of dignity and simple beauty with an outline map of Micronesia superimposed upon a stage-wide map of the world. The occasion was the inauguration of the Congress of Micronesia. This marked a milestone well along the road toward creating a single polity out of divergent peoples widely separated in the past by geography and cultural and linguistic differences. The Mariana Islanders, Marshallese, Palauans, Ponapeans, Trukese, and Yapese have not been submerged as such, but they are more and more referring to themselves as "We the people of Micronesia." The United States cannot brush aside this people it bears responsibility for creating.

I X

The birds return to these island homes each bearing a fish.
Samoan Proverb

The late High Talking Chief of American Samoa, M. T. Tuiasosopo, used the proverb above as a text for his benediction at an early session of the South Pacific Conference of representatives of Pacific Island peoples. In interpreting the proverb and displaying proverbial Samoan dignity and courtesy, he thanked God for bringing the participants together and the administering powers who had made possible that foregathering of brothers from far distant, though neighboring islands. They were now returning home with something of value from the conference. All were grateful for that enriching experience and for the assistance and guidance they had received from the powers responsible for their administration. He hoped that the assistance and guidance would continue, but he also pleaded for the opportunity in a swiftly changing world for peoples to decide for themselves what of their cultures they wished to discard and what they wished to retain. For who could foretell whether mankind in the outside world, which seems rushing on to destroy itself, would not disappear completely from the earth save, perhaps, in the case of some small, remote peoples in the Pacific? There some atoms of civilization might be preserved, and mankind could begin again.

The thrust of Tuiasosopo's pensiveness is enduring and universal in character. It suggests the fears and frustrations of choosing what is good and should be retained and what can well be discarded in a rapidly changing world in which the opportunity to make such decisions is often nonexistent.

I trust that participants here will take home some fish. I have attempted to weave a banana-leaf satchel for you to carry the number of fish I have been obliged to net. The braiding was done by a statesider who would have profited from more time and expertness in banana-leaf weaving, and the heavy burden would have been lessened by netting fewer fish. This, however, would not have lessened the total weight of problems and policy challenges which the American people and their government, in cooperation with peoples in the territories, have to carry. The pragmatic responses the United States has made to challenges arising from its "remnants of empire" in mid-twentieth century have been in keeping with American patterns of thought and experience. These are part and parcel of the total fabric of domestic and foreign politics and policies which the United States continues to unfold from its sprawling, inefficient loom of benevolent democratic government.

Much has been written by students of American constitutional law to point out that when the United States acquired responsibility for island dependencies and set them apart as unincorporated territories, the pattern for territorial government extending back to the Ordinance of 1787 was discarded. This, however, is a conclusion based largely on legalities and not on political and spiritual considerations, which are often decisive in the final analysis. The political ideal that American "government by the people" was an exportable commodity useful to peoples elsewhere, and the *spirit,* derived from long experience and success with United States territorial government, continue to pervade America's relations with its territories.

In all United States territories there is agitation for an advance in political status. In all except the Trust Territory of the Pacific Islands the course seems to be directed toward closer association with the United States. The course to be followed by the trust territory is only now in the process of being charted.

In all the territories, the worldwide problems of urban blight and pollution, fast-growing populations, distasteful aspects of economies built on the tourist business, and high costs of modernization are being felt. In the trust territory and American Samoa, fear of losing title to land to outsiders is extremely acute. In seeking immediate long-range answers to such problems, people in island territories need to consider the extent to which they must rely on the United States for guidance and practical assistance here and now. How are they to deal with the cocoanut palm-destroying rhinoceros beetle, the coral reef-destroying "crown of thorns" starfish, and other natural disasters for which outside help would be imperative? Pacific Islanders might well use their growing political power to strengthen ties of understanding and cooperation, to ensure full and swift response to future needs.

The time is past when the United States can soft-pedal security and defense interests it has in the trust territory, which are compelling and potentially vital. These were spelled out when the Trusteeship Agreement was negotiated, and the price in human lives and material of the conquest of the islands was underlined. Those responsible for the defenses of the United States have reason to cling steadfastly to the belief that it will not relinquish its jurisdiction to manage the external relations of the trust territory, and political leaders are not and could not be unmindful of this.

Competing United Nations principles could receive quite an airing within the United States government, in the Security Council, and in public discussions before a new political status is achieved and the international trusteeship terminated. This could be painful and damaging, and we could and should seek to minimize the dangers by extended and frank joint discussions with the Micronesians.

NOTES

1. *Annals of the American Academy of Political and Social Science* 30 (1907): 137.
2. Ibid., pp. 3–15.
3. Ibid.
4. Ibid., pp. 16–23.
5. Pub. L. No. 204, 80th Cong.; U.S.C. 271, 66 Stat. 397.
6. U.S., Congress, Senate, Committee on Interior and Insular Affairs, *Alaska Statehood, Hearing on H.R. 331 and S. 2036,* 81st Cong., 2d sess., April 24–29, 1950, pp. 68–69.
7. U.S., Congress, House, Committee on Interior and Insular Affairs, *Hawaii-Alaska Statehood, Hearing on H.R. 2535 and 2536,* 84th Cong., 1st sess., January–February 1955, pp. 268–69.
8. Graduate School of Public Health, University of Pittsburgh, *Alaska's Health: A Survey Report to the United States Department of the Interior by the Alaska Health Survey Team* (Pittsburgh, 1954), pp. 1–2.
9. Even though, as Rexford G. Tugwell said, "the New Deal never properly came to Puerto Rico. . . . " Quoted in Carl J. Friedrich, *Puerto Rico: Middle Road to Freedom* (New York, 1959), p. 29.
10. Arnold H. Leibowitz, "The Applicability of Federal Law to the Commonwealth of Puerto Rico," *Georgetown Law Journal,* 56, no. 2 (December 1907): 219–71.
11. For the complete record of the Puerto Rican item during the 1953 General Assembly see United Nations Eighth General Assembly, *Official Records,* Fourth Committee, 321st–322d Meetings (September 30–October 1, 1953), and 348th–356th Meetings (October 30–November 6, 1953); *Official Records,* Eighth General Assembly, 459th Plenary Meeting (November 27, 1953). See also Frances P. Bolton and James P. Richards, "Eighth Session of the General Assembly," report for the House of Representatives Committee on Foreign Affairs (Washington, D.C.: Government Printing Office, April 26, 1954).
12. United States–Puerto Rico Commission on the Status of Puerto Rico, *Status of Puerto Rico: Hearings before the United States–Puerto Rico Commission on the Status of Puerto Rico,* Selected Background Studies, U.S., Senate, 89th Cong., 2d sess., Senate Document 108, vols. 1, 2, 3 (Washington, D.C.: Government Printing Office, 1966).
13. Cordell Hull, *The Memoirs of Cordell Hull,* vol. 2 (New York: Macmillan Co., 1948), p. 1237.
14. U.S., Department of State, *U.S. Participation in the United Nations,* Report

by the President to the Congress for the Year 1952, Publication 5034, p. 199.

15. "Extension of the Territorial Scope of the South Pacific Commission," *South Pacific Commission Quarterly Bulletin* (now *South Pacific Bulletin*) 2, no. 2 (April 1952), pp. 47–51.

16. Hull, *Memoirs,* 2:1237; see also United Nations, *The United Nations and Non-Self-Governing Territories,* United Nations Information Series, no. 18, April 5, 1947, pp. 6 ff.

17. For somewhat later commentary on shortcomings of Virgin Island government, see U.S., Senate, *Virgin Islands Report,* by Sen. Hugh Butler, 83d Cong., 2d sess. (Washington, D.C.: Government Printing Office, 1954).

18. The *1965 Annual Report* by the governor of the Virgin Islands to the United States secretary of the interior (Washington, D.C.: Government Printing Office), pp. 21–42, contains a report on the Virgin Islands constitutional convention.

19. Papers of Harry S. Truman, Harry S. Truman Library, Independence, Mo.

20. Felix M. Keesing to Benjamin Gerig, director, Office of Dependent Area Affairs, Department of State, enclosing three memorandums.

21. U.S., Congress, House, Committee on Interior and Insular Affairs, *American Samoa,* Report of a Special Subcommittee on Territorial and Insular Affairs, pursuant to H.R. 89, November 1954 (Washington, D.C.: Government Printing Office, 1955).

22. U.S., Congress, House, Committee on Interior and Insular Affairs, *Hearings,* February 2, 1967, Serial 90–1 (Washington, D.C.: Government Printing Office, 1967) p. 15.

23. "When We Acquired Guam: Instructions Issued by the President," *Nation,* August 19, 1925, p. 217.

24. U.S., Department of the Navy, *Report on Guam, 1899–1950,* Office of the Chief of Naval Operations (Washington, D.C.: Government Printing Office, 1951), p. 3.

25. Charles Beardsley, *Guam Past and Present* (Rutland, Vt.: Charles B. Tuttle Co., 1964); Paul Carano and Pedro C. Sanchez, *A Complete History of Guam* (Rutland, Vt.: Charles B. Tuttle Co., 1964); Laura Thompson, *Guam and Its People* (Princeton: Princeton University Press, 1947).

26. Harold L. Ickes, "The Navy at Its Worst," *Collier's,* August 31, 1946, p. 67.

27. U.S., Department of the Navy, *Report on the Civil Governments of Guam and Samoa,* by Ernest M. Hopkins, Maurice J. Tobin, and Knowles A. Ryerson (Washington, D.C., 1947), p. 1.

28. U.S., Department of State, *Bulletin,* vol. 16 (June 29, 1947), pp. 1312–13.

29. *New Yorker,* February 13, 1965, pp. 39–74, especially 42.

30. A. B. Won Pat, *Your Washington Report,* vol. 2, no. 12 (December 1968).

31. In *New Yorker,* February 13, 1965, p. 42.

32. See U.S., Congress, Senate, *Congressional Record,* 89th Cong., 1st sess., August 18, 1965, 111, pt. 15: 20066–69.

33. Philip W. Quigg, "Coming of Age of Micronesia," *Foreign Affairs,* April 1969.

34. Interesting in regard to presidential authority with respect to the trust territory are views of the author of a "Law Note," *Michigan Law Review,* 66 (April 1968): 1277. He argues that the president has a free hand to conduct the islands' administration. He believes the president requires no

congressional action to establish a status commission requested by Micronesians, and he sees no barrier for termination of the trusteeship agreement, since the authority to terminate international agreements resides in the executive. The author even believes that the president has authority to annex the islands, based on precedents clearly established.

35. Norman Meller, *The Congress of Micronesia: Development of the Legislative Process in the Trust Territory of the Pacific Islands* (Honolulu: University of Hawaii Press, 1969).

36. Sharon Ruzumna, Thomas L. Whittington, and Donald T. Bliss, eds., *Trust Territory Reports* (Orford, N.H.: Equity Publishing Corporation, 1969).

Discussion of Sources

JOHN P. HEARD

THE COMPLEXITY AND SCOPE of records created by our government in the twentieth century make it difficult to convey in a short period of time what the National Archives really has to offer the researcher. Some of the records are highly significant, and naturally others are less significant. Though there have been fewer territories in this century than in the previous, this fact is more than adequately compensated for by the increase in the volume of records created to document government functions and by the increase in the number of functions themselves. Nineteenth-century functions, though they produced records that are voluminous enough, can be grouped under a relatively few headings such as administration, lands, Indians, military and treasury, with the beginnings of some scientific agencies. The implementation in the twentieth century of new scientific and social concepts has led to the creation of a large number of agencies to carry out the vast number of functions falling broadly under the headings of conserving and using efficiently our national resources, promoting their potential, and ensuring that all of the people share in the bounty—social engineering.

Let me give a few examples of the more interesting records available both here in the National Archives Building and in the federal records centers located throughout the nation. Some of them are of general concern and some relate to specific territories. This selection will lead us to the conclusion that federal records are voluminous and diverse, often yielding information quite apart from the original intended purpose.

Records of the Post Office Department, Record Group 28 (Social and Economic Records Division, National Archives), is an excellent source of detailed information on local history. Among its records are the Postmaster General's Orders (1835–1953, 1,146 volumes, 325 linear feet), which relate to post offices and their services; completed forms submitted by postmasters, giving the location of post offices and other geographical information; the Reports of Site Locations (1865–1946, 292 feet); and several series of postmaster appointment registers and files.

Records of the Bureau of the Census, Record Group 29 (Social and Economic Records Division), contains records of the Division of Territorial, Insular, and Foreign Statistics. Series relating to the territories as a whole are the General Subject File (1935–42, 4 feet); classified files for the fifteenth (1929–34, 5 feet) and the sixteenth (1938–43 and 1946–48, 5 feet) decennial censuses; and Scrapbooks Relating to Territorial Decennial Census (1920–41, 14 volumes, 3 feet). The Archives Branch at the Washington National Records Center, Suitland, Maryland, houses 52 feet of Agriculture Schedules for Outlying Territories and Possessions (1920 and 1930). At the same location are records of special censuses for Puerto Rico and the Virgin Islands: Social and Population Schedules (Puerto Rico, 1935–36, 11 feet); Agriculture Schedules (Puerto Rico, 1936, 24 feet); and Agriculture Schedules for the Virgin Islands (1917, 1 inch), all for the island of St. John.

Records of the Office of the Secretary of the Interior, Record Group 48 (Social and Economic Records Division), is one of the more important sources because of the Interior Department's long-standing role as administrator of the territories. Among its extensive holdings are the Central Files of the Office of the Secretary (1907–53, 1,300 feet) and the records of the various divisions. Examples of these divisional records are the Appointment Papers (Appointments Division, 1849–1907, 390 feet); correspondence of the Lands and Railroads Division (three series, 1849–1907, 250 feet); correspondence of the Indian Division (Letters Received, 1880–1907, 180 feet, and Letters Sent, 1849–1903, 120 volumes, 36 feet); and Records Relating to the Territories (Patents and Miscellaneous Division, 1849–1914, 290 feet), which includes incoming correspondence and copies of executive proceedings of territorial governments. Sources dealing with Oklahoma exclusively are found in the records of the Indian Territory Division (Letters Received, 1898–1907, 105 feet; Letterpress Copies of Letters Sent, 1898–1907, 257 volumes, 26 feet; Special Incoming Correspondence, 1898–1907, 5 feet; Cherokee Census Rolls, 1903–7 and 1914, 5 inches; and Chickasaw Census Rolls, 1902–7 and 1914, 6 inches).

Records of the Bureau of Land Management, Record Group 49, documents the work of another venerable agency. Among its records in the Social and Economic Records Division are the Abandoned Military Reservation Files (1822–1937, 60 feet); Records of the Division of Railroads, Rights-of-Way, and Reclamation (1852–1907, 39 feet); Letters Sent to Surveyors General (1861–1907, 36 feet); and the Townsite Case Files, especially good for Oklahoma and Alaska (1888–1925, 102 feet).

Included in the holdings of the Archives Branch at the Washington National Records Center are Railroad Contest Dockets (1872–1909, 271 feet), with indexes (7 feet); Patented Land Entry Case Files (1908–51, 11,028 feet); and Land Entry Papers (Alaska, 1885–1923, 5 feet; Arizona, 1870–1905, 83 feet; New Mexico, 1858–1925, 230 feet; and Oklahoma, 1889–1911, 797 feet). Other records at this center not yet having archival status, but of high interest, are several equally voluminous series: general correspondence (1910–46); records of canceled and relinquished entries (1908–48); patented land entry serial case files (1952–54); soil and moisture conservation, and improvement program and project records (1935–51); and the special files of the Engineering Division (1910–48).

General Records of the Department of the Treasury, Record Group 56 (Legislative, Judicial, and Diplomatic Records Division), contains the records of an agency whose direct interest in the territories was periodically reduced as functions were transferred to other departments. Even so, its operations were still quite important during the early years of this century. Good examples of Treasury records are Letters Received from the Secretary of the Interior (1850–1910, 15 feet); Records Relating to the Special Commissioners to Puerto Rico and Cuba (1898–1900, 3 inches); Correspondence and Monthly Deposit Lists Relating to the Philippine Islands and Puerto Rico Tariff Funds (1900–1907, 2 feet); Journals of the Contingent Expenses of the Puerto Rican Customs Service (1907–18, 2 volumes, 3 inches); Correspondence Relating to Major Treasury Officers ("Presidential Appointments," 1860–1945, 70 feet); and Letters Received Relating to Appointments and Other Personnel Action in the Customs Service (1841–1910, 411 feet).

Records of the Work Projects Administration, Record Group 69 (Social and Economic Records Division), consists of more than 6,200 feet of records created in the course of the relief work carried on by WPA and its predecessors. Abundant material on the territories occurs throughout. Most of the important administrative correspondence is found in the state series of the central files, in which records on individual states and territories are separated from the general subject series. There is a separate state series for each of the three relief agencies: Civil Works Administration (1933–34, 22 feet), Federal Emergency Relief Administration (1933–36, 137 feet), and WPA (1935–44, 870 feet). Records pertaining to functions are organized under the divisions which carried them out. White-collar relief jobs, for instance, are recorded in a group of 3,030 feet known as the Records of WPA Service Projects. Besides such well-known enterprises as the Federal Writers' Project, WPA and its predecessors devoted much effort towards identifying and listing historical records, both federal and nonfederal. Records of the Historical Records Survey (1935–42, 115 feet) and records of the Survey of Federal Archives (1935–43, 530 feet) contain hundreds of published and unpublished reports on their findings which should not be overlooked.

Records of the Bureau of Indian Affairs, Record Group 75 (Social and Economic Records Division), offers the researcher such volume and diversity that an adequate sampling would require a listing much longer than is possible here. However, a few choice examples will indicate what is available. Among the general records are found Letters Received (1881–1907, 1,559 feet); Letters Sent (1870–1908, 2,668 volumes, 333 feet); Central Classified Files (1907–39, 8,033 feet); Chronological File of Letters Sent (1909–36, 90 feet); and the Central Map File (1800–1939, 16,656 items, 11 feet). Some examples of divisional records are Plats of Townships in Indian Reservations (Lands Division, 1846–1937, 5,730 items, 78 volumes, 8 feet); Annuity Payment Rolls (Finance Division, 1841–1949, 959 volumes, 138 feet); Inspection Reports (Inspection Division, 1908–40, 42 feet); Census Rolls and Supplements (Statistics Division, 1885–1940, 420 feet); Rosters of Agency Employees (Employees Section, 1853–1909, 38 volumes, 7 feet); and General Correspondence (Board of Indian Commissioners, 1899–1918, 6 feet). Records relating to Oklahoma and Alaska are particularly well represented in holdings of the Social and Economic Records Division. Included in Oklahoma records are Docket Books for the Five Civilized Tribes (1897–1910, 41 volumes, 3 feet); Records Relating to Applications for Identification as Mississippi Choctaw (1901–7, 17 feet); Records concerning Affairs of the Mexican Kickapoo (1895–1914, 2 feet); Land Sale Orders for Five Civilized Tribes (1908–13, 3 feet); and Rosters of Employees of the Commission to the Five Civilized Tribes (1899–1909, 2 volumes, 2 inches). The Alaska Division records consist of twenty-seven series, mostly correspondence (1877–1939, 163 feet).

General Records of the Department of the Navy, Record Group 80 (Old Military Records Division to 1917; Modern Military Records Division from 1917), has two series of general files among the records of the Office of the Secretary of the Navy. Each series contains files on territorial and insular subjects (1897–1926, 2,995 feet, with register, 275 feet, index, 202 feet, and special indexes, 12 feet; and 1926–46, several thousand feet, not yet inventoried).

Army records in Records of the Adjutant General's Office, Record Group 94 (Old Military Records Division), include twenty-eight series which constitute the AGO Returns and Station Books, 1790–1916. These contain much detailed and valuable information for the history of territories. The series lending themselves most readily to research are Returns of the Territorial Divisions, Departments, and Districts (1809–1916, 214 feet); Returns of Military Posts (ca. 1800–1916, 856 feet); Returns of Military Organizations (ca. 1800–1916, 400 feet); Memoranda of Returns Received (1861–1917, 15 volumes, 3 feet); and Strength Reports (1890–1941, 10 volumes and unbound material, 40 feet). There are also records relating to individual territories: for Oklahoma and Arizona, Enlistment Papers, Indian Scouts (1866–1914, 15 feet, with index, 4 volumes, 4 inches); for Puerto Rico, Muster Rolls of the Puerto Rico Regiment (1899–1901, 2 feet), and Carded Records, Puerto Rican Regiment, United States Volunteers (1899–1901, 12 feet).

The Office of Territories of the Department of the Interior is the agency specifically assigned the duty of administering United States territories. Records of the Office of Territories, Record Group 126, located in the Social and Economic Records Division, contains about 785 feet of materials related to the areas of interest to us here (1907–53). The bulk of these are the Central Classified Files (1907–51, 608 feet). A separate series of the Central Classified Files was set up to accommodate records relating to the Alaska Railroad when the main series became too cumbersome (1916–51, 76 feet). Extensive indexes to these two series exist. Separate series were also created for some specialized functions; these include the Office Files of the Special Disbursing Officer of Puerto Rico (1920–51, 8 feet); Records of the Puerto Rican Hurricane Relief Commission (five series, 1929–36, 6 feet); Records of the Puerto Rican Hurricane Relief Loan Section (three series, 1935–50, 10 feet); Correspondence Relating to Settlement at the Matanuska Valley Colony, Palmer, Alaska (1934–39, 12 feet); a reference file on Territorial Policy (1941–44, 6 feet); records on food stockpiling in World War II (two series, 1942–45, 7 feet); Records of the Federal Inter-Agency Alaskan Development Committee (1947–49, 4 feet); Records Relating to the Pacific Islands Recruitment Program (1949–51, 4 feet); and records relating to defense material allotment and the establishment of priorities during the Korean War (1950–53, 4 feet). General correspondence (1951–58) is at the Washington National Records Center in Suitland, Maryland.

The Bureau of Insular Affairs of the Department of War acted as a central clearinghouse for information on all of the noncontiguous territories of the United States, though Puerto Rico was the only territory directly under the bureau's jurisdiction that concerns us here. Among the general records of the Records of the Bureau of Insular Affairs, Record Group 350 (Social and Economic Records Division), are the General Classified Files (1898–1945, 527 feet); indexes and record cards to the General Classified Files (four series, 1898–1945, 87 feet); Confidential File (1914–35, 6 feet); Classified Files Relating to Customs Matters in the Island Possessions (1898–1941, 47 feet, with index, 3 feet); Letters

Sent (1899–1913, 399 volumes, 34 feet); and Personal Name Information File (1914–45, 193 feet). The civil affairs of the government of Puerto Rico were under the bureau's supervision during the years 1898–1900 and 1909–34 only. Puerto Rico records consist of: Laws, Ordinances, Decrees, and Military Orders Effective in Puerto Rico (1900–1934, 33 volumes, 1 foot); Legislation Pertaining to Puerto Rico (1911–12, 2 inches); Reports of the Superintendent of Insurance of the Department of Finance of Puerto Rico (1929–32, 3 volumes, 1 inch); and Questionnaires concerning American Citizenship for Puerto Ricans (no date, 6 inches). In addition, two series of the general records relate exclusively to Puerto Rico: Index to the General Classified Files Relating to Puerto Rico (1898–1939, 3 feet); and Record Cards for the General Classified Files Relating to Puerto Rico (1898–1939, 6 feet). Also in the general records are photographic prints (1901–38, 300 items, 7 inches), of which some relate to Puerto Rico.

Records of the Coast and Geodetic Survey, Record Group 23 (Archives Branch, Washington National Records Center, Suitland, Maryland), contains 3,765 feet of scientific field records covering the years 1817–1948. These came from the library and archives of the survey, and they consist of about forty separate types of records compiled by field parties throughout the continental United States, the territories, and the insular possessions.

So much for records located in the Washington area. But we should not ignore the regional archives. They offer the researcher valuable sources which complement holdings available in the capital. Often, in fact, such records are a principal source. Four examples will show how important some of them are. The San Francisco Federal Records Center has recently accessioned 183 feet of the Records of the Government of American Samoa, 1900–1966 (Records of the Office of Territories, Record Group 126). The records fall into three categories: high court, governor's office, and attorney general's office. There are twenty-one series of high court records, the main ones of which are the General Files (1907–66, 22 feet); Census Returns (1900–1945, 2 feet); Proceedings of the Fono, the Samoan legislature (1905–47, 5 inches); and War Damage Claims (1953, 3 feet). Other records include Civil and Criminal Case Files, Regulations and Orders, Annual Reports, Native and Village Affairs Files, and Naturalization and Immigration forms. Governor's office records consist of fifteen series, including the Proceedings of the Fono (1902–49, 2 feet); Annual Reports (1902–56, 2 feet); Subject Files (1900–1958, 7 feet); and Coded Subject Files (1941–61, 79 feet). Of the thirteen series of the attorney general's office files, the main ones are the Island Government Files (1931–64, 21 feet); Police Investigations and Case Files

(1932–62, 5 feet); Immigration and Emigration Records (1937–65, 3 feet); and Records of Boards and Commissions (1941–59, 8 inches).

The researcher of the history of Oklahoma Territory will find a staggering amount of material at the Fort Worth Federal Records Center (Records of the Bureau of Indian Affairs, Record group 75). Volume and dates are not yet available for some records. Records of the Office of the Area Director, 1874–1962, include the Central Files Correspondence (1903–20); Letter Press Copies of Letters Sent (1874–1931, 5,200 volumes, 518 feet); Correspondence (1897–1962, 320 feet); Employee Records of the Dawes Commission (from 1899, bound volumes); Record of Dawes Commission Employees (1899–1907, 3 feet); Records of School Employees (1899–1946, 2 feet); School Records (1902–57, 15 feet); Probate and Heirship Case Files (1904–49, 70 feet); Land Records (Miscellaneous Information, 1900–1918, 21 volumes; Intruder Cases, 1900–1906; Maps and Plats, 1890–1948); and Annuity Payrolls (1904–8). The Dawes Commission itself created about 5,000 feet of records spanning the years 1897–1936. Among these are the land allotment records (General Records, 1900–1905; Tribal Allotment Records, 1898–1918, 500 feet; Land Contest Records, 1899–1911, 210 feet; Removal of Restriction Records, 1904–36, 576 feet; Deeds and Conveyances, 1903–14, 25 volumes; Miscellaneous, 1900–1912; and the records of 300 townsites, 1899–1914), citizenship enrollment records (Applications for Citizenship, Cherokee Freedmen; Citizenship Court Cases, 1896–1907; Applications for Cherokee Freedmen, Contested, 1902; and Citizenship Roll, 1902, 14 volumes), and the Dawes enrollment records (General Records, 1896–1914; and Tribal Rolls, Cards, Schedules, Applications, and Indexes, 1897–1908). Finally, there are agency records: Osage Agency (Osage-Kaw, 1856 to present, 373 feet); Old Quapaw Agency (Seneca, 1867–1900, 13 feet); Kiowa Agency (Anadarko Agency, 1893–1935); Chilocco School (1883–1955); Concho Agency, (Southern Cheyenne-Arapaho, 1873–1965); Miami Agency (Quapaw Agency, 1872 to present); Shawnee Agency (1894–1940); and the Pawnee Agency (1883–1919).

An important group of records relating to Alaska Territory is located at the Seattle Federal Records Center. These are the records of the Office of the Governor (Records of the Alaska Territorial Government, Record Group 348). They cover the years 1884–1958 and amount in volume to 297 feet. The principal series are the Executive Office Central File (1884–1920, 24 feet); General Correspondence File (1909–58, 176 feet); Annual Reports of the Governor of Alaska (1917–57, 5 feet); Territorial Legislative File (1913–39, 13 feet); Reports of Surveys and Studies (1910–58, 10 feet); and Records Relating to Emergency Relief Programs in Alaska (1934–41, 16 feet). Records relating to the Trust Territory of

the Pacific Islands are found at the Federal Records Center at Mechanics-
burg, Pennsylvania. The United States Navy governed the territory from
1943 until the Department of the Interior assumed civil functions in 1951.
The dual responsibility of naval officers as governors and commanders of
naval forces is displayed in the Records of the High Commissioners and
District Administrators of the Trust Territory of the Pacific Islands
(1943–51, 121 feet). These are part of the General Records of the Department of the Navy, Record Group 80.

I hope this listing will give readers new insights into the possibilities
offered by federal records. A more formidable summary is available free of
charge on request, as long as stocks last, by writing to the editor, *Territorial
Papers of the United States,* National Archives, and asking for "A Preliminary List of Twentieth-Century Records in the National Archives
Relating to the Territories of the United States" (36 pages, mimeographed,
November 1969). This list, in turn, makes reference to various finding
aids produced by the National Archives. Preliminary inventories issued as
publications will be sent on request whenever available.

Restrictions are a problem in this period. They may be established by a
number of authorities—by the president, the Congress, the agency, the
donor, or the National Archives itself—for a variety of reasons—national
security or to protect other interests and rights, such as legal and economic
ones, of the government, private companies, or individual citizens. The
right of individuals to privacy in personal matters, in particular, is an area
in which the National Archives must be very careful with documents. If
possible, users should check in advance by mail or telephone before coming
in to see records. The National Archives can advise in each instance on the
nature of restrictions, if any, and the procedure for securing clearance
where that is permitted.

In closing, let me mention the problem of citation of sources. Dr. Larson's paper employs the sources judiciously, but I would like to take issue
with the style of his citations. The sheer bulk of some series requires accu-
rate detail if the source is to be located without difficulty. The "General
Correspondence File, 1907–53," footnote 38 in Dr. Larson's paper, is
1,300 feet long. In such cases the precise file or register should be described
by its number or decimal code, its subject heading, and the inclusive years.
In addition to textual citations, National Archives microfilm should be
cited by title, microfilm publication number, and roll number. The National
Archives has published a pamphlet on citation, which will be provided to
interested persons upon request.

Comment on the Larson and Robbins Papers

WHITNEY T. PERKINS

TERRITORIAL GOVERNMENT in the United States has always been transitional. That middle ground referred to by Professor Boyd earlier, where particular rights and powers are balanced with those of the nation, has been ground not to be held permanently but to be relinquished. The papers just delivered focus on times and modes of change, unfolding a familiar pattern in the case of New Mexico and groping for new forms in the Caribbean and Pacific Islands. They reveal a similar tendency on the part of the national government—hesitation to exert directing influence, delayed and limited recognition of concerns and interests that might necessitate more active planning and direction.

In the case of New Mexico, as was true generally on the continent, limited national action was conducive to flourishing self-government. The territory was quite thoroughly exposed to political life in these United States and gained both by example and by direct transfusion a capacity for politics which qualified it as a full participant. Statehood was already overdue when Governor Curry took office. Curry was not as deeply involved in local affairs as his predecessors had been, and he was faced with stronger demands from Washington; but like them he was a New Mexican. Until the collision with Ballinger, he seems to have succeeded admirably in his dual role as the agent of the federal government and a representative of the clamant constituency which surrounded him, and to which he was responsive and beholden hardly less than an elected official would have been.

Increased concern for the national interest in conservation and use of the resources of New Mexico came much too late, as Professor Larson somewhat regretfully pointed out, to engender a clash between national and local interests of such dimension as to disrupt the pattern of territorial government. It did not give rise to any lasting differentiation and interaction between the whole and the part. Permissiveness (the prevalent translation of laissez faire) may not avoid misery and want but it does cut down controversy. In the continental territories it enabled self-government to flourish before statehood without lasting detriment; and it made possible a smooth if somewhat delayed transition to a status of unquestioned validity.

In the overseas territories, with the partial exception of Hawaii, laissez faire was a potential threat to self-government. It was not to be expected that the continental experience could be repeated—that the part would simply grow within and eventually merge with the whole. These were distinct entities, geographically, historically and culturally separate from the United States. They could not merge with the American whole without losing their selfhood. Even if they should come to have some small share in the government of the larger "self," they could not hope to have significant influence in determining its character and setting its priorities. Moreover, self-government could not simply be implanted in these territories by restless Americans. It had to emerge from the local population, and it might not do so if American rule were either too loose or too tight—either too loose to limit the impact of private economic forces from the United States or too tight to permit self-assertion. At best, there was no assurance that a demand and capacity for self-government would emerge, or that it could survive amidst either the teeming vitality of American national life or the deadening routines of a backwater bureaucracy.

Thus an issue was present in the territories discussed by Professor Robbins which hardly existed for the territories whose future status as states was clear. (One must note, however, in a rueful parenthesis, that this issue did apply to the American Indians and to the Eskimos and Aleuts of Alaska.) Self-government was at stake. The national interest in these territories—the most meaningful criterion of national choice—lay not primarily in safeguarding and developing material resources, but in preserving and releasing the potentialities of human societies.

What shall we call this? Not the problem of empire, because we reject the word with its connotations of pride and self-advantage. Not the task of trusteeship, because this suggests incapacity and prolonged dependency. Perhaps we may refer to it as the duty of constituting self-government, the exercise of a constitutional responsibility which derived both from historical events and from the principles of that Constitution which posits the purposes and the limits of government for the United States. What it required was not just restraint and generosity on the part of the United States, but political creativity.

To such a task the United States responded only with hesitation and reluctance. In the light of continental experience, Americans were inclined to expect that the flourishing of self-government would compensate for neglect, that what might otherwise be regarded as national negligence would go down in history as salutary abstention. The outcome and the judgments of history are still in doubt. But it seems that in paradoxical fashion self-government is winning through, despite the absence of a concerted national strategy for its propagation and nurture.

Professor Robbins has given us several intimate glimpses of policy making. One cannot distill from these an image of principled responsibility, with individual exceptions such as Mrs. Bolton and an unnamed participant with whom Professor Robbins seems to have intimate familiarity. Nor can one discern with any clarity the emerging outlines of a new constitutionalism. Yet there has been constructive and promising innovation. The vigor of self-government in Puerto Rico has overcome grave deficiencies in its formal status, even in the critical forum of the United Nations. (One must doubt that what was done in 1953 could have been done in the 1960s, however, and question the likelihood of similar success in gaining approval of a new status for the trust territory.) The Virgin Islands and Guam will soon be electing their governors. In the trust territory, where for many years it seemed that apathy and distances precluded meaningful self-government on more than a local scale, the Congress of Micronesia is already claiming the status of a "self-governing state" which would negotiate association with the United States—a far cry from the status of a county of Hawaii. It is also disposed to drive bargains with the armed forces of the United States with regard to bases.

Except for American Samoa, then, something has happened similar to that which happened on the continent; perhaps more despite than because of conscious policy decisions, self-government has become a reality in terms of aspiration and demand and has found evident if incomplete political expression. What remains is to work out lasting and workable forms of conjunction between these manifestations of self-government and the larger polity of the United States of America. Such forms are not for the federal government unilaterally to decree. Historical experience and national values are clear in one regard: self-government is not to be denigrated or extinguished. Whatever damage may have been done by inadvertence and neglect in delaying or distorting the emergence of expressions of self-government, the United States has always come to recognize and respect such assertions. Here the older territorial system showed the way, and the past links up with the present.

If there has been success and grounds for optimism do exist, even though there is little evidence that statesmen's wisdom produced such results, what explanation can we find? Perhaps what counted most, and may even have prevailed in the face of neglect and frustration, is the force of example and the often unwitting wisdom of forbearance. Not that permissiveness builds character—that would be going too far—but it may give character the chance to reveal itself.

The American Territories of Today and Tomorrow

HARRISON LOESCH

A NUMBER OF IMPORTANT EVENTS are occurring in the territories, and they will occur with a rising tempo in the near future. Before I discuss the present and future, however, a brief reference to the past may be helpful in setting the scene.

By 1925 the United States had acquired all of the geographic areas which came to be known as the insular possessions or territories of the United States. Cuba already had been granted independence, only four years after the Treaty of Paris.

The territories lying beyond the continental limits were acquired by purchase, conquest, and cession. Alaska and the Virgin Islands were purchased. Hawaii and American Samoa became associated with the United States through acts of cession. Cuba, Guam, Puerto Rico, and the Philippines came to us as a result of the Spanish-American War and its Treaty of Paris. The manner in which these areas were acquired, while interesting historically, bears no relation to how they were and are administered, or to their ultimate destiny.

The Constitution of the United States, Article 4, section 3, vests in the Congress plenary authority with respect to territories. Since 1900 the Congress has dealt with the insular territorial areas on an individual basis, making provision for each according to its needs and, generally, the desires of its people. This action, over the years, has taken various forms resulting in a variety of kinds and degrees of political status. Independence, commonwealth status, organized and unorganized, incorporated and unincorporated, and statehood are the terms we associate with territorial political development.

Independence, granted to Cuba and the Philippines, and statehood, accorded Alaska and Hawaii, are well-understood terms. Between these

238

polar extremes of self-government our system, as implemented by the Congress and by the executive, has had flexibility for accommodation of the varying needs of different cultures, economies, and heritages. The system takes into account the dynamics of social and political development and growth. It has seen simple forms freely evolve into other, more advanced institutional arrangements.

Defining our terms: Whether or not a territory is organized is determined by whether the United States Congress has enacted organic legislation defining the form of the territorial government. Incorporation means that the territory is under the umbrella of the Constitution of the United States, and the term carries with it an implied promise of ultimate statehood.

Commonwealth status has no constitutional basis, but in different forms it was created for the Philippines and Puerto Rico as those areas reached higher stages in their development and capability for independent administration.

Prior to statehood, Alaska and Hawaii were organized, incorporated territories. The Virgin Islands and Guam are organized, unincorporated territories, and American Samoa is unorganized and unincorporated.

Immediately after World War II, the United States became involved in an entirely new sort of territorial concern. Pursuant to a trusteeship agreement between the United States and the Security Council of the United Nations, we assumed full responsibility for and complete jurisdiction over a vast area in the western Pacific called the Trust Territory of the Pacific Islands. But this strategic trust does not result in sovereignty, as such, over Micronesia.

Today, as the overseeing assistant secretary, my involvement is with the present and future of Guam, American Samoa, the Virgin Islands, and Micronesia. The Department of the Interior is charged with responsibility for other small insular possessions, but our concerns with those areas are different. They are largely uninhabited, uninhabitable specks of land as to which, oddly enough, sovereignty is sometimes disputed. The Department of the Interior is not officially concerned with areas administered by the Department of the Army such as the Panama Canal Zone or the Ryukyu Islands, which include Okinawa. The leased Canal Zone and Okinawa are not considered to be American territories.

The four areas which I have said concern us most vitally today fall into three levels of association with the United States. Let us look first at American Samoa.

Situated some twenty-four hundred miles south of Hawaii and twenty-six degrees south of the equator, the territory of American Samoa consists of the principal island of Tutuila, the small island of Annu'u just off the eastern end of Tutuila, the three small islands of the Manu'a group 80 miles away, and, 200 miles from Tutuila, Swains Island, a coral atoll about a mile in diameter. In 1925 Swains Island, geographically part of the Tokelau Islands, was extended United States sovereignty. It was appended to American Samoa for administration in recognition of its private owner- ship by an American citizen.

The population of the territory is about thirty thousand. Its citizens are our nationals. As such, while not citizens, they owe permanent allegiance to the United States. The territory is still heavily dependent upon grants appropriated to it annually by the Congress as part of the Department of the Interior budget. In recent years the ratio between local revenues and appropriated grants has changed. The increasing local revenues will soon equal half the fiscal needs of the territory.

While the territorial government remains the largest single employer, rapid improvement in the private sector accounts for the economic growth. Two major fish canneries process tuna delivered to them by foreign fishing fleets and in turn support an operation by the American Can Company and create a substantial business in supplying petroleum products to the fishing fleets. The newest and still-developing industry is tourism.

Politically, American Samoa is an unorganized, unincorporated territory. Congress decrees that the president shall be responsible for the govern- ment of the territory. That responsibility has been delegated to the secre- tary of the interior, and was discharged initially through the promulgation of secretarial orders creating a three-branch government for the territory patterned upon our own democratic form. Secretarial direction has been superseded now, however, by secretarial sanction and promulgation of a constitution created through the efforts of a constitutional convention held by the people of American Samoa. That constitution, locally drafted and rati- fied by the electorate, is the basis for the government of the territory today.

The Virgin Islands and Guam illustrate another level of status or devel- opment. The territory of Guam is a single island, with a population of approximately one hundred thousand. The Guamanians are citizens of the United States, as of course are the considerable numbers of military per- sonnel and their dependents who are stationed there. The Virgin Islands— St. Thomas, St. John, and St. Croix, in the Caribbean about eighty miles east of Puerto Rico—have a population in excess of sixty thousand. The Virgin Islanders, too, are United States citizens.

These territories are alike insofar as political status is concerned. Each is an organized, unincorporated territory. The Congress enacted organic legislation for the Virgin Islands in 1936 and added a major revision in 1954. The Guam organic act dates from 1950. Since 1954, these two acts have been uniformly amended to maintain virtually identical treatment for the two territories.

Economically, Guam is dependent largely upon a private sector devoted to serving the extensive military activities situated there. Light industry and tourism are areas of development yet in their infancy. The Virgin Islands, on the other hand, have been the beneficiaries of a ten-year economic boom, due largely to the amazing influx of tourists which has stimulated growth in almost every facet of the economy. This is supplemented by the substantial development of the watch movement assembly industry. Heavy industry is limited to an oil refinery and an alumina facility. Neither territory seeks appropriated federal funds to support governmental operations, but a special category of funds is appropriated annually to Guam under the terms of the Guam Rehabilitation Act which followed the devastating typhoon of 1962.

That Guam and the Virgin Islands do not seek appropriated funds does not mean that these two territories have achieved fiscal self-sufficiency. Each is heavily subsidized. The Congress has extended the federal income tax to each of the areas with the provision that the tax shall be in the nature of a territorial levy. Collection is made locally and the proceeds are retained by the island governments. In addition, Guam receives the federal withholding taxes collected by the United States from persons living or stationed there. That return in fiscal year 1970 will approximate $7 million.

In the case of the Virgin Islands, federal law provides for the return annually of federal excise taxes collected on products of the Virgin Islands shipped to the United States, to the extent that such funds are matched by local revenues. In recent years such local revenues have risen to far exceed the amount of excise taxes collected, with the result that each year the territory receives the entire amount of such excise tax collections, less only refunds and costs of collection. In fiscal year 1970 the return to the Virgin Islands of the so-called matching funds will reach $11.2 million.

The Trust Territory of the Pacific Islands, or Micronesia, occupies a third category. Spread over an area of the western Pacific slightly larger than the United States, it consists of about two thousand islands, of which approximately one hundred twenty are inhabited. The total population is about ninety-four thousand. The responsibility for discharging our trust obligations with respect to Micronesia is vested in the secretary of the interior, who consults with the Departments of State and Defense on matters involving foreign policy and defense.

The government of Micronesia has its basis in secretarial orders promulgated by the secretary of the interior. The form of government is like that of the territories of the United States: an executive branch, an independent judiciary, and an elected legislature, called the Congress of Micronesia.

Economically, Micronesia is the most underdeveloped of the areas with which we are concerned. It must rely upon federally appropriated grants for 98 percent of its annual budget. Economic growth in the private sector, while improving, still leaves much to be desired, and this is an area on which we shall concentrate in the next few years.

This, then, is where we are today.

Within the framework of the governments I have described, each of the areas administers its own affairs with a minimum of federal intervention. This is consistent with our policy of according the maximum degree of home rule consistent with the level of development and ability in each of the areas.

As we consider the existing relationship between the territories and the United States and speculate upon the future of these areas, we cannot escape awareness of the international concern with "colonialism," old or new. In the parlance of the United Nations, American Samoa, Guam, and the Virgin Islands are categorized as non-self-governing territories. As such, they are of concern to the United Nations General Assembly's "Special Committee on the Situation with Regard to the Implementation of the Declaration on the Granting of Independence to Colonial Countries and Peoples." This mouthful is better known as the "U.N. Committee of 24."

Micronesia and its development are under the particularly close scrutiny of the Trusteeship Council, to which the Security Council has delegated its review responsibilities for this strategic trusteeship.

The United States, usually as a part of an international political ploy, is charged from time to time with maintaining a colonial posture. It is said we are not doing enough soon enough in the discharge of our "obligation" to permit the peoples of the territories and Micronesia to choose their destiny through self-determination. I cannot agree with such charges. An examination of our history will prove that we have never been a colonial power in any traditional sense. People in the offshore areas have been, and are, free to work out political relationships with the United States best suited to their circumstances. It would be difficult to document an instance which might be construed as exploitation of those peoples or their resources. Over the years an element of our territorial policy has been to give rather than to take.

Neither has our policy been static nor directed toward maintenance of the status quo. As time, circumstances, and most particularly the wishes of the people of the territories have required changes in our relationships, those changes have been made. Not all at once and not always in the fullness the people desire at any given time, perhaps, but they do occur. Our policy does not lay down inflexible rules requiring a certain level of "progress" before making changes. If it did it could not be responsive as it must be to the wishes of the people. Our past performance is illustrative of how our system works, but it is not binding precedent.

This policy, system, or approach is not a newly enunciated one in response to our critics. It is basic to the American philosophy of government and the rights of the people. In 1900 President McKinley, in speaking of the Philippines, said, "The government they are establishing is designed not for our satisfaction nor the expression of our theoretical views, but for the happiness, peace and prosperity of the people of the Philippine Islands."

I need not rely upon a quotation from 1900, however, to support my thesis. In the weeks just past we have participated in an extended series of meetings here in Washington with representatives of the people of Micronesia. Those representatives were charged with responsibility for negotiating with the federal establishment a course of substantive action which will ultimately determine the future political status of Micronesia. The course of action can only succeed if the Micronesians on the one hand, and the executive branch and the Congress on the other, are successful in efforts to meld the aspirations of the people of Micronesia with national and international considerations arising from the realities of today's world. There is no question in my mind but that we will succeed.

Since my involvement in territorial affairs is of quite recent date, it is especially gratifying to me to be able to participate in this intimate way in deliberations concerning the future political status of Micronesia, starting as we are almost at the beginning of the process. The unique experience is possible only because, as in other areas of modern life, we are moving faster on a geometrical progression.

Our concerns are not, by any means, limited to the future of Micronesians. We are equally as interested in the other areas I have mentioned. A major political development involving the Virgin Islands and Guam was the recent enactment, in 1970, of legislation permitting the people to elect their own governors. This significant increment of home rule is an example of the flexibility of our system. The people of Alaska and Hawaii were at no time prior to statehood allowed to elect their governors. On the other hand, the citizens of Alaska and Hawaii were bent on achieving statehood.

The peoples of Guam, American Samoa, and the Virgin Islands have not spoken out with respect to their views of the desired ultimate status of those territories, although it is a matter of concern and contemplation.

Several years ago the people of the Virgin Islands convened a constitutional convention, and the report of that body made known to us the views of the people concerning recommended changes and amendments in the revised organic act.

In September, an American Samoa Status Commission appeared in Washington after visiting in the Virgin Islands and Puerto Rico. The report of that group is not yet available to us.

In Guam a "constitutional" review group has recently been organized. But a different kind of question also occupies the attention of the people. It has been suggested by some that the time has come to reunify the Marianas in Micronesia with Guam, in view of historical ties and the present community of interest.

A reunification plebiscite to test local sentiment is being held in the islands of the Northern Marianas, and at this very moment the people of Guam, through a plebiscite, are expressing their wish in this regard. Incorporation of the Marianas into the territory of Guam, if that be the wish of the peoples concerned, could not be accomplished without action by the Congress—and the United Nations would certainly take a position on the question. Furthermore, a satisfactory solution for the rest of the Trust Territory would have to be developed. If the people of the two areas strongly favor such a course, the United States government would doubtless consider it.

I cannot tell you what the future holds for the territorial areas of the United States. We do not have a grand scheme which plots by day and year the course of their development and their ultimate status. I submit that it is not for us to devise such a scheme. Their destiny will, I am certain, be more the product of the will of the people than of our judgment as to what is good—or better—or best for them. That is the way it should be.

Our immediate goals are less sweeping than the issue of ultimate status.

The United States citizens resident in the territories are not able to vote in the national elections for president and vice president. That should be remedied.

None of the territories is represented before the Congress. A nonvoting delegate to the House of Representatives may be appropriate.

While the federal courts in Guam and the Virgin Islands, created by the organic acts of those territories, offer access to the Supreme Court of the United States, the citizens of American Samoa and Micronesia, within those areas, do not have recourse to the federal courts. Perhaps they should.

At the local level we intend to assist in every way to insure that the people of the territories, during the period of growth and development, have a government strong enough to serve their needs and an environment conducive to the happiness, peace, and prosperity of which President McKinley spoke, and conducive, as well, to rapid and worthwhile growth politically, economically, and socially.

The environment we envision presupposes the absence of fear—fear of corrupt government, fear of economic instability, fear of adverse external influences, and fear of shortages in physical necessities.

So there we are—our challenge is, where do we go from here?

Biographical Sketches

THOMAS G. ALEXANDER. Native of Utah, educated at Weber College, Utah State University, University of Utah, and University of California at Berkeley (Ph.D., 1965) . . . member of history faculty of Brigham Young University (1964 to present) . . . specialist in United States history, late nineteenth and early twentieth centuries . . . author of articles published in *Pacific Historical Review; Utah Historical Quarterly; Dialogue: A Journal of Mormon Thought; Journal of the West;* and *Arizona and the West.*

ROBERT F. BERKHOFER, JR. Native of New Jersey, educated at New York State College for Teachers and Cornell University (Ph.D., 1960) . . . member of history faculties of Ohio State University, University of Minnesota, University of Wisconsin at Madison (1969–73), and University of Michigan (from 1973) . . . specialist in the American West and in synthesis and methodology in history . . . author of books and articles, including *Salvation and the Savage* (1965) and *A Behavioral Approach to Historical Analysis* (1969).

ARTHUR EUGENE BESTOR. Native of New York, educated at Yale University (Ph.D., 1938) . . . member of history faculties of Yale University, Columbia University, Stanford University, University of Wisconsin, University of Illinois, and University of Washington (1962 to present) . . . specialist in United States constitutional, intellectual, and social history . . . author of many books and articles, including *Backwoods Utopias* (1950) and *Educational Wastelands: The Retreat from Learning in Our Public Schools* (1953), and coauthor of *The Heritage of the Middle West* (1958).

NANCY JO TICE BLOOM. Native of California, educated at University of Chicago, Reed College, Northwestern University, University of Wisconsin (Ph.D., 1967) . . . Director of Research, Business and Professional Women's Foundation (1968–69) . . . member of history faculties of University of Wisconsin at

Whitewater (1965–68) and Bowie State College (1969 to present) . . . specialist in history of United States territories and the United States frontier.

JOHN D. W. GUICE.   Native of Mississippi, educated at Yale University, University of Texas at El Paso, and University of Colorado (Ph.D., 1969) . . . member of history faculties of University of Texas at El Paso, University of Colorado, and University of Southern Mississippi (since 1969) . . . specialist in territorial legal history . . . author of articles published in *Colorado Magazine* (State Historical Society).

JOHN PAUL HEARD.   Native of England, educated at San Francisco State College (B.A., 1965; M.A. in progress) . . . United States Army (1957–60) . . . Archivist, Federal Records Center, San Francisco, and National Archives (1967–71) . . . Department of Housing and Urban Development (since 1971) . . . specialist in social change theories . . . article published in *Forest History* (1968), others pending.

ROBERT W. JOHANNSEN.   Native of Oregon, educated at Reed College and the University of Washington (Ph.D., 1953) . . . member of history faculties of Universities of Washington, Kansas, and Illinois (since 1959) . . . awards include Pelzer Award (1952), Guggenheim Fellowship (1967–68) . . . specialist in mid-nineteenth-century United States territorial history, the West . . . editor and author of many articles, reviews, and books, including *Frontier Politics and the Sectional Conflict* (1955; paperback edition, 1966), *Letters of Stephen A. Douglas* (1961), and *Democracy on Trial, 1845–77* (1966).

MARION M. JOHNSON.   Native of Tennessee, educated at George Washington University (M.A., 1959, history) and University of Alabama (J.D., 1969) . . . Archivist, National Archives (1948 to present), subject specialist for legal records.

PHILIP DILLON JORDAN.   Native of Iowa, educated at Northwestern University and University of Iowa (Ph.D., 1935) . . . member of history faculties of Long Island University, Miami University of Ohio, and the University of Minnesota (1945–69) . . . specialist in nineteenth-century America, the history of medicine and public health, and frontier law and legal thought . . . author of many books and articles, including *The National Road* (1948) and "Scholar and Archivist: A Partnership," *American Archivist* (January 1968).

WILLIAM LEE KNECHT.   Native of New Jersey, educated at Brigham Young University (B.S., 1951) and Harvard Law School (J.D., 1958) . . . Southern

States Mission, Church of Jesus Christ of Latter-Day Saints (1947–49) . . .
military service (1951–54) . . . private practice in Berkeley, California, and
Director, Public Utilities Department, California Farm Bureau Federation
(1958 to present) . . . specialist in history of Utah Territory . . . author of
several publications.

ROBERT W. LARSON.   Native of Colorado, educated at the University of Denver and the University of New Mexico (Ph.D., 1961) . . . member of history
faculty of Colorado State College (1960 to present) . . . specialist in southwestern history and populism-progressivism in the West . . . author of *New
Mexico's Quest for Statehood, 1846–1912* (1968) and articles in *Mid-America*
and the *New Mexico Historical Review*.

HARRISON LOESCH.   Native of Illinois, educated at Colorado College, Denver
University Law School, Yale University (LL.B., 1939) . . . United States Army
(1942–45, major) . . . President, Seventh Judicial District Bar Association,
1956; President, Colorado Bar Association, 1961–62 . . . Assistant Secretary,
United States Department of the Interior (1969–73); minority counsel, Senate
Committee on Interior and Insular Affairs (from 1973).

KENNETH N. OWENS.   Native of Washington State, educated at Lewis and
Clark College and University of Minnesota (Ph.D., 1959) . . . member of
history faculties of Northern Illinois University (1959–67) and Sacramento
State College (1967 to present) . . . specialist in American frontier history and
ethnohistory . . . author of *Galena, Grant, and the Fortunes of War* (1963).

WHITNEY T. PERKINS.   Native of Massachusetts, educated at Tufts College,
Fletcher School of International Law and Diplomacy (Ph.D., 1948) . . . United
States Army Air Force (1942–45, captain) . . . member of political science
faculties of University of Denver (1948–53) and Brown University (1953 to
present); Fulbright Fellow (1950–51); consultant, United States Commission
on Status of Puerto Rico (1965–66) . . . specialist in United States policy in
administration of dependent areas, and intervention . . . author of *Denial of
Empire: The United States and Its Dependencies* (1962) and of various articles.

LEONARD RAPPORT.   Native of North Carolina, educated at University of
North Carolina and George Washington University (M.A., 1957) . . . member
of editorial staff, University of North Carolina Press (1935–38) and the Southern Regional Writer's Project (1938–41) . . . United States Army (1941–48,
Captain) . . . Archivist, National Archives, (1949–58 and 1969 to present) . . .
associate editor, *Ratification of the Federal Constitution and Bill of Rights,* a
documentary history, National Historical Publications Commission (1958–69)

248   BIOGRAPHICAL SKETCHES

. . . author, coauthor, editor, compiler of books and articles, including *Rendez-vous with Destiny* (1948, 2d edition, 1965) and revised edition of Max Farrand's *Records of the Federal Convention of 1787* (in progress).

KENT D. RICHARDS. Native of Wisconsin, educated at Knox College and University of Wisconsin (Ph.D., 1966) . . . member of history faculty of Central Washington State College (1966 to present) . . . specialist in Pacific Northwest and territorial history . . . author of articles published in *Pacific Northwest Quarterly* and *Arizona and the West.*

ROBERT R. ROBBINS. Native of Ohio, educated at Ohio State University (Ph.D., 1941, political science), with master's degrees from Ohio State University (1934, political science), Fletcher School of International Law and Diplomacy (1940), and Columbia University (1943, military government and civil affairs) . . . civil affairs officer, United States Navy, London, (1943–46) . . . member, Office of Dependent Area Affairs, United States Department of State (1946–56) . . . Jackson Professor of Political Science, Tufts University, and Professor of Dependent Area Affairs, Fletcher School of International Law and Diplomacy (1957 to present); President, New England Political Science Association (1969).

HAROLD W. RYAN. Native of Illinois, educated at Quincy College (B.A., 1934), postgraduate studies at George Washington University . . . Archivist, National Archives, research and editorial assistant for the *Territorial Papers of the United States* (1941–61 and 1964 to 1973) . . . military service (1943–46) . . . author and editor of articles and documents in *Journal of Southern History,* Missouri Historical Society *Bulletin,* and other journals.

JOHN WELLING SMURR. Native of California, educated at University of Montana and Indiana University (Ph.D., 1960) . . . member of history faculties of University of Montana, Moorhead State College, and Stanislaus State College (1968 to present) . . . specialist in United States territorial government and comparative civilizations . . . coeditor, *Historical Essays on Montana and the Northwest in Honor of Paul C. Phillips* (1957); completed Phillips's *Fur Trade* (1961, two volumes).

CHARLES E. SOUTH. Native of Texas, educated at University of Texas at Austin (M.A., 1966) . . . high school instructor, Abilene, Texas . . . member of history faculty of University of Southwestern Louisiana (1966–67) . . . Archivist, National Archives, Legislative, Judicial, and Diplomatic Records Division (1967–73); Coordinator of Regional Archives (from 1973).

An ORDINANCE for the GOVERNMENT of the TERRITORY of the UNITED STATES, North-West of the RIVER OHIO.

BE IT ORDAINED by the United States in Congrefs affembled, That the faid territory, for the purpofes of temporary government, be one diftrict; fubject, however, to be divided into two diftricts, as future circumftances may, in the opinion of Congrefs, make it expedient.

Be it ordained by the authority aforefaid, That the eftates both of refident and non-refident proprietors in the faid territory, dying inteftate, fhall defcend to, and be diftributed among their children, and the defcendants of a deceafed child in equal parts; the defcendants of a deceafed child or grand-child, to take the fhare of their deceafed parent in equal parts among them : And where there fhall be no children or defcendants, then in equal parts to the next of kin, in equal degree; and among collaterals, the children of a deceafed brother or fifter of the inteftate, fhall have in equal parts among them their deceafed parents fhare; and there fhall in no cafe be a diftinction between kindred of the whole and half blood; faving in all cafes to the widow of the inteftate, her third part of the real eftate for life, and one third part of the perfonal eftate; and this law relative to defcents and dower, fhall remain in full force until altered by the legiflature of the diftrict. ——— And until the governor and judges fhall adopt laws as herein after mentioned, eftates in the faid territory may be devifed or bequeathed by wills in writing, figned and fealed by him or her, in whom the eftate may be, (being of full age) and attefted by three witneffes; — and real eftates may be conveyed by leafe and releafe, or bargain and fale, figned, fealed, and delivered by the perfon being of full age, in whom the eftate may be, and attefted by two witneffes, provided fuch wills be duly proved, and fuch conveyances be acknowledged, or the execution thereof duly proved, and be recorded within one year after proper magiftrates, courts, and regifters fhall be appointed for that purpofe; and perfonal property may be transferred by delivery, faving, however, to the French and Canadian inhabitants, and other fettlers of the Kaskaskies, Saint Vincent's, and the neighbouring villages, who have heretofore profeffed themfelves citizens of Virginia, their laws and cuftoms now in force among them, relative to the defcent and conveyance of property.

Be it ordained by the authority aforefaid, That there fhall be appointed from time to time, by Congrefs, a governor, whofe commiffion fhall continue in force for the term of three years, unlefs fooner revoked by Congrefs; he fhall refide in the diftrict, and have a freehold eftate therein, in one thoufand acres of land, while in the exercife of his office.

There fhall be appointed from time to time, by Congrefs, a fecretary, whofe commiffion fhall continue in force for four years, unlefs fooner revoked, he fhall refide in the diftrict, and have a freehold eftate therein, in five hundred acres of land, while in the exercife of his office; it fhall be his duty to keep and preferve the acts and laws paffed by the legiflature, and the public records of the diftrict, and the proceedings of the governor in his executive department; and tranfmit authentic copies of fuch acts and proceedings, every fix months, to the fecretary of Congrefs : There fhall alfo be appointed a court to confift of three judges, any two of whom to form a court, who fhall have a common law jurifdiction, and refide in the diftrict, and have each therein a freehold eftate in five hundred acres of land, while in the exercife of their offices; and their commiffions fhall continue in force during good behaviour.

The governor and judges, or a majority of them, fhall adopt and publifh in the diftrict, fuch laws of the original ftates, criminal and civil, as may be neceffary, and beft fuited to the circumftances of the diftrict, and report them to Congrefs, from time to time, which laws fhall be in force in the diftrict until the organization of the general affembly therein, unlefs difapproved of by Congrefs; but afterwards the legiflature fhall have authority to alter them as they fhall think fit.

The governor for the time being, fhall be commander in chief of the militia, appoint and commiffion all officers in the fame, below the rank of general officers; all general officers fhall be appointed and commiffioned by Congrefs.

Previous to the organization of the general affembly, the governor fhall appoint fuch magiftrates and other civil officers, in each county or townfhip, as he fhall find neceffary for the prefervation of the peace and good order in the fame: After the general affembly fhall be organized, the powers and duties of magiftrates and other civil officers fhall be regulated and defined by the faid affembly; but all magiftrates and other civil officers, not herein otherwife directed, fhall, during the continuance of this temporary government, be appointed by the governor.

For the prevention of crimes and injuries, the laws to be adopted or made fhall have force in all parts of the diftrict, and for the execution of procefs, criminal and civil, the governor fhall make proper divifions thereof——and he fhall proceed from time to time, as circumftances may require, to lay out the parts of the diftrict in which the Indian titles fhall have been extinguifhed, into counties and townfhips, fubject, however, to fuch alterations as may thereafter be made by the legiflature.

So foon as there fhall be five thoufand free male inhabitants, of full age, in the diftrict, upon giving proof thereof to the governor, they fhall receive authority, with time and place, to elect reprefentatives from their counties or townfhips, to reprefent them in the general affembly; provided that for every five hundred free male inhabitants there fhall be one reprefentative, and fo on progreffively with the number of free male inhabitants, fhall the right of reprefentation increafe, until the number of reprefentatives fhall amount to twenty-five, after which the number and proportion of reprefentatives fhall be regulated by the legiflature; provided that no perfon be eligible or qualified to act as a reprefentative, unlefs he fhall have been a citizen of one of the United States three years and be a refident in the diftrict, or unlefs he fhall have refided in the diftrict three years, and in either cafe fhall likewife hold in his own right, in fee fimple, two hundred acres of land within the fame :—Provided alfo, that a freehold in fifty acres of land in the diftrict, having been a citizen of one of the ftates, and being refident in the diftrict; or the like freehold and two years refidence in the diftrict fhall be neceffary to qualify a man as an elector of a reprefentative.

The reprefentatives thus elected, fhall ferve for the term of two years, and in cafe of the death of a reprefentative, or removal from office, the governor fhall iffue a writ to the county or townfhip for which he was a member, to elect another in his ftead, to ferve for the refidue of the term.

The general affembly, or legiflature, fhall confift of the governor, legiflative council, and a houfe of reprefentatives. The legiflative council fhall confift of five members, to continue in office five years, unlefs fooner removed by Congrefs, any three of whom to be a quorum, and the members of the council fhall be nominated and appointed in the following manner, to wit: As foon as reprefentatives fhall be elected, the governor fhall appoint a time and place for them to meet together, and, when met, they fhall nominate ten perfons, refidents in the diftrict, and each poffeffed of a freehold in five hundred acres of land, and return their names to Congrefs; five of whom Congrefs fhall appoint and commiffion to ferve as aforefaid; and whenever a vacancy fhall happen in the council, by death or removal from office, the houfe of reprefentatives fhall nominate two perfons, qualified as aforefaid, for each vacancy, and return their names to Congrefs; one of whom Congrefs fhall appoint and commiffion for the refidue of the term; and every five years, four months at leaft before the expiration of the time of fervice of the members of council, the faid houfe fhall nominate ten perfons, qualified as aforefaid, and return their names to Congrefs, five of whom Congrefs fhall appoint and commiffion to ferve as members of the council five years, unlefs fooner removed. And the governor, legiflative council, and houfe of re-